THE CATHOLIC BIBLICAL QUARTERLY MONOGRAPH SERIES

20

THE RHETORIC OF POLITICAL PERSUASION
The Narrative Artistry
and Political Intentions of 2 Kings 9–11

by
Lloyd M. Barré

THE RHETORIC OF POLITICAL PERSUASION
The Narrative Artistry and Political Intentions of 2 Kings 9–11

by
Lloyd M. Barré

The Catholic Biblical Association of America
Washington, DC 20064
1988

THE RHETORIC OF POLITICAL PERSUASION
by Lloyd M. Barré

©1988 The Catholic Biblical Association of America
Washington, DC 20064

PRODUCED IN THE UNITED STATES

Library of Congress Cataloging-in-Publication Data

Barré, Lloyd M.
  The rhetoric of political persuasion

  (The Catholic Biblical quarterly. Monograph series; 20)
  Bibliography: p.
  Includes index.
  1. Bible. O.T. Kings, 2nd IX–XI—Criticism,
interpretation, etc. I. Title. II. Series.
  BS1335.2.J37   1988   222'.54066   87-15878
  ISBN 0-915170-19-1

TABLE OF CONTENTS

ACKNOWLEDGMENTS

The present monograph represents a modest revision of my 1986 doctoral dissertation submitted to the Graduate Department of Religion at Vanderbilt University. During the course of my graduate studies at Vanderbilt, I was often the glad recipient of the stimulation and the encouragement provided by both colleagues and faculty. Among these I would especially like to thank my fellow student and friend, Mr. Gordon Matties, for his interest in this project, and for his sustained willingness to serve as my sounding board. I would also like to express a special indebtedness to my dissertation adviser, Dr. Douglas Knight, whose remarkable freedom from academic bias was a constant source of challenge. It has also been my good fortune to befriend Dr. Ronald Hendel, who kindly read the entire manuscript and offered a number of valuable suggestions. And finally, I will remain profoundly indebted to my wife, Ellen, who both read the manuscript and offered able assistance throughout the duration of this project. Her continued support made the completion of this project possible, and it is to her and to my daughter Linda that I wish to dedicate this work.

ABBREVIATIONS

*In addition to those abbreviations listed in *CBQ* 46 (1984) 401–08, the following abbreviations are used in this monograph.

AJBI	Annual of the Japanese Biblical Institute
BAT	Botschaft des Alten Testaments
FOTL	Forms of Old Testament Literature
HS	Die Heilige Schrift des Alten Testaments
HSAT	Die Heilige Schrift des Alten Testaments
KeH	Kurzegefasstes exegetisches Handbuch zum Alten Testament
KHC	Kurzer Hand-Commentar zum Alten Testament
LXX	Septuagint
LXX^L	Lucian's recension
MT	Masoretic Text
Q	Qumran manuscripts
S	Syriac Peshitta
T	Targums
ThSt	Theologische Studien
V	Latin Vulgate version

N.B. All translations found in this monograph are those of the author.

INTRODUCTION

Anyone who has developed an appreciation of the artistic subtleties of Hebrew narration will not be disappointed by the engaging story found in 2 Kings 9–11. Here one encounters a vigorous and dramatic recital of the events that led to the overthrows of Jehoram king of Israel, and of Athaliah queen of Judah. The assault against Jehoram's regime was commanded by a high-ranking army officer, Jehu ben Nimshi, who is most remembered for the pitiless way in which he decimated the house of Ahab. The overthrow of Athaliah, although not characterized by the extreme violence to which Jehu often resorted, was nonetheless equally effective in attaining its political goals. This coup was led by the high priest Jehoiada, whose great achievement was that he not only restored Judah's throne to its rightful heir, but also dislodged Athaliah from power with a modicum of bloodshed.

Although it takes only a cursory reading of this account to appreciate something of its fine literary quality, it is much more difficult to isolate the essential theme of this piece. One of the principal problems that engages the interpreter of this story concerns a determination of the narrator's disposition toward Jehu's rampant violence. At times it seems that the narrative is supportive of Jehu's butchery. Jehu is commissioned by none other than Elisha the prophet, who sends him forth to annihilate the house of Ahab. Furthermore, as he goes about killing the members of Ahab's house, we are told either by Jehu or by the narrator that these assassinations were carried out to satisfy the judgment that Yahweh had pronounced through the prophet Elijah. A positive portrayal of Jehu's coup is further reinforced by Jehu's alliance with the zealous Yahwist, Jehonadab, and especially by Yahweh's explicit statement in 2 Kgs 10:30 that by eradicating the house of Ahab, Jehu had satisfied Yahweh's wrath.

But in spite of those aspects of the story that place Jehu's actions in a favorable light, one also receives the strong impression that other aspects Jehu's character were presented in order to evoke the reader's condemnation. Although one may find it acceptable that the murders of Jehoram and Jezebel were done out of political necessity, it is much more difficult to be comfortable with a coup that resulted in several mass murders. According to our text, Jehu was either directly or indirectly responsible for the slaughter of the

1

seventy princes of Samaria (2 Kgs 10:1–9), for the slaying of the forty-two Judean princes (2 Kgs 10:12–14), for the purge of the members of the house of Ahab in Jezreel (2 Kgs 10:11), for the eradication of the remaining members of house of Ahab in Samaria (2 Kgs 10:17), and for the massacre of the worshipers of Baal (2 Kgs 10:18–25). It is therefore not surprising that Hosea's ancient condemnation of Jehu's violence (Hos 1:4–5) has been echoed by modern interpreters.[1]

It seems, then, that we are facing a narrative that reflects contrary views toward Jehu's personality. At times he is depicted as Yahweh's obedient servant; at times as an vehement killer. It is clear, therefore, that a valid interpretation[2] of this account must come to terms with this apparently contradictory portrayal of the story's protagonist.[3]

As for Jehoiada's overthrow of Athaliah, the major interpretive problem does not revolve around a determination of the narrator's attitudes toward the leading characters. Jehoiada is clearly held up as the hero, while Athaliah is unquestionably depicted as the villain. Here the major problem concerns the question of the literary relationship of 2 Kings 11 to 2 Kings 9–10. Ostensibly, 2 Kings 11 continues the account contained in the two preceding chapters, but most commentators regard 2 Kings 9–10 and 2 Kings 11 as independent literary entities. We shall argue that this majority opinion is in fact mistaken, and that by treating 2 Kings 9–11 as the original literary unit it becomes possible to provide a more adequate understanding of fundamental interpretive issues. Among these we include: (1) a demarcation of the material that comprised the original version of the story; (2) the identification of its literary genre; (3) a profile of its author; (4) the place and date of composition; (5) the intended audience; (6) and the purpose for which this material was written.

Our interests in dealing with this work, however, will not be restricted to questions about the text's composition. Although the attempt to come to terms with the author's message does define the basic concern of this investigation, it would be remiss to neglect the literary dimensions of this work, especially since it is widely acknowledged to be one of the finest examples of

---

[1] For example, J. Bright (*A History of Israel* [2d ed.; Philadelphia: Westminster, 1972] 247) observes that Jehu's coup ". . . rapidly turned into a bloodbath," and that the murder of the worshipers of Baal ". . . was a purge of unspeakable brutality, beyond excuse from a moral point of view. . . ." A similar view is expressed by W. Harrelson (*Interpreting the Old Testament* [New York: Holt Reinhart and Winston, 1964] 215), who maintains that "Jehu was no faithful servant of Yahweh, nor is he portrayed as one."

[2] For a discussion of the theoretical principles that underlie the interpretation of texts, see E. D. Hirsch, *Validity in Interpretation* (New Haven: Yale University, 1967).

[3] A desperate attempt to come to terms with these contradictory elements is found in J. Ellul, *The Politics of God & the Politics of Man* (Grand Rapids: Eerdmans, 1972).

classical Hebrew narrative.[4] A significant portion of our discussion will therefore be devoted to an appreciation of the artistic techniques that the author employed to convey his message effectively.

Our attempt both to clarify and to appreciate 2 Kings 9–11 will utilize a broad range of methodological procedures. Following the introduction, the first chapter will be dedicated to source-critical matters where we shall attempt to define the limits of the original composition by separating primary and secondary material. In the second chapter, the original narrative recovered in chapter one will be subjected to a form-critical analysis in which we shall endeavor to determine its structure, intention, genre and setting. The third chapter will offer a detailed analysis of this primary material, with special consideration being given to textual and grammatical matters and to the artistic techniques of character portrayal and plot development. This close reading of this material will be offered in order to substantiate the findings of chapter three. The fourth chapter will return to the secondary material isolated in chapter two where we shall explore the identity of the redactors responsible for these expansions. An effort will be made to grasp the significance of their attempts to make earlier traditions applicable to the needs of their own day.

[4] H. Gunkel, ("Die Revolution des Jehu," *Deutsche Rundschau* 40 [1913] 289-308) saw 2 Kings 9–10 as an example of "the highly developed art of Hebrew narration" (289), and his praise has been repeated by several commentators. For example, J. Skinner (*Kings* [NCB; Sack, 1904] 230) writes that this narrative ". . . arises at times to a height of descriptive power which is unsurpassed in the pages of the O.T."

I

THE COMPOSITION OF 2 KINGS 9–11

One of the most significant contributions of the nineteenth century source critics was their discovery that the Hebrew Bible's compositional complexity reflects the historical processes that brought it to its final form. Critical scholarship now recognizes that both the Tetrateuch and the Deuteronomistic (Dtr) History are multi-layered documents that have been subjected to one or more redactional revisions.[1] The complicated nature of this literature obligates the interpreter of a portion of these larger composite works to give vigilant consideration to matters of composition. In this chapter, we shall explore the literary composition of 2 Kings 9–11, addressing the three major concerns that have previously commanded scholarly consideration: the literary relationship of the pre-Dtr material contained in these chapters to other pre-Dtr sources found elsewhere in Kings; the relationship between 2 Kings 9–10 and 2 Kings 11; and the boundaries of the original narrative as opposed to later textual accretions.

A. *The Original Literary Context of 2 Kings 9–11*

Three main views have been taken with regard to the literary relationship of 2 Kings 9–10 to another pre-Dtr source. Some maintain that the original pre-Dtr portions of this material belong to a literary stratum that centers on Elisha. O. Eissfeldt writes:

Evidently the attempt has been made twice to group around an eminent personage the tremendous events which shook Israel about the middle of the ninth century B.C., namely the prophetic revolutionary movement directed against the dynasty of Ahab because of its favoring of a foreign cult, and the Aramean wars which pressed so terribly upon Israel. In one of these attempts Elijah stood in the centre, with Elisha as one of his instruments; in the other it was Elisha

[1] For a summary of Noth's foundational study of the Dtr History and of subsequent critical discussion, see S. L. McKenzie, *The Chronicler's Use of the Deuteronomistic History* (HSM 33; Atlanta: Scholars, 1985) 1–15.

himself. The first found expression in I xvii, I-xix, 18; the second in II viii, 7–15 + ix-x(xi).[2]

I. Benzinger also links material in 2 Kings 9–10 to a larger literary complex, but he differs from Eissfeldt in that he assigns only 9:1–13 to what he labels *"Die Elisageschichten"*:

> The stories narrated in the section in 2 Kings 2–8 are doubtlessly indicated as related in content in that they all deal with Elisha as the principal character. Closer examination shows that the redactor did not create these accounts from living tradition, but that he had written material before him. . . . Furthermore, the account of Elisha's death and of the miraculous powers of his bones (13:4–21) and the account of the anointing of Jehu (9:1–13) belong here; . . . .[3]

Other endeavors have been made to relate these chapters to a larger literary complex that is not reconstructed on the basis of a principal focus on the figure of Elisha. Based on similarities of vocabulary, style, and perspective, J. Wellhausen proposed that 2 Kings 9–10 was originally a portion of a literary source that he found in 1 Kgs 20, 22; 3:4–27; 6:24–7:20; 9:1–10:27.[4] M. Noth likewise rejects the attempt to relate this material to a literary strand that places Elisha at the center. He differs from Wellhausen, however, in that he assigns these chapters to a pre-Dtr stratum that centered on the interaction between the prophets and the kings of Israel:

> There are grounds for believing that the story of the anointing of Jehu by one of Elisha's "prophetic disciples" and of the accession of Jehu to the kingship (2 Kings 9:1–10:27) is not from the cycle of stories about Elijah and Elisha, since here Elisha is very much in the background, and that instead, the stories of the prophetic interventions in the succession of Israelite kings and dynasties formed a cycle of their own. In that case, 1 Kings *11, *12, *14 and 1 Kings (20) 22 and 2 Kings 9–10 would have belonged to this cycle; but it cannot be proved since these sections are not specifically linked with each other and they have in common only the subject and the idea of the word of the prophet and its effect.[5]

A bolder synthesis has been undertaken by some who connect 2 Kings 9–10 to the Elohistic source.[6] R. Kittel writes, "Our passage constitutes the

---

[2] O. Eissfeldt, *The Old Testament. An Introduction* (New York: Harper & Row, 1965) 292. See also his "Die Komposition von I Reg 16:29 – II Reg 13:25," in *Das Ferne und Nahe Wort* (ed. Fritz Maass; Berlin: Töpelmann, 1967) 49-58.

[3] I. Benzinger, *Die Bücher der Könige* (KHC; Leipzig: Mohr [Siebeck], 1899) 129. G. Fohrer (*Introduction to the Old Testament* [Nashville: Abingdon, 1968] 234) similarly regards 9:1–10 as a separate Elisha tradition that has been fused with Jehu narrative.

[4] J. Wellhausen, *Die Composition des Hexateuchs und der historischen Bücher des Alten Testaments* (4th ed.; Berlin: Reimer, 1963) 285-87.

[5] M. Noth, *The Deuteronomistic History* (JSOTSup 15; Sheffield: JSOT, 1981) 69.

[6] G. Hölscher, *Geschichtsschreibung in Israel. Untersuchungen zum Jahvisten und*

continuation and the conclusion of that Ephraimite account (E) that informs us of King Ahab's success and objective, and that here also tells of the ruin of his dynasty."[7]

Against these attempts to relate 2 Kings 9-10 to a pre-Dtr literary stratum, many scholars regard these chapters as an independent unit of tradition.[8] Several arguments have been put forward to question the views that consider 2 Kings 9-10 to be a part of a larger pre-Dtr literary stratum. Benzinger's attempt to separate 9:1-13 from what follows, and to then relate this episode to the "Elisha stories" has been convincingly refuted by Kittel and A. Šanda. The latter writes:

> It [i.e. 9:1-13] constitutes an integrated component of ch. 9. Beginning from 9:1, the account (apart from the additions of the redactor) continues smoothly through v. 13. V. 15b attaches directly to 13. The assembled commanders in v. 13 are presupposed in v. 15b, and their enthusiasm in v. 13 is explained only on the basis of what precedes.[9]

Wellhausen's suggestion, that 2 Kings 9-10 originally was a part of a literary source found in 1 Kgs 20, 22; 3:4-27; 6:24-7:20; 9:1-10:27, has also evoked criticism. Šanda contends that while it is true that 1 Kings 20, 22 and 2 Kings 9-10 show a remarkable objectivity, the latter differs from the former in its strong Yahwistic bias.[10] Šanda therefore concludes that the two texts come from different authors. Similarly, Benzinger points out that in the two texts, differing attitudes toward Ahab prevail:

Elohisten (Lund: Gleerup, 1952) 173-77. D. N. Freedman, "Pentateuch," *IDB* 3. 711-27, esp. p. 715.

[7] R. Kittel, *Die Bücher der Könige* (KHAT I/5; Göttingen: Vandenhoeck & Ruprecht, 1900) 228.

[8] Benzinger (only the *Jehugeschichte* in 9:14ff) 147-48; J. Skinner, 27-28; A. Šanda, *Die Bücher der Könige. Das Zweite Buch der Könige,* EHAT (Aschendorffsche Verlagsbuchhandlung, 1911) 122-23; H. Gunkel, 209; H. Gressmann, *Die älteste Geschichtsschreibung und Prophetie Israels* (SAT; 2nd ed; Göttingen: Vandenhoeck & Ruprecht, 1921) 310-12; A. Jepsen, *Nabi. Soziologische Studien zur alttestamentlichen Literatur und Religionsgeschichte* (München: C. H. Beck'sche Verlagsbuchhandlung, 1934); P. Ellis, "1-2 Kings," *JBC* #10.56. J. A. Montgomery, *A Critical and Exegetical Commentary on the Book of Kings* (ed. H. S. Gehman; ICC; Edinburgh: T. & T. Clark, 1951) 399. S. Olyan ("*Haššālôm*: Some Literary Considerations of 2 Kgs 9," *CBQ* 46 [1984] 652-68) stands alone in seeing 2 Kings 9 as a self-contained unit of tradition, distinct from the two subsquent chapters. Unfortuantely, he does not discuss those references in chapters 10 (10:4, 9) and 11 (11:1) that refer back to events described in chapter 9.

[9] Šanda, 121. In his *Jahwist und Elohist in den Königsbüchern* (BWANT NF 2; Berlin: Kohlhammer, 1921) 57-59, Benzinger abandons this view and comes to the conclusion that 8:28-29, 9:1-13, 15bff. is to be attributed to the Jahwist and that 9:14-15a is to be assigned to the Elohist.

[10] Šanda (122) sees this bias reflected in the prophetic designation of Jehu, the repeated allusions to Elijah's prophecies, and in the presentation of the destruction of the temple of Baal.

. . . it is from the start highly unlikely that one and the same narrator, who recounted the story of Ahab with such warmth and affection for his hero, is now here supposed to have presented with a certain satisfaction the destruction of the house of Ahab as the righteous judgment of God for Ahab's wickedness.[11]

The acceptance of these criticisms to a certain degree depends upon how the limits of the original narrative are defined. As our subsequent analysis will argue, both the prophetic viewpoint reflected in the citations of Elijah's prophecies and the strongly negative attitude toward the house of Ahab are Dtr additions. But since a negative evaluation of the Omride regime is still perceptible even when the Dtr additions are removed, Benzinger's criticism remains valid. It is not likely, therefore, that 2 Kgs 9-10 can be linked convincingly to a pre-Dtr literary stratum.

As with chapters 2 Kings 9-10, endeavors have been made to relate 2 Kings 11 to a larger literary stratum. Wellhausen wanted to link 2 Kgs 11:1-12, 18b-20 to a *Tempelgeschichte* that also included 2 Kings 12, 2 Kgs 16:10ff and 2 Kings 22.[12] But Kittel and J. Gray point out that these texts do not reflect a common "Priestly" viewpoint.[13] Additional considerations make Wellhausen's view difficult to maintain. First of all, it presupposes the correctness of B. Stade's division of 2 Kings 11 into two sources.[14] But as we shall see below, this position is open to serious doubt. Second, Kittel correctly observes that in 2 Kings 11, the temple is merely the setting of the action, not its focus. In his view, Wellhausen confuses a thematic redactional link with the contents of the source material. As an alternative, he and others ascribe 2 Kings 11 to the "History of the Kings of Judah."[15] Third, as we shall contend, 2 Kings 11 contains many implicit and explicit connections with 2 Kings 9-10, strongly suggesting that together these three chapters are the original literary unit.

B. The Relationship of 2 Kings 9-10 and 2 Kings 11

Although conceding that 2 Kgs 11:1-20 ostensibly continues the story presented in the two preceding chapters, several scholars maintain that the two sections come from different sources. In their view, chapters 9-10 represent northern traditions while chapter 11 is thought to be of southern origin.[16] The "apparent" continuity between chapters 9-11 and chapter 11

---

[11] Benzinger, *Könige,* 148-49.

[12] F. Bleek and J. Wellhausen, *Einleitung in das Alte Testament* (4th ed.; Berlin: Reimer, 1878) 115-16.

[13] J. Gray, *I & II Kings: A Commentary,* (OTL; Philadelphia: Westminister, 1977) 568.

[14] B. Stade, "Anmerkungen zu 2 Kö. 10-14," *ZAW* 5 (1885) 275-97.

[15] Kittel, 243-44; Skinner, 29, 336.

[16] Kittel, 243; Eissfeldt, "Die Bücher des Könige," (*HSAT*; Tübingen: Mohr [Siebeck], 1922) 559; W. Rudolph, "Die Einheitlichkeit der Erzählung vom Sturz der Atalja (2 Kön 11),"

must then be explained. Eissfeldt accounts for it with a conjecture:

> The connection of 11:1 to what precedes is to be explained by the view that chapter 11 is an extract from a larger account which also reported the information in chapters 9–10, especially that of the death of Ahaziah.[17]

This position has been criticized by G. Hölscher[18] and especially by H. Hoffmann.[19] Hoffmann accurately observes that the events described in chapter 11 clearly presuppose those of chapters 9–10, and that Athaliah's attempt to destroy the royal offspring of Judah was stimulated by Jehu's coup. Moreover, as evidence of the unity of the three chapters, K. Fricke points out that the theme of the destruction of the house of Ahab developed in 2 Kings 9–10 continues into 2 Kings 11. Two Omrides, Athaliah and Jehoram, are removed from power.[20] Finally, not only do the parallel literary structures of chapters 9–10 and chapter 11 provide evidence of common authorship,[21] but also one can perceive a calculated attempt to contrast the characteristics of the northern and southern coups.[22] Thus, the attempt to deny the ostensive continuity of 2 Kings 9–11 is not justified.

C. Secondary Material[23]

All commentators agree that 2 Kings 9–11 has undergone redactional revision. Yet there are significant differences concerning precisely which material is to be ascribed to the original narrative. In the following, we shall

---

in *Festschrift für Alfred Bertholet*, eds. W. Baumgartner, O. Eissfeldt, K. Elliger, L. Rost (Tübingen: Mohr [Siebeck], 1950) 473; Montgomery, 417–18; C. Levin, *Der Sturz der Königin Atalja. Ein Kapitel zur Geschichte Judas im 9. Jahrhundert. v. Chr.* (Stuttgart: Katholisches Bibelwerk, 1982) 79–82. Levin also asserts that a greater use of dialogue and a higher artistic style in the Jehu narrative distinguish it from chapter 11.

[17] Eissfeldt, *Könige*, 559. In his *Introduction*, Eissfeldt (295) concedes that one of the strands in chapter 11 may continue the preceding chapters.

[18] G. Hölscher "Das Buch der Könige, seine Quellen und seine Redaktion," in *Eucharisterion* (FRLANT 36; ed. Hans Schmidt; Göttingen: Vandenhoeck & Ruprecht, 1923) 158–213, esp. pp. 186–87.

[19] H. Hoffmann, *Reform und Reformen: Untersuchungen zu einen Grundthema der deuteronomistischen Geschichtsschreibung* (ATANT 66; Zurich: Theologischer Verlag, 1980) 104–6.

[20] K. Fricke, *Das Zweite Buch von der Königen* (BAT 12/11; Stuttgart: Calwer, 1972) 144.

[21] Levin's observations about the greater use of dialogue and about the distinctive dramatic style expressed in the Jehu account are correct, but these differences can be explained in terms of the intention of the account. As will be discussed below, the author sought to develop a critical presentation of Jehu and his coup. One need not take this as an indication of two original narratives.

[22] See chapter II for a discussion of the structure of the original narrative.

[23] Source-critical findings are represented with various typefaces in the translation given in the "Conclusions" section of this chapter.

examine those passages commonly thought to reflect alterations of the original work.[24]

1. 2 Kgs 9:7–10a

Other than Noth, who regards v 7 as a part of the original account, virtually every commentator agrees that these verses expand the original account.[25] Although some are not explicit concerning the tradition to which the redactor belonged,[26] others connect him with the Dtr tradition.[27]

---

[24] Source criticism, particularly as it was practiced by some with regard to the analysis of Pentateuchal sources, has been rightly criticized as being artificial and too refined to command conviction. However, apart from those who subscribe to certain hermeneutical presuppositions such as those who align themselves with the "New Literary Criticism," it seems that most scholars regard the tendency of earlier source critics to multiply the number of Pentateuchal sources to be an abuse of a valid interpretive method, and continue to maintain the position that an adequate exegetical approach must take into account the fact that much of the Hebrew Bible has been subjected to redactional revision. The charge that a given analysis is "artifical" or "too refined" should take into consideration the Chronicler's handling of 2 Kings 9–11. As our analysis will show, the types of revisions that we see in the earlier redactions of these chapters are similiar in character to those that we find that the Chronicler has made. In addition to the evidence provided by the Chronicler, studies of the literary evolution of the Gilgamesh Epic have shown that Mesopotamian scribes engaged in the same sort of redactional activities that source critics have detected through their analyses of OT narratives. On the literary evolution of the Gilgamesh Epic, see S. N. Kramer, "The Epic of Gilgamesh and its Sumerian Sources, a Study in Literary Evolution," *JAOS* 64 (1944) 7–23, and especially J. H. Tigay, *The Evolution of the Gilgamesh Epic* (Philadelphia: University of Pennsylvania, 1982). Tigay has also defended the methods of source criticism in his "An Empirical Basis for the Documentary Hypothesis," *JBL* 94 (1975) 329–42.

[25] Noth's position is adopted by I. Plein, "Erwägungen zur Überlieferung von I Reg 11, 26–14, 20," *ZAW* 78 (1966) 8–24, esp. p. 15.

[26] Wellhausen, 288; Hölscher, *Geschichtsschreibung*, 145, 398; Montgomery, 400; Skinner, 322; Gunkel, 293–94; Šanda, 94, 121; Gressmann, 313; W. Dietrich, *Prophetie und Geschichte: Eine redaktionsgeschichtliche Untersuchung zum deuteronomistischen Geschichtswerk* (FRLANT 108; Göttingen: Vandenhoeck & Ruprecht, 1972) 47–48; R. de Vaux, *Les Livres des Rois* (JB; Paris: Cerf, 1958) 164; A. Jepsen, *Die Quellen des Königsbuches* (Halle: Niemeyer, 1956) 74.

[27] Benzinger, *Könige*, 150; Eissfeldt, *Könige*, 555; Kittel, 229; N. Snaith, "The First and Second Book of Kings: Introduction and Exegesis" *IB* 3 (1954) 3–338, esp. p. 232; Gray, 539; M. Weinfeld, *Deuteronomy and the Deuteronomic School* (Oxford: Clarendon, 1972) 20; H. Schmitt, *Elisa: Traditionsgeschichtliche Untersuchungen zur vorklassischen nordisraelitischen Prophetie* (Gütersloh: Gerd Mohn, 1972) 20–21; O. Steck, *Überlieferung und Zeitgeschichte in den Elia-Erzählungen* (WMANT 26; Neukirchener-Vluyn, 1968) 38–39; R. Bohlen, *Der Fall Nabot: Form, Hintergrund und Werdegang einer alttestamentlichen Erzählung (I Kön 21)*, TTS 35 (Trier: Paulinus, 1978), 291–95; Hoffmann, 98; S. Timm, *Die Dynastie Omri. Quellen und Untersuchungen zur Geschichte Israels im 9. Jahrhundert vor Christus* (Göttingen: Vandenhoeck & Ruprecht, 1982) 137; M. Rehm, *Das zweite Buch der Könige* (Würzburg: Echter, 1982) 98; Olyan, 655–66. E. Würthwein (*Die Bücher der Könige* [ATD; Göttingen:

Considerable evidence supports this virtual consensus. It is clear that the verses interrupt the flow of the narrative; removing them reestablishes the intended correlation between the commission given in vv 1–3 and its execution in vv 4–6, *10b*. In vv 1–3, Elisha commissions his disciple to search out Jehu in Ramoth-Gilead and to anoint him as king while delivering the brief message, "Thus says Yahweh, 'I have anointed you king over Israel.'" The disciple is then to flee without delay. Verses 4–6 describe the disciple's meticulous execution of his master's first two directives. But rather than reporting that he fled immediately as instructed, the present text states that the disciple supplemented his master's instructions by charging Jehu to exterminate the whole house of Ahab (vv 7–10a). It is not until v 10b that we read that the disciple carried out Elisha's final exhortation to flee the scene immediately.

2 Kgs 9:12 provides additional support. When Jehu is questioned by his fellow officers about the visit from the "madman," Jehu repeats only the brief message found in verses 3 and 6, making no reference to the contents of vv 7–10a. Although this observation is not conclusive in itself, the lack of a reference to vv 7–10a offers an additional indication of the secondary nature of these verses.

Both the form and the content of these verses betray their Dtr origin. Weinfeld calls the form of this section a Dtr "prophetic oracle," and cites other examples of this distinctively Dtr method of expanding an underlying source (1 Kgs 14:7–10, 16:1–4, 21:21–24 and Jer 19:3–9).[28] Also, the Dtr content of this material is reflected in its distinctive vocabulary.[29] Additional confirmation is found in the Dtr additions in 10:11, 10:17b and 10:31. Together with vv 7–10a, they portray Jehu as obediently executing the prophetic commission that resulted in Yahweh's reward of dynastic longevity.

Some doubts persists, however, about v 10, in which Jezebel's ghastly fate is predicted. When other Dtr passages are examined, we find that apart from 1 Kgs 16:31, the mention of Jezebel within these passages appears to be secondary. In the Dtr oracle directed against the house of Ahab (1 Kgs 21:20b–24), an oracle directed specifically at Jezebel begins with its own messsenger formula, and severs the connection between vv 22 and 24. Verses 25–26 of the same chapter, which are commonly regarded as an addition,[30] emphasize that it was Jezebel who incited Ahab's wickedness. Again, in 2 Kgs 9:36 the fulfillment of the prophecy given in 1 Kgs 21:23 is noted, and

Vandenhoeck & Ruprecht, 1984] 325) thinks that the mention of Jezebel in vv 7 and 10 are post-Dtr.

[28] Weinfeld, 15.

[29] Bohlen, 291–95; Schmitt, 20–21; Weinfeld, 351–52.

[30] Benzinger, *Könige*, 116; Skinner, 260; Gray, 443; Snaith, 177; Würthwein, 246.

this too appears to be an insertion since it breaks the connection between v 36a1 and v 37.[31] It appears that the same post-Dtr redactor who introduced the prophecy against Jezebel in 1 Kgs 21:23 also included the fulfillment notice in 2 Kgs 9:36.

All of this indicates that 2 Kgs 9:10 represents the activity of this post-Dtr redactor who had a special interest in insisting that Jezebel was punished for her heinous crimes. But what about the mention of Jezebel in 9:7? Here the source-critical problem is tied to a text-critical decision. While the MT reads *wĕ'ābad,* the LXX presupposes *ûmiyyad.* Of the two, the MT offers a reading that reflects a certain banality due to its use of an intransitive form[32] and to its repetitive content. On the other hand, the LXX reading, which adds to the syntactical complexity of the clause, seems less likely to be the adjustment of a copyist.[33]

The acceptance of the LXX reading allows an explanation of the presence of a phrase in v 7 that has been regarded as a gloss.[34] The phrase, "and the blood of all the servants of Yahweh," appears to expand upon the preceding, "the blood of my servants the prophets." By reading with the LXX, the expansion appears to be an attempt to make reference to Jezebel's persecutions of the non-prophetic devotees of Yahweh. In that case, the original Dtr text would have concerned only crimes committed against the prophets by the house of Ahab: "And I will avenge the blood of my servants the prophets . . . [which was shed] at the hand of the whole house of Ahab." But a later redactor, who was especially interested in specifying Jezebel's crimes against non-prophetic followers of Yahweh, expanded the text with the addition, "and the blood of all the servants of Yahweh [which was shed] by the hand of Jezebel." It seems then, some post-Dtr redactor made several minor additions (1 Kgs 21:23, 25-26; 2 Kgs 9:7*, 10, 36*) in order to single out Jezebel from among the members of Ahab's house as a special object of Yahweh's wrath, and to show that this wicked woman was indeed punished for her crimes.

2. 2 Kgs 9:14-15a

Contrasting the consensus about 9:7-10a, the source-critical assessments of 9:14-15a are complex and varied. To clarify the various positions, the following discussion will deal first with those who assign all of 9:14-15a

---

[31] See the discussion below on 9:36-37.

[32] The S and V compensate for this by reading the first person hiphil form, *wĕ'ôbîd.*

[33] So also Schmitt, 226.

[34] Benzinger, *Könige* (150) and Schmitt (225-26) note the redundancy of the phrase following the preceding, *dĕmê 'ăbāday hannĕbî'îm,* and switch to a third person reference to Yahweh (*'ăbdê yhwh*).

to the same source, and then treat those who ascribe v 14a to a different source than 14b–15a.

Benzinger argues that these verses were the original introduction to the *Jehugeschichte*, a source which he distinguishes from the preceding account in vv 1–13.[35] But the majority view regards these verses as secondary within their present context. Disagreement emerges when the attempt is made to assign them to their original sources. Some think that these verses originally preceded 9:1 where they served as an introduction, but that they were subsequently interpolated to their present position.[36] Others see them as an extract from official annals,[37] or as a late addition.[38] As for those who distinguish v 14a from the following, Gray thinks v 14a constitutes the concluding verse of the "prophetic source" consisting of 9:1–14a, while Kittel regards v 14a as a redactional interpolation. Steck also thinks v 14a has been added, but goes beyond Kittel in attributing it either directly or indirectly to the Dtr redactor.[39]

As for vv 14b–15a, Steck, Kittel and Gray agree in assigning vv 14b–15a to a different source than v 14a, but differ in identifying their source. Steck argues that these verses are properly positioned and that they belong to the original account.[40] Kittel and Gray, on the other hand, think that they were transposed from an earlier position. Gray accounts for the positioning of these verses as follows:

> This fragment, itself perhaps a précis, served no doubt as the original introduction to the reign of Jehu. The editor adapted it at 8:28f. in his introduction of Ahaziah of Judah, who was associated with the death of Joram, and in consequence of its appearance at that point it was omitted before the account of the call of Jehu at the beginning of ch. 9. It was reintroduced at this point at vv. 14b–15a to account for the absence of Joram when Jehu was anointed and acclaimed king at Ramoth Gilead.[41]

The complexity of the issues and the diversity of opinions concerning these verses caution us against thinking we can resolve this issue with certainty. Yet it seems likely that vv 14–15a have been inserted into the original account, since v 15b follows directly from v 13. As Kittel observed, this is

---

[35] Benzinger, *Könige*, 149.

[36] Gunkel, 290; Gressmann, 310; Šanda, 94, 121; Montgomery, 400.

[37] Schmitt, 22–23; M. Sekine, "Literatursoziologische Beobachtungen zu den Elisaerzählungen," *AJBI* 1 (1975) 39–62, esp. p. 55; Jepsen, 72; Fricke, 122–23.

[38] Rehm, 99.

[39] Steck, 32. Jepsen's view (*Quelle*, 33) is similar except he thinks that all of v 14 is an extract from a synchronistic Chronicle.

[40] Steck, 32. Also Plein, 15; Timm, 138.

[41] Gray, 543.

indicated by Jehu's reference in v 15b to the supportive attitude of his fellow officers previously described in v 13. Furthermore, vv 14–15a are in fact editorial comments, and their present position disrupts the interaction between Jehu and his comrades.

While it is reasonably clear that vv 14–15a have been inserted into the text, it is difficult to assign v 14a and vv 14b–15a to their original source or sources. It seems that v 14a should probably be attributed to the Dtr redactor since he often mentions the various conspiracies (*qešer*) that plagued the Northern Kingdom.[42] Regarding vv 14b–15a, Gray's conclusion is attractive since it explains the relationship of 9:14b–15a to 8:28–29, and can account for its present position. Additional considerations support this position. It should be observed that 9:1–13 presupposes the situation described in these verses since Elisha knows that Jehu can be found at Ramoth-Gilead. Furthermore, a corresponding literary arrangement of 2 Kings 9–10 and 2 Kings 11 suggests that, like its counterpart in 11:1–3, 9:14b–15a originally served as a description of the setting from which a coup emerged.[43] Moreover, placing 9:14b–15a at the beginning of the story provides the reader with an explanation for Elisha's actions: Jehoram's separation from his troops provided Elisha with an opportune moment to instigate a rebellion. And finally, the narrative found in 1 Kgs 20:1–34 contains introductory verses that are similar in style and content to 2 Kgs 9:14b–15a:

> Now Ben-Hadad king of Aram mustered his entire army. Accompanied by thirty-two kings with their horses and chariots, he went up and besieged Samaria and attacked it.[44]

These considerations suggest that v 14a is a Dtr addition and that vv 14b–15a represent the original introduction. Among the alternatives, this view best accounts for the relevant factors.

3. 2 Kgs 9:25–26

A source-critical assessment of these verses has also generated several different conclusions. Some think these verses belong to the original narrative,[45] while others regard either all or a part of them as secondary. C. F. Whitley maintains that v 25b is ". . . obviously an interpolation to connect this incident with the circumstances of Ahab's death as told in 1 Kgs."[46] S.

---

[42] 1 Kgs 16:9; 16:20; 2 Kgs 12:20; 14:19; 15:10; 15:15; 15:30; 17:4; 21:23.

[43] A full discussion of the structure of the narrative is given below.

[44] 1 Kgs 20:1.

[45] Hölscher, *Geschichtsschreibung*, 145; Montgomery, 402; Noth, 72; Dietrich, 50; Olyan, 658–59.

[46] C. F. Whitley, "The Deuteronomic Presentation of the House of Omri," *VT* 2 (1952)

Timm argues that only v 25a is original, thereby attributing vv 25b–26 to a redactor.[47] But H. Schmitt and R. Bohlen regard all of vv 25–26 as an addition.[48]

The following considerations support the latter alternative. First of all, Bohlen points out that these verses disrupt the connection between v 24 and v 27. Verse 27 states, "When Ahaziah the king of Judah saw what had happened, he fled . . ." What did Ahaziah see that moved him southward in such haste? The scene described in v 24 is the natural antecedent. Second, it is unlikely that the original narrative, concerned as it is with picturing the rapid pace and secrecy of Jehu's assault against the ruling dynasty, would have included the scene described in vv 25–26. Here Jehu pauses to give instructions about the treatment that Jehoram's corpse is to receive even as Ahaziah, a certain threat to success of his coup, flees southward to safety. Third, as Schmitt notes, these verses reflect an "apologetic" tendency in that they relate Jehu's actions to prophetic pronouncements.[49] As the discussion of 10:10 will show, the portrayal of Jehu as one who consciously related his own acts of violence against the house of Ahab to prophetic oracles of judgment constitutes the central concern of the Dtr redactor.

Yet concluding that vv 25–26 have been inserted into the text does not exhaust the source-critical issues surrounding them. It is acknowledged that v 26a contains details that differ from 1 Kings 21, and this has led Steck, Schmitt, and Bohlen to conclude that it is an early prophetic oracle that has been inserted here by the Dtr redactor. The redactor's contributions are found in vv 21b, 25 and 26b, and serve as the explanatory framework by which an older oracle found in v 26a was incorporated into the narrative.[50] By means of this framework, the oracle is applied to a later situation in which Jehoram, rather than Ahab, is made the object of Yahweh's judgment.[51] The redactor's purpose was to portray Jehu favorably, and to promote the view that Yahweh's oracle against the house of Ahab was realized through Jehu's murdering Jehoram.

137–52, esp. p. 149. So also J. M. Miller, "The Fall of the House of Ahab," *VT* 17 (1967) 307–24, esp. p. 308.

[47] Timm, 141.

[48] Schmitt, 26–27; Bohlen, 282–84.

[49] Schmitt (24–27) attributes vv 9:21b, 25–26, 10:19b, 23 to what he calls an "apologetische Bearbeitung," a redactional layer that is regarded by him as independent of the Dtr redactor's contributions. But with Timm (139–40), I do not find the tendency of these verses to be significantly distinctive to justify the postulation of a separate redactional layer.

[50] The mention of "Bidkar" need not indicate that the verse cannot be ascribe to the Dtr redactor. In 2 Kgs 11:18b it is clear that the Dtr redactor makes a reference to another otherwise unknown person, the priest Mattan.

[51] This framework also explicitly identifies the "property" mentioned in the original account as "the property of Naboth the Jezreelite."

4. 2 Kgs 9:28-29

The only question requiring a decision is whether v 28 along with v 29 should be regarded as an addition. The majority of scholars maintains v 28 as original,[52] but the opinion that v 28 is an addition also has several adherents.[53] What is striking about v 28 is that it bears a close resemblance to the account of Josiah's death and burial, who also died at Megiddo and was also subsequently transferred in a chariot by his servants back to Jerusalem for the royal burial.[54] This suggests that both vv 27bβ and 28 depend upon the account of Josiah's death, marking them as post-Dtr additions.[55] In that case, the original text placed Ahaziah's death at the ascent of Gur.[56] It appears that to make the circumstances of Ahaziah's death and burial conform to Josiah's, the redactor exploited the ambiguity of the word nākâ, and took it to mean that Ahaziah did not die when he was "struck," but was only wounded at Ibleam, who then somehow managed to elude Jehu's men and to reach Megiddo where he died.

5. 2 Kgs 9:36-37

An earlier view saw either a portion or all of vv 36–37 as part of the original narrative,[57] but it has given way to the opinion that both verses should be regarded as additions.[58] The fulfillment statement in v 36 is clearly

---

[52] Kittel, 233; Skinner, 326; B. Stade and F. Schwally, *The Book of Kings* (Leipzig: Hinrichs'sche Buchhandlung, 1904), 41; Šanda, 100; Eissfeldt, *Könige*, 555; Jepsen, 74; de Vaux, 167; Montgomery, 400; Hölscher, *Geschichtsschreibung*, 398; Snaith, 236; Gray, 549; Fricke, 126; Hoffmann, 104–6; Timm, 138–39; Rehm, 100.

[53] Wellhausen, 288; Gunkel, 300; Gressmann, 313; Schmitt, 24; Sekine, 55; Würthwein, 332; Olyan, 656.

[54] 2 Kgs 23:30.

[55] Because of the paucity of evidence, it is not my intention to ascribe all of the post-Dtr additions to Dtr². It does seem likely, however, that a Josianic edition of the Dtr History was updated by an exilic redactor. Fresh arguments supporting this older view are found in F. M. Cross, "The Themes of the book of Kings and the Structure of the Deuteronomistic History," in *Canaanite Myth and Hebrew Epic* (Cambridge: Harvard University 1973) 274–89; R. D. Nelson, *The Double Redaction of the Deuteronomistic History* (JSOTSup 18; Sheffield: JSOT, 1981); R. D. Friedman, *The Exile and Biblical Narrative: The Formation of Deuteronomistic and Priestly Works* (HSM 22; Chico: Scholars, 1981) 1–43.

[56] Commentators have puzzled over why Ahaziah turned northwest to travel to Megiddo. The conjectures that Jehu hoped to gain the protection of the governor (Kittel, 233), or of the garrisons stationed there (Gray, 548) are not persuasive since any protection that Megiddo offered could have been received at Samaria.

[57] Kittel, 235; Skinner, 327–28; Eissfeldt, *Könige*, 555; Noth, 72; Montgomery, 399. Benzinger (*Könige*, 149, 152) thinks that only v 36b has been added while Stade/Schwally (41), Šanda, (121) and Hölscher, *Geschichtsschreibung*, (145, 398) view only v 37 as secondary.

[58] Wellhausen, 288; Gunkel, 301; Gressmann, 313; Steck, 37; Dietrich, 36–37; Weinfeld,

an addition since, as we noted above, it was added by the same post-Dtr redactor who inserted its corresponding prophecy in 1 Kgs 21:23. When it is removed, a coherent scene describing Jezebel's aborted burial remains. After Jehu brutally tramples Jezebel, he enters the palace and dines. He then summons some servants to bury her, explaining that although she is an "accursed woman," her royal status requires that she be buried. But the servants discover that her trampled body is so mangled that they are only able to identify the hands, feet, and skull of her corpse, making it impossible for them to carry out Jehu's instructions. When they report the situation to Jehu, he reverses himself, pronouncing that the mutilation of her corpse was justified, since nothing, not even a grave, should serve to keep alive the memory of Jezebel.[59]

Arguments for regarding v 37 as an addition are not convincing. They rest on the assumptions that v 37 presupposes v 36, that the mention of *ḥēleq yizrĕ'e'l* reflects a theological interest, and that the verses are similar to passages in Jeremiah.[60] But there is no reason to suppose that v 37 presupposes the fulfillment statement in v 36. Only the opening clauses ("And they returned and told him. And he said . . .") are required to produce a coherent text. As for the mention of "the vicinity of Jezreel," this phrase looks suspiciously like a gloss since it appears to be superfluous following *haśśādeh*.[61] Finally, similarities to Jeremiah's prediction of a judgment that will see numerous unburied corpses shows only that conventional curse formulae are used in both places, so that the similarities cannot be convincingly regarded as indicating literary dependence.[62] In addition, the point of the scene is to reveal Jehu's deep-seated hatred of Jezebel, which is precisely the point of the preceding scene. Only the fulfillment notice in v 36 should be attributed to a later redactor.

21; Schmitt, 21–22; Sekine, 55; Bohlen, 295–99; Hoffmann, 99; Timm, 137; Würthwein, 334–35; Olyan, 656.

[59] The conclusion that this scene in the original narrative ended with v 35 seems unjustified. Without Jehu's final pronouncement on the suitableness of Jezebel's fate, the scene would have a truncated appearance.

[60] Jer 8:2; 9:21; 16:4; 25:33.

[61] So also Schmitt, 230.

[62] Thus Dietrich (37–38) argues that a reader of the book of Jeremiah, who was connected with Dtr groups, associated the formula about "a corpse lying on the field like dung" with the account of the death of Jezebel, and therefore added v 37 to v 36. But the curse of receiving no burial is common to vassal treaties. For example, in Esharhaddon's Vassal Treaty (*ANET*, 534–41), we read, ". . . may the earth not receive your body for burial, may the bellies of dogs and pigs be your burial place. . . ."

6. 2 Kgs 10:1a

This half-verse has given pause to some careful readers since it repeats information given in v 6b.[63] That v 1a is the gloss and not v 6b rests on the consideration that Jehu's target was not the children of Ahab, but Jehoram's offspring, who are designated as "the children of the king."[64] The addition of v 1a is probably Dtr, since according to the programmatic Dtr passage (2 Kgs 9:7–9), Jehu is commanded to destroy the "house of Ahab." It seems that this redactor wished to make it explicit that Jehu's attack on Jehoram's sons was also an attack on Ahab's descendants.[65]

7. 2 Kgs 10:10–11

Although some take v 10 to belong to the original narrative,[66] most commentators ascribe it to the Dtr redactor on the basis of stylistic and ideological considerations.[67] Schmitt states, "The saying about the 'not-failing of the word of Yahweh concerning what he has promised' in v. 10 is typically Dtr."[68] Weinfeld also notes the historical and theological significance that the Dtr redactor assigned to the word of Yahweh:

> Every event of religio-national significance must occur as a result of the word of God which foreordained that event and to which historical reality must exactly conform, so that in the phraseology of the Deuteronomist 'nothing shall fall to the earth of the word of the Lord.' . . .[69]

Concerning v 11, stylistic considerations suggest that it should also be attributed to the Dtr redactor. Schmitt points out that ". . . like v. 17aβb, v. 11a declares 'he struck all who were left of the house of Ahab,' and the formula in v. 11b, 'until he left him without a survivor,' indicates a Dtr origin."[70] Also, the redactor's positive attitude toward Jehu over against the negative portrayal in the underlying narrative supports this conclusion. A positive depiction manifests itself here by presenting the usurper as an obedient servant of Yahweh, who faithfully executed the (Dtr) commision

---

[63] B. Stade, "Anmerkungen zu 2 Kö. 10–14," *ZAW* 5 (1885) 275; Eissfeldt, *Könige*, 557; Benzinger, *Könige*, 152, Gressmann, 308.

[64] Verses 6 and 7 mention the *bĕnê hammelek*.

[65] The same redactor seems also responsible for the presence of the unsyntactical mention of Ahab in v 1b noted by Montgomery (413) and Schmitt (230).

[66] Kittel, 237; Skinner, 329; Šanda, 107; Eissfeldt, *Könige,* 555; Noth (except for the mention of Elijah), 72.

[67] Wellhausen, 288; Gunkel, 308; Gressmann, 313; Hölscher, *Geschichtsschreibung,* 145, 398; Steck, 34; Gray, 538; Dietrich, 25; Schmitt, 22; Weinfeld, 22; Robinson, 95; Timm, 138; Würthwein, 337.

[68] Schmitt, 22. This linguistic evidence is also documented by Weinfeld, 350.

[69] Weinfeld, 22.

[70] Schmitt, 23. So also Sekine (55), Timm (135), and Würthwein (337).

given in vv 7–10a. Here we find a radical reinterpretation of the original account, in which Jehu is depicted as deceiving the people by disclaiming responsibility for the death of the seventy princes (v 9). But the Dtr redactor, who wished to relate Jehu's murders to Yahweh's judgment of the house of Ahab, added vv 10–11 in order to portray Jehu's actions as motivated by Jehu's desire to carry out Yahweh's decision to exterminate this wicked dynasty.

8. 2 Kgs 10:12–14

These verses have been regarded as original,[71] but Stade's influential article[72] has led many to conclude either that these verses are out of order[73] or that they are a fragment taken from another source.[74] The evidence indicates that these verses are indeed foreign to their present context. Stade observes that the form of the passage indicates the presence of an insertion because v 12 is overloaded with verbs: *wayyāqom wayyābō' wayyēlek*.[75] Taking the first verb as original, the story line again emerges in v 17: "And he arose . . . and came to Samaria." Contextual tensions created by vv 12–14 also betray the presence of an insertion. How is it that Jehu, while traveling from Jezreel to Samaria, would encounter the Judean party traveling from Jerusalem to Jezreel? If one accepts the unlikely conclusion that they were not coming from Jerusalem, but from Samaria, then this leaves unexplained the Judeans' ignorance of earth-shaking events that had taken place in Samaria at least one day before.[76]

While it is evident that these verses are secondary to their present context, the episode is characterized by a specificity lacking in passages composed by the Dtr redactor. This suggests that they were taken from another source and inserted here. But the final clause in v 14 may have come from the Dtr redactor since similar notices about the thoroughness of Jehu's violent acts are found in other Dtr passages.[77] Indeed, this clause reads as if it were tacked on,[78] and it conforms to the Dtr redactor's interest in

---

[71] Skinner, 330; Gunkel; Šanda, 110; Gressmann, 309; Hölscher, *Geschichtsschreibung*, 145; Plein, 15; Steck, 61; Schmitt, 28–29, 232; Würthwein (except for the last clause in v 14), 339.

[72] Stade, "Anmerkungen," 275–97.

[73] Montgomery, 400; de Vaux, 170; Gray, 556; Ellis, 201.

[74] Stade, 277; Benzinger, *Könige*, 149; Kittel, 227.

[75] See also C. Burney, *Notes on the Hebrew Text of the Book of Kings* (Oxford: Clarendon, 1903) 303.

[76] 2 Kgs 10:1–9 makes it clear that at least one day had transpired before Jehu's trip to Samaria since Jehu addresses the people the morning after the arrival of the heads of the Israelite princes.

[77] Vv 10:10, 10:17b.

[78] Cf. Levin, 80, n. 3.

picturing not only Jehu's commitment to exterminate the members of Ahab's house, but also Jehu's desire to execute all who were sympathetic to this reign. It is also striking that v 14b takes a very abrupt turn. Jehu specifically orders his men to take the Judean princes alive, and the text states that his men complied to this order. But then v 14b suddenly states that Jehu's men slaughtered them! Apparently, in the original source the reason for Jehu's desire to take the Judeans as prisoners was explained. But the Dtr redactor, intent on presenting Jehu as the obedient exterminator of the anyone connected with the house of Ahab, had Jehu's men kill the princes on the spot by adding v 14b.

Taking these considerations together, that vv 12-14 interrupt the progress of the account, that the material creates tensions within its present context, and that the insertion of the material serves the interests of the Dtr redactor, it appears that the Dtr redactor drew this material from another source and added v 14b to emphasize Jehu's thoroughness in eradicating all who were related to the hated house of Ahab.

9. 2 Kgs 10:15-16

For the most part, the conclusion adopted about vv 12-14 influence a source-critical assessment of vv 15-16.[79] It was noted above that vv 15-16, along with vv 12-14, disrupt the flow of the narrative. Besides this, Jehonadab does not play any role in the events that follow, indicating that this material is not well integrated into the content of the story. Jehonadab is indeed mentioned again in v 23, but this verse also betrays the same lack of integration and has therefore been regarded as an addition.[80] A clear indication that this episode stands in tension with its present literary context is the fact that it presupposes events that are nowhere reported. Jehu's dialogue with Jehonadab reveals that the two are not strangers, and that they had previously acted together in some common cause. Evidently, it is this unreported former alliance that would explain why Jehonadab comes *seeking out* Jehu. This implicit reference to an event that is not reported elsewhere provides a strong indication that we are here confronted with a fragment.[81]

---

[79] Those who take these verses as original include: Skinner, 330; Gunkel, 305; Hölscher, *Geschichtsschreibung*, 398; Kittel , 239; Eissfeldt, *Könige*, 555; Montgomery, 400. Those who regard them as an addition are: Stade, 276; Benzinger, *Könige*, 149; Jepsen, 74; Robinson, 99-100; Würthwein, 327. Those who see the passage as misplaced are: de Vaux, 170; Gray, 559; Ellis, 201.

[80] See below.

[82] A contradiction in the narrative's logic may provide another indication that these verses are foreign to their content. Stade rightly observes that a public demonstration of Jehu's

Although this episode was not authored by the Dtr historian, it was included because it served his editorial concerns. That Jehonadab and his followers were held in high esteem by Dtr circles is shown by Jeremiah 35, a chapter that is filled with Dtr phraseology.[82] This same admiration appears to have motivated the Dtr redactor's use of this fragment. By using an episode that portrays the Yahwistic zealot Jehonadab as supportive of Jehu's coup, the redactor sought to relate Jehu's political motives to the highest ideals of traditional Yahwism as embodied in Jehonadab, the venerable founder of the Rechabites.

10. 2 Kgs 10:17aβb

Although some retain this verse as original,[83] the prevailing opinion regards this verse as a Dtr addition.[84] The following reasons support the majority view. First, v 18 follows smoothly from v 17aα. Removing the secondary material in vv 12–16 and in v 17aβb allows the flow of the original account to reemerge: "Then he arose . . . and came to Samaria. . . . Then Jehu gathered all the people and said to them. . . ." Second, the language of this verse is clearly Dtr,[85] and third, the addition serves the Dtr redactor's primary concern: to present Jehu as obediently executing the (Dtr) commission given in 9:7–10. The Dtr additions note that Jehu first exterminated the members of the house of Ahab first in Jezreel (10:11), and then in Samaria (10:17aβb). These explicit Dtr notices emphasize Jehu's obedience and transform the original narrative's negative presentation of Jehu's exploits into a depiction of his dedication to Dtr ideals.

11. 2 Kgs 10:19b

It is not difficult to understand why several scholars regard this half-verse as a gloss.[86] Its editorial style distinguishes it from its context, and its content reflects an obvious apologetic intention.[87] Moreover, the clause,

---

solidarity with a Yahwistic zealot would certainly undermine Jehu's intended masquerade as a patron of Baal. Considering the consistency and realism of the original account, the departure from these traits here in vv 15–16 creates a problem.

[82] See Weinfeld, 320, 336–37, 350–54.

[83] Kittel, 237; Skinner, 332; Šanda, 121; Eissfeldt, *Könige*, 555; Jepsen, 74.

[84] Gunkel, 303; Gressmann, 309, 313; Hölscher, *Geschichtsschreibung*, 145, 398; Plein, 15; Steck, 40; Dietrich, 61–62; Schmitt, 22; Robinson, 98; Timm, 138; Würthwein, 327. Benzinger (*Könige*, 153) takes only v 17b as the addition and Noth (72) thinks that only the mention of Elijah is secondary.

[85] Schmitt, 22.

[86] Gunkel, 306; Gressmann, 309; Schmitt, 25; Sekine, 55; Timm, 139; Würthwein, 340.

[87] Gunkel (306) perceptively noted that this addition detracts from the dramatic tension of the episode: "A scrupulous reader added that he [Jehu] would only have done this out of

lema'an ha'ăbîd 'et-'ōbĕdē habbā'al, shows affinities with Dtr usage.[88] As in other Dtr passages, Jehu is favorably represented as the agent of Yahweh's wrath upon Ahab's dynasty which it had earned for its failure to obey Deuteronomic legislation.[89]

12. 2 Kgs 10:23

It was concluded previously that the Dtr redactor inserted 10:15–16 into its present position. Some who adopt this conclusion see only the mention of Jehonadab in v 23 as a gloss.[90] But Schmitt, following H. Gressmann, takes the whole verse as secondary since it manifests obvious apologetic purposes: to link Jehu to the religious commitments of the zealous Yahwist Jehonadab, and to portray Jehu's concern for "his fellow Yahwists" in the face of an imminent massacre.[91] Also, the statement that Jehu and his party "entered the temple of Baal" repeats information stated previously in v 21, thereby betraying a tension with the context.[92] Verse 23 is a Dtr addition intended to picture Jehu as a committed Yahwist who not only acted in cooperation with a leading Yahwist zealot, but also took care to preserve "his fellow Yahwists" from the violent death awaiting the worshipers of Baal. Here the redactor wished to make explicit that Jehu had not committed the crime of which Ahab's house was accused—the murder of the servants of Yahweh.[93]

13. 2 Kgs 10:25b–27

Hoffmann has argued that 10:25b–27 is an addition of the Dtr redactor who sought to present Jehu's massacre of the worshipers of Baal as a radical cult reform.[94] In support of this view, he observes that vv 18–25a constitute stylistically a detailed "Erzählung," parallelling 1 Kings 18, but that vv 25b–27a contain an "Aufzählung," that catalogues the actions taken to destroy the temple of Baal and its cultic personnel.[95] Linguistic evidence also supports this view.[96] Once again the Dtr redactor here depicts Jehu as a zealous promoter of Deuteronomic ideals.

deception, and by doing so destroyed the suspense of what follows."

[88] Weinfeld, 346.

[89] The Dtr redactor's portrayal will be more fully discussed in chapter IV.

[90] Stade, 277; Benzinger, Könige, 154; Šanda, 115; Würthwein, 340.

[91] Gressmann, 301; Schmitt, 25.

[92] The plural subject of wayyābō'û in v 21 refers to Jehu and the worshipers of Baal just as it does in v 24.

[93] See 2 Kgs 9:7.

[94] Hoffmann, 99–102.

[95] Ibid., 100. This addition is similar to the Dtr expansion in 2 Kgs 11:18a.

[96] Ibid., 101–2.

14. 2 Kgs 10:28–36

These verses, for the most part, are widely acknowledged to be of Dtr origin.[97] One source-critical question that needs to be addressed concerns vv 28–31: do we have here two Dtr conclusions (vv 28–29 and vv 30–31),[98] or has the original Dtr conclusion in vv 28, 30–31 been expanded with the addition of v 29?[99] The following considerations speak in favor of the latter conclusion. First of all, following v 28, a positive statement from the Dtr redactor is expected since he has exerted considerable effort to present Jehu as the champion of Dtr principles. Verse 30 satisfies this expectation. Second, the transition from v 29 to v 30 is awkward. The negative content in v 29 does not prepare the reader for the positive statement in v 30. Third, v 29 is distinctive in that it employs the masculine noun *ḥēṭe'* instead of the feminine noun *ḥaṭṭā't* that one usually finds in Dtr passages.[100] It is likely, therefore, that the Dtr conclusion in vv 28, 30–31 was subsequently expanded by v 29.[101]

Another problem is raised by the double mention of Gilead in v. 33. This has led some commentators to suspect that the verse has been expanded. Attempts to isolate the added material has produced two main solutions. Either the expansion follows the first mention of Gilead and extends through v. 33,[102] or it is comprised of *'ēt qol-'ereṣ haggil'ād* through *'al-naḥal 'arnōn*.[103] The latter interpretation is preferable since it allows a general description of the east Jordan to be separated from one that specifies the region according to tribal allotments. Accordingly, its seems that the Dtr description followed a general east-west, south-north scheme, but a later scribe — perhaps motivated by such texts as Numbers 32 and Deut 3:12–13 —

---

[97] Wellhausen, 288; Benzinger, *Könige*, 154; Kittel, 242; Skinner, 335; Gressmann, 313: Eissfeldt, *Könige*, 559; Snaith, 243; Noth, 72. Many also suppose the Dtr redactor probably took the information given in vv 32–33 from an annalistic source: Benzinger, *Könige*, 155; Kittel, 249; Skinner, 335; Šanda, 124; Eissfeldt, *Könige*, 559; Snaith, 243; Gray, 562.

[98] Stade/Schwally, 41; Montgomery, 411–12; Gray, 562; Robinson, 103.

[99] Šanda, 117–18; Landsdorfer, *Die Bücher der Könige* (HS; Bonn: Peter Hanstein, 1927) 176; Hölscher, *Geschichtsschreibung*, 398. Dietrich (34) sees the situation differently. He ascribes vv 29a, 31b to DtrG and vv 30–31a to DtrN (29b is a later gloss).

[100] The masculine noun occurs only here in the Book of Kings.

[101] In addition, it seems that v 31 had been expanded with the clause that Jehu "was not careful to walk in the law of Yahweh, the God of Israel with all his heart," since the reference to the "law of Yahweh" is unique in the Dtr verdict statements but is common in the work of the Chronicler (1 Chr 16:40; 22:12; 2 Chr 12:1; 17:9; 31:3, 4; 35:26; Ezra 7:10; Neh 9:3). Dietrich's solution (34) is to take 29a, 31b as DtrG and 30–31a as DtrN. But v 30 must certainly be attributed to the same redactor that inserted 2 Kgs 9:7–9 since v 30 is predicated upon it.

[102] Kittel, 242; Würthwein, 343.

[103] Montgomery, 412.

felt compelled to specify what he called "the whole land of Gilead" according to tribal boundaries.

15. 2 Kgs 11:6

Most commentators follow Wellhausen's suggestion that this verse is probably a gloss.[104] But C. Levin has recently departed from this consensus. According to him, the original text arranged the division of the guards according to the structure "one third . . . one third . . . one third. . . ."[105] To make sense of this reconstructed text, however, Levin excises parts of vv 5 and 6 and all v 7, and also removes subsequent references to the excised portions of these verses. The simplicity of Wellhausen's solution is more satisfying. The removal of v 6 not only restores the sense of the passage, but also allows the use of parallelism in the reporting of Jehoiada's instructions to emerge:

> A One third of you,
>   B [all] who come in on the Sabbath,
>   C those who keep guard on the house of the king,
>
> A' and two thirds of you,
>   B' all who go out on the Sabbath,
>   C' those who keep[106] guard on the house of
>   Yahweh, ...

This analysis is confirmed by v 9 where again reference is made to "those who go out on the Sabbath" and to "those who come in on the Sabbath."

Besides restoring the parallelism, the removal of v 6 recovers the sense of an otherwise confused passage. Skinner offers the following lucid explanation of the details of Jehoiada's plan:

> The guard was divided into three companies. On weekdays two of these were on duty in the palace and the third in the temple. On the Sabbath the order was reversed, two companies being on guard in the temple and one in the palace. The essential feature of Jehoiada's scheme is the assembling of the whole guard within the temple at the critical time, so as to leave the palace entirely denuded of troops. For this purpose he chooses the moment when on the Sabbath the two companies have come up from the palace to relieve the third, which ought

---

[104] Wellhausen, 292; Benzinger, *Könige*, 157; Kittel, 247; Skinner, 338–39; Šanda, 128; Eissfeldt, *Könige*, 560; Gressmann, 314; Landsdorfer, 178; de Vaux, 175; Rudolph, 474; Montgomery, 419–20; Snaith, 246; Gray, 570–71; Fricke, 149; Robinson, 110; Würthwein, 344.

[105] Levin, 24.

[106] Reading *smrw* for *smry*.

immediately to return to its quarters. By detaining this third division he attains his end: the whole guard (as verse 9 clearly shows) is present, and takes part in the coronation of the king.[107]

Verse 6, which blurs the focus of the story, reflects a technical and pedestrian interest in locating the guard in precise locations. Since we have not seen any evidence indicating that the Dtr redactor was concerned with such matters, we are cautioned against assigning v 6 to this redactional layer. Its concern, in fact, is more akin to priestly sources.[108]

16. 2 Kgs 11:10

Most are sympathetic to Wellhausen's suggestion that this verse is a gloss.[109] The scene in vv 9 and 11 depicting the guards' execution of Jehoiada's command is abruptly interrupted v 10. Furthermore, this verse falls outside of the symmetrical structure of the episode:

The Instruction:

    A (5) Then he commanded them saying, "This is what you shall do:
        B (7) One third of you, those who enter on the Sabbath to guard the palace,
            C And two thirds of you, those who leave [the palace] on the Sabbath to guard the temple
                D (8) shall station yourselves around the king,
                    E each man with his weapon drawn.
                        F Anyone entering your ranks shall die and you shall be with the king when he leaves [the temple] and enters [the palace].

The Execution:

    A' (9) Then the commanders of a hundred did all that Jehoiada the priest commanded them:
        B' The commanders of those who enter on the Sabbath
            C' along with those who leave on the Sabbath and came to Jehoiada the priest.

---

[107]Skinner, 338.

[108]See Chapter IV for a discussion of the Chronicler's handling of this text.

[109]Benzinger, 157; Kittel, 248; Stade/Schwally, 41; Skinner, 339; Stade/Schwally, 41; Eissfeldt, *Könige,* 560; Gressmann, 314; de Vaux, 175; Rudolph, 475; Montgomery, 420; Hölscher, *Geschichtsschreibung,* 398; Snaith, 247; Levin, 25; Würthwein, 344.

D' (11)   Then the guard stood on the left wing
and right wing of the temple stretching
from altar to the temple to surround the
king,

E' each man with his weapon drawn.

Besides disrupting the symmetry of the passage, Levin has noted that the reference to Jehoiada as simply "the priest" relates this verse to others that also show indications that they are additions (vv 15b, 18b).[110] It has also been noted that v 8 presupposes the guards are already armed, making the dispensing of weapons superfluous.[111]

The reasons for the insertion of this verse are not completely clear. It has been attractively suggested that this verse is a late addition based on 2 Chr 23:9 since the interest in David is much more at home in Chronicles than in Kings. But it is unlikely that this verse is based on Chronicles since 2 Chr 23:9 expands 2 Kgs 11:10.[112] The gloss therefore predates the Chronicler. It probably should be regarded as a post-Dtr addition because it severs the description of the execution of Jehoiada's directives to the guard, shares characteristics with other secondary elements in the chapter, and apparently injects a superfluous element into the story.

17. 2 Kgs 11:13–18a

Stade has argued that vv 13–18a were taken from another source and conflated with an account now found in vv 1–12, 18b–20.[113] This thesis has been widely accepted[114] on the merits of the following arguments. First, according to 11:1–12, 18b–20, Jehoiada plays the role of the instigator of the conspiracy, but in 11:13–18a the people play this part in the overthrow of Athaliah. Accordingly, the former is designated as the "priestly" account and the latter the "popular" source. Second, one uses the long form of the queen-mother's name, *'ătalyāhû,* while the other employs the short form, *'ătalyāh.* And last, the repeated statements about Athaliah's death (v 16, v 20) and about the making of a covenant (v 4, v 17) are seen as additional indications of two sources.

---

[110] Levin, 23.

[111] It is possible, however, that the weapons were for ceremonial purposes, as some have suggested.

[112] Chronicles' expansions include the naming of *yĕhôyādā'* and the mention of *hammăginôt.*

[113] Stade, "Anmerkungen," 280–88.

[114] So Benzinger, *Könige,* 155–56; Kittel, 244–45; Skinner, 336; Šanda, 134–37; Eissfeldt, *Könige,* 559, *Introduction,* 142, 295; Montgomery, 417–18; Snaith, 246; Ellis, 201; Gray, 556; Fricke, 145; Robinson, 109.

Although popular, Stade's thesis has not convinced everyone.[115] Hoffmann, for example, argues forcefully against Stade's view, noting that no conflict exists between the two references to the death of Athaliah. Its mention in v 20b is actually a summarizing statement about the state of affairs that prevailed following the removal of Athaliah.[116] Also, separating the two sources on the basis of linguistic criteria falters since ". . . 'Exceptions' must be conceded whenever a defined typical word at times verifies the other account."[117] And finally, the mention of two covenants in vv 4 and 17 does not indicate two sources since the two covenants are different in kind. The one described in v 4 is clearly a secret pact made among those committed to restoring the rightful king to the throne, while the one presented in v 17 is a public agreement, made between the people and their new king. The two complement one another and do not indicate the conflation of two sources.

Additional considerations argue against Stade's analysis. The alleged literary seam between v 12 and v 13 does not exist. Verse 13 clearly presupposes the events described in vv 11–12 since the "noise of the crowd" (*qôl hā‘ām*) mentioned in v 13 refers back to the acclamation of the new king by "the guard" (*hārāṣîm*) that is described in the two preceding verses. As for the discontinuity created by the break between v 18a and v 18b, this is not a result of the conflation of two sources. As we shall shortly argue, v 18a is part of a Dtr insertion, while v 18b is an addition of a subsequent redactor who was especially concerned with matters of Temple protocol.

18. 2 Kgs 11:15b

The commitment to Stade's two-source theory has evidently led commentators to overlook evidence of textual expansion in 11:13–18a. Levin offers compelling reasons for regarding v 15b as a gloss:

> This is an explanatory comment of the foregoing command to lead Athaliah out in the center of the ranks and to kill her potential supporters. The sentence is joined with *kî* "for" and is a new introduction to an utterance. Indeed, it stands outside the sequence of the narrative. It is not on the level of action, but on the

---

[115] Hölscher, *Könige*, 187; *Geschichtsschreibung*, 398; Rudolph, 473–78; de Vaux, 174; Hoffmann, 106–8.

[116] Even Gray (556), who accepts the two-source theory, realizes that this evidence is not convincing ". . . since v. 16 and 20 agree on the death of Athaliah in the palace, and either 16 may be proleptic of 20 or 20 may be a circumstantial amplification of 16."

[117] Hoffmann, 107. Again Gray (566) realizes that the inability to apply consistently such linguistic criteria robs the argument of its cogency: "In vv. 13–18a the queen-mother's name is spelled in the short form *Athalyah*, while in vv. 1–12 and 18b–20 the longer form *Athalyahu* is used. But in vv. 1–4, dealing with Athaliah's reign before the *coup d'etat*, both forms are found, so that this argument is unconvincing."

level of interpretation. What Jehoiada ordered is interpreted from the outside:
. . . This "compensating parenthesis" (Thenius) is a clear break in style. It is
literally secondary in its relationship to the context.[118]

Levin further notes that the title "the priest" appears in two other places (v 10
and v 18b) that for other reasons are to be regarded as additions.

19. 2 Kgs 11:17–18a

Recent studies agree that these verses reflect Dtr concepts and
phraseology.[119] Levin, H. Spieckermann and E. Würthwein concur that the
original text is found in v 17 in the words "and Jehoiada made a covenant . . . between the king and the people." Thus the prepositional phrase,
". . . between Yahweh and the king and the people to be the people of
Yahweh . . ." is considered by them to be a Dtr addition.[120] The sentence as
it stands is clearly overloaded with prepositional phrases, and this phrase
along with v 18a reflects both theological concerns and linguistic usage
typical of the Dtr historian. Furthermore, v 19 follows smoothly from v
17a,[121] thus providing additional evidence that these verses are a Dtr
expansion.

20. 2 Kgs 11:18b

There is widespread agreement that v 18b does not follow smoothly
from what precedes it. This conclusion is acknowledged both by those who
adhere to Stade's two-source theory and by those who do not. But Levin
points out the similarity of this verse to 15b: both half-verses employ the title
"the priest" for Jehoiada, and both are concerned with matters of Temple
protocol.[122] Moreover, the scene described in vv 19–20a follows smoothly
after v 16. With Athaliah under arrest and with a threat of death hanging
over potential supporters of Athaliah (vv 15–16), Jehoiada was free to enact
a covenant (v 17aα, 17b) and then to proceed with the enthronement of Joash
(v 19). It is likely, therefore, that v 18b is an addition stemming from the
same redactor who inserted vv 10 and 15b.[123]

---

[118] Levin, 23.

[119] Hoffmann, 109–10, Levin, 59–66; H. Spieckermann, *Juda unter Assur in der Sargonidenzeit* (Göttingen: Vandenhoeck & Ruprecht, 1982), 177–79; Würthwein, 350.

[120] Hoffmann differs only in that he regards all of vv 17–18a as Dtr.

[121] Note the subject of *wayyiqqah* in v 19 refers back to the last mention of Jehoiada as
the subject of a verb in v 17aα.

[122] Levin, 24–25.

[123] The interests reflected in v 6 suggests that this verse also belongs to this redactional
layer.

21. 2 Kgs 11:20b

For those who follow Stade, v 20b belongs to the "priestly source" found in 11:1–12, 18b–20.[124] Levin and Spieckermann, however, see v 20b as a late expansion dependent on v 16, since, like the gloss in v 15b, this statement emphasizes the "proper" location for the queen's execution.[125] In addition, v 20a reads like the conclusion of the account, while v 20b looks like an appendage. Its emphasis on the "proper" location of Athaliah's death indicates that it is an expansion based on v 16b. It also reflects a priestly interest similar to that detected in the additions discussed above (vv 6, 10, 15b, 18b).

22. "The People of the Land"

The phrase, *'am hā'āreṣ,* occurs four times in the chapter (14a, 18a, 19a, 20a). W. Rudolph examined each of these occurrences and concluded that only the last should be regarded as part of the original text.[126] But certain considerations show that the last occurrence is also suspect. In the preceding discussion of vv 17–18a, we concluded that these verses come from the hand of the Dtr redactor. Since one of the four instances is found here, we are prompted to consider the possibility that the other occurrences also originate from him. Examining its presence in v 14a confirms our suspicions about its originality since the phrase severs the connection between the subject of the clause (*haššārîm wĕhahaṣĕrôt*) and its verb (*wĕtōqēaʿ*). Moreover, the sudden appearance of "the people of the land" seems to violate the logic of the story. Jehoiada had taken special precautions to reveal his plans to a select few — the captains of the palace and the temple guards. Now the "people of the land" suddenly emerge alongside them as initiated participants.

This observation leads us to doubt their appearance in v 19a. Here they are named as accompanying the two groups with whom Jehoiada had originally planned the coup — *hakkārî* and *hārāṣîm* — as he leads the throng from the temple to the palace. Since the mention of "the people of the land" in both v 14a and v 18a are suspect, we may infer that the same hand included them in the story at this point also.

Naturally, the final mention of this group in v 20a is also dubious. In this case, however, the story does not demand that "the people of the land" were active participants in the overthrow of the queen. They may have heard of the events at a later time when the news became public knowledge.

---

[124] Rudolph (476) argues the unity of the text by suggesting that v 20b summarizes what is narrated in v 16. Even so, he finds it necessary to place v 20 before v 18. Gray (512) also leans toward this view.

[125] Levin, 23–24; Spieckermann, 178, 414.

[126] Rudolph, 478.

Although this is a defensible position, the fact that the clause in which it occurs is almost identical to the clause in v 14a suggests that its presence is a result of the same redactor. Furthermore, the addition of the phrase in v 19 seems to serve no purpose by itself. But its presence is explained if it is understood to place "the people of the land" at the palace so that they may "rejoice" over Joash's enthronement. It therefore appears that all four occurrences of the phrase are additions made by the Dtr redactor whose special fondness for this group moved him to portray them both as religious reformers and as political supporters of Joash. Accordingly they are presented as rejoicing over both his acclamation and enthronement.

D. Conclusions

In the first section of this chapter, we examined the question of a possible literary relationship of 2 Kings 9–10 to other pre-Dtr sources and concluded that the attempts to link these sources to the pre-Dtr portions of 2 Kings 9–10 (11) have failed. The original narrative underlying 2 Kings 9–11 was, in all likelihood, an autonomous literary entity. On the question of the relationship of 2 Kings 9–10 and 2 Kings 11, we have seen that the view that distinguishes them as separate traditions is also unjustified. Chapter 11 manifests several traits that indicate that it constitutes a continuation of the events narrated in the two preceding chapters. And finally, our inspection of 2 Kings 9–11 has led us to conclude that the original narrative has been expanded in several places. According to our analysis, the original narrative is to be found in 2 Kgs 9:14b–15a, 1–6, 10b–13, 15b–21abα, 22–24, 27abα, 30–36aα*, 37; 10:1b–9, *wayyāqom* at the beginning of v 17, 18–19a, 20–22, 24–25a; 11:1–5, 7–9, 11–15a, 16–17aα*, 17b, 19–20a. The following translation illustrates our conclusions with regard to the literary layers present in 2 Kings 9–11:

The typefaces below indicate the various redactional layers:

Roman = Original Narrative
Bold = Dtr additions
Italics = redactional extractions from pre-Dtr sources
<u>Underlining = post-Dtr additions</u>

(9:14b) Now Jehu and all Israel were defending Ramoth Gilead against Hazael, king of Aram. (15a) And Jehoram the king had returned to Jezreel to recover from the wounds the Arameans had inflicted on him while battling Hazael, the king of Aram.

(9:1) Now Elisha the prophet summoned one of the prophetic disciples and instructed him, "Tuck your cloak into your belt, take this vial of oil with you and go to Ramoth Gilead. (2) When you get there, search out Jehu ben Nimshi. When you find him, get him away from his fellow commanders and take him into a secluded room. (3) Then take the vial, pour oil on his head and declare, 'Yahweh says this: "I anoint you king over Israel."' Then open the door and flee without delay!"

(4) Then the young man went to Ramoth Gilead. (5) When he entered he looked and there were the army officers sitting together. He said to them, "Commander, I have a message for you." Jehu responded, "For which of us?" "For you, Commander," he answered. (6) So Jehu arose and entered a house. Then the young man poured oil on Jehu's head and declared, "Yahweh says this: 'I anoint you king over Yahweh's people over Israel. (7) **You are to destroy the house of Ahab your lord. Thus I will avenge the blood of my servants the prophets,** and the blood of all my servants [that was shed] by Jezebel's hand. (8) and [that was shed] by the hand of the whole house of Ahab. I will destroy every male in Israel related to Ahab, both child and adult. (9) I will destroy the house of Ahab just as I destroyed the house of Jeroboam ben Nebat, and the house of Baasha ben Ahijah.** (10) As for Jezebel, no one will bury her. Dogs will devour her corpse at a place in Jezreel.'" Then he opened the door and fled.

(11) Then Jehu went out to the commanders, the servants of his lord, and they asked, "Is everything all right? What did that madman have to say?" "You know the kind of things these people say," Jehu replied. (12) "Don't try to deceive us," they said. "Tell us what he said!" Jehu responded, "This is exactly what he said: 'Yahweh says this: "I anoint you king over Israel."'" (13) Then each man quickly took his cloak and covered the landing of the steps before him, blew a trumpet and shouted, "Jehu is king!" (14a) **So Jehu ben Nimshi conspired against Joram.** (15b) So Jehu said, "If this is what you want, let no one slip out of the city to go to Jezreel to report what has happened here." (16) Then he mounted his chariot and rode toward Jezreel because Jehoram was recovering there. Now Ahaziah king of Judah had come down to see Jehoram.

(17) The watchman who was standing on the tower in Jezreel saw Jehu's band as it approached and reported, "I see some troops coming." Jehoram ordered, "Summon a rider and send him out to meet them, and have him ask, "Is all well?" (18) Then the rider rode out to meet them. Arriving he said, "The king says this: 'Is all well?'" Jehu replied, "What do you care? Fall in behind me!" Then the watchman reported, "The messenger met them but did not return." (19) So Jehoram send a second rider out to them. When he

arrived he said, "The king says this, 'Is all well?'" Jehu replied, "What do you care? Fall in behind me!"

(20) The watchman reported, "He met them but did not return. But the way the leader drives his chariot is just how Jehu ben Nimshi drives his — like a madman." (21) Then Jehoram ordered, "Prepare my chariot!" And when it was prepared, Jehoram king of Israel and Ahaziah king of Judah both rode out, each in his own chariot, to meet Jehu. **And they met him at the property of Naboth of Jezreel.** (22) When Jehoram saw that it was Jehu he asked, "Is all well, Jehu?" Jehu answered, "How can all be well as long as the seductions and sorceries of your mother Jezebel are so many?"

(23) Then Jehoram reared about and fled, calling out to Ahaziah, "It's an ambush, Ahaziah!" (24) But Jehu took his bow and shot Jehoram in the back, and Jehoram slumped down dead in his chariot.

(25) **Then Jehu said to Bidkar, his officer, "Pick him up and throw him onto the field that belonged to Naboth the Jezreelite. For I recall that when you and I were riding behind Ahab his father, Yahweh pronounced this oracle against him: (26) 'As surely as I have seen yesterday the blood of Naboth and the blood of his sons,' says Yahweh, 'I will make you pay for it on this property,' says Yahweh." So pick up his body and throw it on that plot in accordance with the word of Yahweh.**

(27) When Ahaziah realized what was happening, he fled on the road toward Beth Haggan, and Jehu pursued him and ordered, "Shoot him also!" And they shot him in his chariot on the road to Gur near Ibleam. But he escaped to Megiddo and died there. (28) Then his servants took him by chariot to Jerusalem and buried him with his fathers in his tomb in the city of David. (29) In the eleventh year of Joram son of Ahab, Ahaziah became king of Judah. (30) Then Jehu rode into Jezreel.

When Jezebel heard about it, she painted her eyes, arranged her hair and waited for Jehu at her window. (31) When Jehu entered the city she asked him, "Is all well my champion, slayer of his lord?" (32) Then he looked up and called out, "Who supports me? Who?" Some eunuchs looked down (33) and Jehu said, "Throw her down!" So they threw her down and some of her blood splattered on the wall and on the horses. Then Jehu trampled her body, entered the palace and dined.

(34) Then Jehu said, "Take care of that accursed woman and bury her, for she was of royal blood." (35) But when they went out to bury her, they found

nothing except her skull, her feet and her hands. (36) And they went back and told Jehu who said, "This fulfills the word of Yahweh that he spoke through his servant Elijah the Tishbite: 'The dogs will devour Jezebel's flesh in the vicinity of Jezreel.' (37) Jezebel's body will be like excrement on the field so that no one will be able to say, 'This is Jezebel's corpse.'"

(10:1) Now seventy of Ahab son's lived in Samaria. Then Jehu wrote letters and sent them to Samaria to the rulers of the city, to the elders, and to the royal guardians. The first said, (2) "Since you are with the king's sons and possess chariots and horses, and fortified cities and weapons, as soon as this letter arrives, (3) choose the best and most worthy from among your lord's sons and set him upon his father's throne. Then defend your lord's house!" (4) But they were terrified and said among themselves, "Since two kings could not resist him, how can we?" (5) So the palace administrator and the city governor, the elders, and the royal guardians replied, "We are your servants and will do anything you say. We will not appoint anyone as king. Do as you wish."

(6) Then Jehu wrote them a second letter, saying, "If you do indeed support me and will do what I command, take the heads of your lord's sons and deliver them to me in Jezreel by this time tomorrow." (Now the royal princes, seventy of them, were under the care of the leading men of the city whose task it was to rear them.) (7) When the letter arrived, these men took the princes and slaughtered all seventy of them. Then they put the heads in baskets and sent them to Jehu in Jezreel. (8) Then a messenger came to Jehu and told him, "They have brought the heads of the princes." Then Jehu ordered, "Put them in two piles at the entrance of the city until morning." (9) When morning arrived, Jehu went out and stood before all the people and said, "You can judge fairly. I admit that I indeed conspired against my lord and killed him. But who struck down all these people? (10) **Know then, that Yahweh's pronouncement against the house of Ahab is not idle. Yahweh has carried out what he predicted through his servant Elijah." (11) Then Jehu killed everyone in Jezreel who were sympathetic toward Ahab, all his chief men, his close friends and his priests, leaving no survivor.** (12) Then he set out. . . .

Then he left, traveling toward Samaria. (13) On the road at Beth Eked Haroim, Jehu met some relative of Ahaziah king of Judah and asked, "Who are you?" They answered, "We are relatives of Ahaziah, and we have come down to greet the family of the king and queen mother." (14) Then he said, "Take them alive." And they took them alive. **And they slaughtered them by the well of Beth Eked, all forty-two, leaving no survivor.**

(15) After he left there, he came upon Jehonadab ben Recab who was on his way to meet him. Jehu greeted him and said, "Are you willing to support me as I have supported you?" Jehonadab answered, "I am willing." Jehu said, "Then take my hand." And he did so and Jehu helped him up into his chariot. (16) "Come with me," he said, "and witness my zeal for Yahweh." So Jehonadab rode with him in his chariot.

(17) . . . and came to Samaria. And he struck down those remaining of Ahab's family and destroyed it in accordance with what Yahweh predicted through Elijah.

(18) Then he assembled all the people and told them, "Ahab's patronage of Baal was insignificant compared to the patronage Jehu will show." (19) Now let all of the prophets of Baal and all of his priests be assembled before me. Let no one be missing, for I have a great sacrifice for Baal. Any who do not attend will forfeit their lives!" (Now Jehu was acting deceptively in order to destroy the servants of Baal). (20) [When they arrived] Jehu said, "Convene the assembly for Baal." And they proclaimed it. (21) So Jehu had it announced throughout Israel, and all the servants of Baal came; no one was absent.

Then they entered the temple of Baal and filled it from one end to the other, (22) and Jehu told the keeper of the ritual garments, "Bring robes for all the servants of Baal," and he did so. (23) Then Jehu and Jehonadab ben Recab went into Baal's temple, and Jehu instructed the servants of Baal, "Check everyone. Search and see that there is none among you who are the servants of Yahweh, but only the servants of Baal." (24) Then they proceeded to make sacrifices and burnt offerings. Now Jehu had posted eighty men outside whom he had threatened saying, "The man who allows to escape any of those whom I am delivering into your hands will pay for it with his one life." (25) So as soon as Jehu had completed making the burnt offering, he ordered the guards and officers: "Go in and kill them. Let no one escape!" So they went in and struck them down with their swords.

Then they cast them out into the third court and went into the innermost shrine of the temple of Baal, (26) and they brought out the sacred pillar and burned it. (27) Then they tore down the altar of Baal, and they tore down the temple of Baal and made it into latrine which stands to this day. (28) Thus Jehu destroyed Baal worship from Israel. (29) However, he did not turn away from the sins of Jeroboam ben Nebat, who made Israel worship the golden calves at Bethel and Dan. (30) So Yahweh said to Jehu, "Inasmuch as you have done well in executing what is right in my sight, and have done to the house of Ahab according to all that I desired, your sons will occupy the throne of Israel to the fourth generation." (31) Yet Jehu was not careful to keep the law of Yahweh, the God of Israel, with all his heart did not abandon the sins of Jeroboam, who made Israel commit sin.

(32) At that time Yahweh began to reduce the size of Israel's territory. (33) Hazael defeated Israel in the area east of the Jordan throughout all the land of Gilead, the land of the Gadites and the Reubenites and the Manassites, from Aroer which is by the valley of the Arnon, in both Gilead and Bashan.

(34) As for the other events of Jehu's reign, all he did, and all his achievements, are they not written in the book of the annals of the kings of Israel? (35) Jehu died and was buried in Samaria and Jehoahaz his son succeeded him as king. (36) Jehu reigned over Israel from Samaria for twenty-eight years.

(11:1) When Athaliah, the mother of Ahaziah, learned of the death of her son, she set out to exterminate the royal family. (2) But Jehosheba, daughter of King Joram and sister of Ahaziah, took Joash, Ahaziah's son, and stole him away from among the royal princes who were about to be murdered. She put him in a bedroom with his nurse and hid him from Athaliah so that he was not killed. (3) For six years he remained hidden in Yahweh's temple while Athaliah maintained her rule over the land.

(4) But in the seventh year, Jehoiada sent for the commanders of a hundred comprised of the Karites and the guards and had them brought to Joash in the temple of Yahweh. There he made a pact with them and put them under an oath, making them swear by Yahweh's temple, and revealed the king's son to them.

(5) Then he gave them the following instructions: "This is what you shall do: one third of you, those who go on duty on the Sabbath to keep guard at the palace, (6) and a third of you, those at the Horse Gate, and a third of you, those at the Guard's gate, shall keep watch over the temple for defense. (7) And two thirds of you, those who go off duty [at the palace] on the Sabbath to keep guard at the temple, (8) shall station yourselves around the king with drawn swords. Kill anyone who approaches your ranks and remain with the king when he leaves [the temple] and when he enters [the palace].

(9) The commanders of the garrisons carried out the instructions of Jehoiada the priest. The commander of those who went on duty on the Sabbath along

with the commander of all those who went off duty on the Sabbath took their men and came to Jehoiada the priest. (10) <u>Then the priest gave the commanders the spears and shields that belonged to King David and were kept in the temple of Yahweh.</u> (11) The guards, with their weapons drawn, stationed themselves on the right and left wing of the temple precincts, stretching from the altar to the temple, in order to surround the king. (12) Then Jehoiada brought out the king's son and placed on him the crown and the royal armband, proclaimed him king, and anointed him. Then they clapped their hands and shouted, "Long live the king!"

(13) When Athaliah heard the noise made by the crowd, she went to the temple of Yahweh where the crowd was gathered. (14) She looked and there was the king standing by the pillar in accordance with custom, while the singers and the trumpeters beside the king, **while all the people of the land rejoiced,** sounded the trumpets. Athaliah tore her garment and cried out, "Treason! This is treason!"

(15) Then Jehoiada the priest commanded the officers of the army: "Escort her out and anyone who follows her kill with your swords." <u>For the priest had said, 'Let her not be killed in the temple of Yahweh.'</u> (16) So they arrested her. And when she had gone as far as the entrance where the horses enter the palace grounds, there she was executed.

(17) Then Jehoiada mediated a covenant between **Yahweh, the king and the people to be the people of Yahweh, and between the king and the people.** (18) **Then all the people of the land entered the temple of Baal and tore it down. And the altar and its images they completely smashed, and they killed Mattan the priest of Baal in front of the altar.** <u>And the priest stationed guards over the temple of Yahweh.</u> (19) And he took the officers of a hundred, the Karites, and the guards, **and all the people of the land,** and together they brought the king down from the temple of Yahweh and entered the palace through the Guard's gate. Then they set him on the royal throne (20) **and all the people of the land rejoiced** and the city remained undisturbed. <u>And they killed Athaliah with the sword at the palace.</u>

II

FORM-CRITICAL CONSIDERATIONS
OF THE ORIGINAL NARRATIVE

The preceding examination of 2 Kings 9–11 has shown that the original version of the narrative contained in these chapters has been worked over extensively by subsequent redactors who altered its message to serve their own aims. This attempt to make traditional materials relevant to a later situation has left its mark on the narrative, making it difficult to grasp the artistic and conceptual integrity of the original work.[1] Having concluded the preliminary task of restoring the underlying story to its original form, we may now endeavor to hear the message as the author originally intended it. The first step toward this goal will be taken by considering the original version of the text from a form-critical perspective. Here issues concerning the text's structure, intention, genre and setting will be addressed.

A. Structure

In order to grasp the author's essential message or "intrinsic genre,"[2] it is necessary to examine the literary structure of the story. Literary works that exhibit a high degree of artistic sophistication indicate that their authors took considerable care to integrate the various parts of the composition under a controlling idea in order to achieve that power of expression that results from an integrated presentation. Here we shall examine the various parts of the narrative and chart the hierarchy of their conceptual relationships. In the end we will arrive at the fundamental message that has informed

---

[1] It is not uncommon today to find that those who are interested in exploring the aesthetic dimensions of the Hebrew Bible find fault with source-critical method. But Gunkel's sensitivity to and appreciation of the literary aspects of OT literature did not place him at odds with the source critics of his day. On the contrary, for Gunkel they performed a vital task (294): "The purifying of the texts from such additions, which we owe to Wellhausen and his school, for the first time restores them to their original life."

[2] See Hirsch's discussion on "Intrinsic Genres," 78–89.

the organization of the various parts of the text. The following outline
provides a schematic overview of the literary architecture of our narrative:

Part One: The Establishment of Jehu's Reign through the Eradication of
Omride Rule in Israel (2 Kgs 9:1–10:25a*).

 I. The Setting (2 Kgs 9:14b–15a).

   A. Jehu's military command in Ramoth-Gilead (9:14b).
   B. Jehoram's recovering in Jezreel (9:15a).
 II. The Instigation of the coup (2 Kgs 9:1–6, 10b, 11–13, 15b–16).
   A. Covert preparations (9:1–6, 10b, 11–12).
     1. Elisha's designation made known to Jehu (1–6,10b).
       a. Commission (1–3).
       b. Execution (4–6, 10b).
     2. Elisha's designation made known to the officers (11–12).
       a. Dialogue between Jehu and officers: message concealed
          (11).
       b. Dialogue between Jehu and officers: message revealed (12).
   B. Jehu is acclaimed King of Israel (9:13, 15b–16).
     1. The officers' reaction to the message (13).
       a. "Ceremonial" preparations (13a).
       b. The acclamation (13b).
     2. Jehu's response (15b–16).
       a. Jehu orders the sealing off of Ramoth-Gilead (15b).
       b. Jehu departs for Jezreel (16).

 III. The Extermination of the Old Regime (2 Kgs 9:17–10:17aα).

   A. The Murder of Jehoram and Ahaziah (9:17–21bα, 22–24, 27abα).
     1. Jehoram and Ahaziah confront the conspirators (17–21bα,
        22–23).
       a. Jehoram is drawn from the palace (17–21a, 22).
       b. Jehoram's realization of the conspiracy (23).
     2. The Murder of the Kings (24, 27abα, 30a).
       a. Jehu kills Jehoram (24).
       b. Jehu orders Ahaziah's death (27abα¹).
       c. Ahaziah is hunted down and killed (27abα²).
     3. Jehu enters Jezreel (30a).

   B. The Murder of Jezebel and her Aborted Burial (9:30b–34a,
      34b–36*,37).
     1. The Murder of Jezebel (30b–34a).

     a. Jezebel's Seduction (30b–31).
        i. Her deeds: Cosmetic preparations (30b).
        ii. Her words: Seductive greeting (31).
     b. Jehu's Response (32–34a).
        i. His words: Jehu orders Jezebel's murder. (32a–33a).
        ii. His deeds: Jehu tramples her body, enters palace and dines (33b–34a).
   2. The Aborted Burial of Jezebel (34b–36*, 37).
     a. Jehu's orders Jezebel's burial (34b).
     b. Complication (35–36*).
     c. Jehu's response (37).
 C. The Murder of the Princes of Samaria (10:1–9, 17aα).
   1. Jehu's first letter (1b–5).
     a. The challenge to battle (1b–3).
     b. The challenge declined (4–5).
   2. Jehu's second letter (6–7).
     a. Jehu orders the slaughter of the princes (6).
     b. The leaders of Samaria execute the orders (7).
   3. Jehu's deceptive self-justification (8–9).
     a. Jehu orders the public display of the dismembered heads (8).
     b. Jehu denies responsibility for the deaths of the princes (9).
     c. Jehu departs for Samaria (17aα).

IV. The Consolidation of the New Regime (2 Kgs 10:18–22, 24–25a).

   A. Jehu convenes a cultic assembly (10:18–20a)
   B. The sacrifice and its outcome (10:20b–22, 24–25a)

Part Two: The Establishment of Joash's Reign through the Eradication of Omride Rule in Judah (2 Kgs 11:1–20*).

  I. The Setting (2 Kgs 11:1–3).

   A. Athaliah murders the princes of Judah (11:1).
   B. Jehosheba rescues Joash (11:2).
   C. Joash's secret rearing (11:3).

  II. The Instigation of the Coup (2 Kgs 11:4–6, 8–9, 11–12).

   A. Covert Preparations (11:4–6, 8).
     1. The pact with the captains of the Karites and the guards (4).
     2. Jehoiada's instructions concerning the coup (5–6, 8).

    B. Joash is acclaimed King of Judah (11:9, 11–12).
      1. The execution of Jehoiada's instructions (9, 11).
      2. The crowning and acclamation of Joash (12).

III. The Extermination of the Old Regime (2 Kgs 11:14–15a, 16).

    A. The Execution of Athaliah (11:14–15a, 16).
      1. Athaliah confronts the conspirators (14–15).
        a. Athaliah is drawn from the palace (14).
        b. Athaliah's realization of the conspiracy (15).
      2. The Execution of Athaliah (15a, 16).
        a. Jehoiada orders her arrest and execution (15a).
        b. Athaliah is escorted from the temple and executed (16).

IV. The Consolidation of the New Regime (2 Kgs 11:17, 19–20a).

    A. Jehoiada mediates a covenant between the king and the people
      (11:17*).
    B. Jehoiada leads Joash's enthronement procession to the palace
      (11:19a).
    C. Joash is enthroned without resistance (11:19b-20a).

The basic structural feature the account is its bipartite arrangement. The narrative juxtaposes two events of similar character. Both describe a political coup through which Omride rule was terminated and in its place a new political order was established. The author's purpose in creating this scheme is obvious. By juxtaposing the two events, he was inviting his audience to compare them and, on the basis of the similarities and differences, to formulate certain conclusions. The following discussion will show that the fundamental interests of the author lie in emphasizing what distinguishes the two revolts. Similarities are important only to the extent that they set in relief what separates Jehoiada's coup from Jehu's.

Before proceeding to an investigation of specific similarities, certain general correspondences should be observed. In addition to the presentation of two events that share a family resemblance, a comparative reading of the two is fostered by portraying the coups as directed against a common enemy — the royalty of the Omride dynasty. In the North, the Omride royalty who die in the course of the coup include Jehoram, Ahaziah, Jezebel, and the princes of Samaria. So also in the South, another member of the Omride dynasty meets her demise — Athaliah, the mother of Ahaziah and sister of Jezebel. The two major parts of the account describe how it happened that Omride rule was terminated in both Israel and Judah.

A second general correspondence between the two parts of the account is seen in the way the events are ordered. Both contain four main sections. The first is comprised of a brief note that sets the scene for a revolt, followed by a section that describes the gathering of anti-establishment forces. The third section sustains the parallelism by narrating the events that led to the extermination of the old regime, while the concluding section completes the symmetry by reporting the actions taken by both Jehu and Jehoiada to consolidate their new regime. Coupled with the common theme of the eradication of Omride rule, this parallel arrangement of the plot structure promotes the reader's comparison of the two rebellions.

Complementing these general similarities are the specific parallelisms that are present within each of the four sections. Although the differences that distinguish the two coups are prominent, the similarities warrant consideration.

1. The Setting for the Coup

Comparing 9:14b–15a to 11:1–3 shows that the two passages resemble one another in tone and content. Both perform the parallel function of setting the stage for a coup by describing briefly the circumstances that surrounded its instigation. In the first part, Elisha's entry into the story is anticipated with a description of the battlefront at Ramoth-Gilead; in the second, the temporal context for Jehoiada's decision to move against the present regime is provided. In both cases, the tone is reportorial, providing the information that explains the motives that drove the instigator to incite a coup.[3]

In the sections that describe the coup's instigation, the author continues to draw a comparison of the northern and southern coups. Both tell of an instigator's successful efforts to incite a group to rally against the ruling power. It is portrayed as a two-stage process. First, instigator makes covert preparations to install a new king; next, the preparations are executed, climaxing in the acclamation of the new king. A confrontation between the newly acclaimed king and the current ruler now becomes inevitable.

Besides this complementary arranging of the plot, both sections include the introduction of characters who play analogous roles. In both sections the instigator emerges on the scene. In the account of the northern revolt, this role is played by Elisha the prophet; in the southern coup, Jehoiada the priest is cast as the instigator. Both are portrayed as the character who designs the plan of attack and marshalls opposition to the present regime.

---

[3] Note, however, that unlike 9:14b–15a, 11:1–3 does not serve as the introduction to a separate narrative. This is evident from the reference in 11:1 to the death of Ahaziah which was described in part one.

In these sections the instigator's support group is also introduced. Elisha chooses Jehu and his fellow army officers to be the instrument of the prophet's political designs; Jehoiada enlists the captains of the Karites and the guards.

The narrator's portrayal of the extermination of the old regime sustains a parallel presentation. In both parts, the acclamation of the new king is followed by an account of the overthrow of the ruling power. One notable difference between the two parts is that the destruction of Omride rule in the North covers three episodes, while the eradication of Omride rule in the South only one is required. In spite of this difference, structural and thematic similarities are noticeable. Both sections report how it happened that the usurpers were able to kill the reigning monarch. First given is the dramatic confrontation of the rulers with the conspirators, followed by an enumeration of the events that culminated in their deaths. Even the strategy adopted by the usurpers is the same. Both Jehu and Jehoiada realized that in order to achieve their goal, the targeted royalty had to be drawn from the protective confines of the palace. Accordingly, both were lured away from the palace into a vulnerable position. Both accounts then portray the rulers' sudden realization that a coup is afoot. The fateful confrontations conclude with the victim's last words, Jehoram shouting, "It's a conspiracy, Ahaziah!" and Athaliah rebuking the conspirators with "This is treason, treason!"

In both accounts, these episodes climax with the slaying of the monarchs. Jehu himself kills Jehoram and then orders his men to hunt down the fleeing Ahaziah. Likewise, Athaliah's realization is followed by Jehoiada's order to have Athaliah executed. The two scenes conclude with the assassination of the ruler.

At this point in the story, the plot lines of the two parts do not maintain a strict parallelism. Rather than immediately proceeding to an account of the consolidation of the new regime as the second part does, the account of Jehu's coup reports his murdering of Jezebel and the princes of Samaria. But the narrator eventually does return to the parallelism in the last sections.

The author does not end the account of either coup with the extirpation of the old regime. The final section of both parts contains a description of how both Jehu's and Jehoiada's took steps to consolidate their newly acquired power. Although the emphasis here falls upon what distinguishes the conduct the two protagonists, certain similarities are detectable.

These final episodes describe royal ceremonies — Jehu's sacrifice for Baal, and Jehoiada's installation of Joash. The plot progresses in three stages. First, the leader of the coup calls upon the new subjects to join him in proclaiming their loyalty to the new regime by participating in a royal ceremony. Upon his arrival in Samaria, Jehu announces his ardent support of Baalism and orders that the preparations be made for the royal sacrifice.

This action corresponds to Jehoiada's mediation of a covenant between the king and the people. Next, the ceremony commences, with the leader of the coup gathering the throng at a special location. In the first part, the scene switches from the palace[4] to the temple of Baal where Jehu sees that the worshipers are properly attired, and then leads them into the temple. In the second part, the movement is in the reverse direction. Jehoiada leads the king and the subjects in procession from the temple to the palace. Finally, the act that constitutes the heart of the ritual is performed and its outcome is reported. After Jehu presents his sacrifice to Baal, the guards ruthlessly slaughter the servants of Baal. In the parallel account, the climactic act of enthroning the new king results in bringing peace to the city.

This examination of the structure of the narrative shows that the author has artfully constructed two parallel presentations. The two parts are integrated not only by the explicit transitional statement in 2 Kgs 11:1, but also by the presence of several structural and thematic correspondences.

B. Intention

The author's interest in showing the similarities of Jehu's and Jehoiada's coups serves the important function of fostering a comparative reading of the two events. Complementing this function is the role that the element of contrast plays in conveying the author's fundamental message. Up to now structural and thematic similarities have been emphasized. We now turn to an examination of the contrasts that the author has drawn. Examining them allows us to isolate the central message that the narrator sought to convey. We shall see that it is what distinguishes the coups that lies at the heart of the narrator's intention.

As instigators of a political coup, Elisha and Jehoiada play parallel roles. In our text Elisha is called "the prophet" who serves as the "father" of a group known as the *běnê něbî'îm*. Elisha and his prophetic guild occupy a social location that differs sharply from the position occupied by Jehoiada the priest, who performed his service as part of the religious establishment under the regimes of both Ahaziah and Athaliah. The fact that Elisha was a prophet from the North while Jehoiada was a priest from the South may partially account for the portrayal that Elisha receives in our narrative. For as the instigator of the coup, this northern prophet, when compared with his southern counterpart, is placed in an unflattering light.[5] He appears only at

---

[4] Although the location of Jehu's call for an assembly for Baal is not explicitly stated, it may be deduced since it is from the palace that one would receive official orders to appear before the king.

[5] An antagonism between priests and prophets is reflected in Hosea's many attacks against the priesthood (Cf. Hos 4:1–5:7). Amaziah the priest of Bethel also shows an attitude that is

the beginning of the narrative and then quickly disappears from the story, leaving Jehu to execute the assault against the house of Omri. Jehoiada, on the other hand, not only serves as the instigator of the coup but also directs its execution from start to finish.

Elisha's non-involvement in the coup is a result of the strained relationship that he had with Jehu and his fellow officers. It is significant that Elisha himself did not deliver the oracle that ignited the coup. Rather, he chose to send one of his prophetic disciples, warning him that the mission was a dangerous one, and that he should complete his task and leave Jehu's presence without delay. Elisha was keenly aware of the possibility that Jehu might regard the oracle as an act of treason and turn against its messenger. It is clear that the author wished to show that a very uncertain relationship exists between Elisha and those he seeks to enlist in his cause. Here he depicts the prophet as acting shrewdly, choosing to send a messenger rather than delivering the politically explosive oracle himself.

The distrust that Elisha shows toward Jehu and his men is reciprocated. Although the army officers ultimately act as Elisha had hoped, the narrator informs the reader that they did not do so out of respect for the prophets. On the contrary, these men are presented as possessing nothing but disdain toward these "madmen" and their irritating ravings. Indeed, it was Elisha's knowledge of their hostile attitude toward prophetic concerns that led him to instruct his disciple to fled immediately once the message had been uttered. The narrator has chosen to portray the relationship between the prophets and the officers as one of mutual distrust.

The opposite conception governs the portrayal of Jehoiada's relationship with his support group. Unlike Elisha, Jehoiada marshalls his forces directly, inviting the guard to come to the temple where Joash has remained hidden for seven years. The priest is fully confident about their commitment to his cause. His only demand is that they maintain secrecy about what he is about to show them. Once they are shown the king, he issues his instructions, fully confident that they will carry out his plans explicitly. Such solidarity contrasts sharply with uncertain and strained relationship of Elisha and Jehu's officers.

The situation that stimulated Elisha and Jehoiada are also contrasted. Elisha chose to act because he sought to exploit a situation that resulted from a military crisis, not because Jehoram had committed a crime. To the contrary, the introduction to the account states that Jehoram had been wounded while defending Israel's border. Elisha's decision to act was purely tactical. With Jehu in charge of Jehoram's troops, Elisha guessed correctly that the officers would realize that the situation could be exploited to Jehu's

hostile toward prophets, especially toward Judean prophets (Amos 7:10–13).

advantage. But Jehoiada's coup was not stimulated by an opportune moment to seize power. The account sets Athaliah's bloody seizure of the throne as the background for Jehoiada's actions, thereby imputing to him a moral impetus that for Elisha is conspicuously absent.

Jehu's character fares even more poorly than Elisha's when compared to that of this heroic priest. In the portrayal Jehu's reception of and response to Elisha's message, certain criticisms of Jehu are registered. When Jehu learned that he was selected to be Israel's king, he initially tried to conceal this from his fellow officers. His reason for doing so was an attempt to extricate himself from a difficult situation. Jehu knew that the content of the oracle was nothing less than treason, and yet he had allowed the messenger to leave. In an effort to conceal this fact from his comrades, Jehu made light of the whole matter, hoping to dismiss it. It was only after Jehu learned that his men were also traitors did he "accept" the prophetic designation. This depiction is so constructed as to reveal the opportunistic motive that drove Jehu against his king.

Jehoiada's motives, on the other hand, are shown to be above reproach. The account presents a priest of Yahweh who had secretly cared for the boy Joash, awaiting the moment when he could replace the murderous Athaliah with Judah's legitimate king. Jehoiada is set before the reader as a paradigm of piety and patriotism. Unlike Jehu, who sought to seize political power for himself, Jehoiada is shown to be solely motivated by the righteous desire to see Judah's rightful king returned to the throne.

Jehu's self-serving ambition was not his only character flaw. The author has exerted much effort to portray him as an extremely violent man. His savagery is indicated not only by the sheer number of persons that die at his hands, but also by the gruesome manner by which they were killed. Of all Jehu's victims, Jehoram and Ahaziah died most mercifully. Jezebel, however, experienced Jehu's wrath by being thrown from a window and trampled to a bloody mass of flesh. Jehu then turned his murderous intentions toward the seventy princes of Samaria, whom he ordered massacred by those charged to care for and to protect them. The death toll of Jehu's coup climbed still higher after he had a great number of Baal worshipers slaughtered within the temple. It is clear that the narrator chose to report those incidents that would convince the reader that Jehu obtained Israel's throne by means of a bloodbath.

In contrast to Jehu's rampant bloodshed, Jehoiada achieved his goal with an absolute minimum of violence. Indeed, it seems that the manner by which Jehoiada's coup was executed was intended to avoid bloodshed. Unlike Jehu, who continually acted as an aggressor, Jehoiada ordered his men to adopt a defensive posture, instructing them to kill only if they were attacked. As a result of this tactic, Jehoiada's coup produced only one well-deserved death. Jehoiada's avoidance of bloodshed places him in stark contrast to Jehu who is conspicuous for his willingness to use violence as a means to attain his political goals.

Jehu is contrasted with Jehoidada by the former's propensity to use threat and intimidation to obtain his ends. Several parties felt the fear inspired by this vicious officer. Through intimidation Jehu detained the king's messengers, forced the palace eunuchs to murder Jezebel, manipulated the leaders of Samaria into slaughtering the princes, secured the cooperation of the priests and prophets of Baal, and insured that the guard would kill the worshipers of Baal. In each case, Jehu made it clear that failure to comply to his demands would carry the most serious consequences—usually death to the disobedient party. By contrast, Jehoiada never resorted to threat and intimidation to achieve his goals. All involved in removing Athaliah from power cooperated with him willingly.

One final contrast that was important to the narrator concerns ritual protocol. We have already noted that both accounts of the instigation of the coup conclude with the acclamation of a new king. But the manner in which this important ritual is compared shows that while Jehu's acclamation was a makeshift, spontaneous affair, Joash's acclamation was carried out in line with sacral protocol. Jehu was acclaimed in a moment of frenzied ambition as the officers realized that the situation was indeed ripe for the overthrow of their king. By contrast, the description of Joash's acclamation is permeated by a sense of ritual propriety. The time, the place, and the acclamation itself are presented as proceeding in full accord with traditional practice. The purpose behind this sort of presentation is clear. It was intended to question the legitimacy of Jehu's acclamation and by contrast to emphasize that Joash's acclamation was fully sanctioned by sacred tradition.

The preceding examination of the contrasts drawn between the two parts of 2 Kings 9–11 makes it evident that the author's fundamental orientation is ardently anti-Jehu and pro-Jehoiada.[6] The fact that the account is double-edged suggests that this narrative was not written only to justify Jehoiada's coup. It also seeks to distinguish it from Jehu's bloody coup that preceded it seven years earlier. This in turn suggests that when this text was composed, some were indeed identifying the southern coup with the northern one, and that the author, while conceding similarities, was deeply concerned

---

[6] Only Kittel (228) and Würthwein (341) have concluded that Jehu is presented in a negative light. Most other commentators, influenced by Elisha's role in the narrative and by what I consider to be mostly Dtr additions to the original story, think that the narrative presents Jehu in a positive light. Indeed, it is commonly suggested that the story was written to legitimate Jehu and his dynasty.

to emphasize their differences.[7] The original text therefore reflects an apologetic purpose,[8] written to justify Jehoiada's takeover by favorably contrasting it with Jehu's bloody purge.[9]

C. Genre

Gunkel's foundational works on OT narrative genres[10] have remained a standard from which most subsequent treatments of the subject depart only in certain details.[11] Regarding 2 Kings 9-10 as a distinct unit from 2 Kings 11, Gunkel classified it as "History" (*Historie*) or "Historical narrative" (*Geschichtserzählung*) in a strict sense.[12] Historical narrative stands over against a genre that he designates as *"poetische Erzählung"* in which he includes Myth, Saga, *Märchen*, Fable, Novella and Legend.[13]

[7] That Jehu's coup was the object of continued criticism throughout the duration of his dynasty is evidenced by Hos 1:4-5, a passage that H. H. Wolff (*Hosea: A Commentary on the Book of the Prophet Hosea* [Philadelphia: Fortress , 1974] 17) dates to 750 B.C.E. If Hosea was moved to condemn Jehu and his dynasty for events that transpired nearly a century earlier, then it seems entirely reasonable to suppose that criticisms of Jehu's coup were voiced soon after these events took place.

[8] Works written for the purpose of political legitimation are not uncommon in the ancient Near East. Discussion of royal propaganda in connection with Mesopotamian, Egyptian and Hittite literature are found in H. Hoffner, "Propaganda and Political Justification in Hittite Historiography," *Unity and Diversity: Essays in the History, Literature and Religion of the Ancient Near East* (ed. Hans Goedicke and J. J. M. Roberts; Baltimore: Johns Hopkins University, 1975) 49-62; H. W. Wolf, "Apology of Hattusilis Compared with other Political Self-Justifications of the Ancient Near East," (Ph.D. dissertation, Brandeis University, 1967) 99-117; G. Posener, *Littérature et politique dans l'Egypte de la XIIe dynastie* (Paris: Bibliothèque del l'Ecole des Hautes Etudes, 1956); R. J. Williams, "Literature as a medium of political propaganda in ancient Egypt," *The Seed of Wisdom: Essays in Honor of T. J. Meek* (Toronto: University of Toronto, 1964) 14-30; J. Finkelstein, *Propaganda and Communication in World History* (ed. Harrold D. Lasswell, Daniel Lerner and Hans Speier; Honolulu: University, 1979),1. 50-110; A. Oppenheim, *Propaganda and Communication in World History* (ed. Harrold D. Lasswell, Daniel Lerner and Hans Speier; Honolulu: University, 1979),1. 111-44; J. A. Wilson *Propaganda and Communication in World History* (ed. Harrold D. Lasswell, Daniel Lerner and Hans Speier; Honolulu: University, 1979),1. 145-74; H. Tadmor, "Autobiographical Apology in the Royal Assyrian Literature," *History, Historiography and Interpretation: Studies in Biblical and Cuneiform Literatures* (ed. H. Tadmor and M. Weinfeld; Jerusalem: Magnes, 1983) 36-57.

[9] The propagandistic intentions of the account of Jehoiada's coup has been perceived by M. Liverani ("L'Histoire de Joas," *VT* 24 [1974] 438-51) who observes that 2 Kings 11 shows some thematic similarities with "The Statue of Idri-mi" and "The Apology of Hattusilis."

[10] H. Gunkel, *Die israelitische Literatur* (Darmstadt: Wissenschaftliche Buchgesellschaft, 1963); *idem, The Legends of Genesis* (New York: Schocken, 1964).

[11] Especially G. Fohrer, 85-95 and O. Eissfeldt, *Introduction*, 32-56. For a survey of this development see J. Wilcoxen, "Narrative," in *Old Testament Form Criticism*, ed. John H. Hayes (San Antonio: Trinity University, 1974) 57-98.

[12] Gunkel, *Die Revolution*, 289.

[13] Gunkel, *Die Israelitische Literatur*, 15-16.

Gunkel describes historical narrative in terms of its intention, audience, perspective and authorship. In contrast to poetic narrative, the purpose of historical narrative is not to entertain or inspire, but to report past events based on objective observation. The intended audience is the educated class, not the general populace. Unlike Saga, events are depicted in a realistic manner without recourse to divine intervention. Furthermore, the material utilized by historical narrative is not derived from oral tradition. Rather, it is a self-conscious literary creation of an individual.

A. Bentzen employs the terms "history-narrative" and "historiography" to describe this type of literature.[14] Like Gunkel, he sees it as the product of an educated class, some of whom were "court historiographers." It is characterized by a realistic depiction of events in which divine activity is portrayed as acts of providence rather than as miraculous interventions of a deity. Also, its compositional techniques are relatively sophisticated. Techniques such as developing main characters through dialogue and action, contrasting the main characters, building and resolving narrative tension, and retarding action to create suspense are commonly employed. Bentzen also observes that although the characters and events are realistically depicted, this type of narration often reflects a biased perspective.

Drawing primarily on the work of H. Gressmann, J. Wilcoxen provides a summary of the literary traits of historical narrative.[15] He compares and contrasts historical writing with a species of poetic narrative—the Saga. The two share several literary techniques:

> Both follow the narrative law of putting the less important before the more important; both increase the suspense by "retarding" moments, by inserting extra incidents prior to the anticipated ending; both love to pair up their heroes, whether in friendship or emnity; both extend the action slowly to a high point, then move rapidly to the conclusion; both often leave certain things unclear for the hearer at first in order to later relieve the aroused curiosity; and both often use repetition of an action, only slightly altered, in order to fully exploit the kind of situation involved.[16]

The two genres, however, may be distinguished on the basis of content and by the way the subject matter is presented:

> History chooses its subject from the present or recent past. Its heroes are kings, crown princes, prophets—in short, the leading persons of the nation. Saga, on the other hand, portrays events from the more distant past. Its heroes are patriarchs, their wives and children, or the mighty men of old time, Moses,

---

[14] A. Bentzen, *Introduction to the Old Testament* (Copenhagen: Gad, 1958), 1. 243–44.
[15] Wilcoxen, 74–76.
[16] Ibid., 75.

Joshua, and the judges. In treating its subjects, history portrays what actually happened, the unique and individual. Saga, on the other hand, is fond of the marvelous and the typical. This does not mean, however, that history writing has no religious character. It simply presents its piety differently, by discerning the hand of God working behind human deeds instead of in *Märchen*—like interventions. It also shows a remarkable objectivity toward its subjects; that is, judgments about the moral character of persons or deeds are always implicit, not explicit.[17]

One of the more recent treatments of narrative genres is found in G. Coats's form-critical treatment of the book of Genesis.[18] Coats, however, appears to introduce a new term, using "novella" to describe what others have labeled "historical narrative." The novella, like the "tale," contains a plot that is constructed to create and resolve dramatic tension. But what distinguishes the plot of the novella from that of the tale is its comparatively complex structure. Unlike the tale, the novella may contain a series of sub-plots that support the principal theme. In order to achieve this complexity, the "pattern of narration" is not controlled by an attempt to reproduce historical cause and effect. Events are related with the primary purpose of maintaining the integrity of the plot.

In spite of the role that imagination plays in the forging of the plot, the novella reflects a realistic orientation, depicting the world as it is normally experienced. Characters are portrayed with more subtle and psychological sophistication than one finds in tales or legends, and unlike the tale, a scene in the novella often involves more than two characters.

This literary complexity indicates that the novella did not arise from oral tradition. It is the product of an individual who created as an original piece of art. Although traditional elements may be employed, the author thoroughly integrates them into the work and transforms them to suit his own purposes. This type of literature is not without an interest in providing entertainment, but the specific intention of a work is defined by the particular goals of the author, and thus may vary.

B. Long's form-critical treatment of First Kings also includes a discussion of narrative genres.[19] Long's designation for this type of narrative is "(historical) story," which he describes as ". . . a self-contained narrative mainly concerned to recount what a particular event was and how it happened, but with more literary sophistication than is usually evident in simple reports."[20] This recounting of events reflects a realistic perspective, but the

---

[17] Ibid., 75–76.
[18] G. Coats, *Genesis, with an Introduction to Narrative Literature*, FOTL, Vol. I, 5–10.
[19] B. Long, *1 Kings, with an Introduction to Historical Literature*, FOTL, Vol. IX, 3–8.
[20] Long, 6.

role of imagination is clearly detectable. Although the author seeks to report how things happened, he is not necessarily ". . . oblivious to the pleasure to be gained from exploring the artistic and literary imagination, and even on occasion a blatant bias of one kind or another."[21] This mixing of fact and imagination is a recollection of the past by "imaginative reenactment."

The plot of historical story is controlled by imagination and designed to arouse and resolve tension. Such narratives typically begin by describing the background and setting for the action, and proceed to description of a problem. As the narrative continues, tension increases until some climactic turn of events leads to a relaxation of the tension, followed by a sense of rest. The artistic sophistication indicates that these works are written compositions probably produced by "the literate scribal classes at work in the royal court and religious institutions." They often entertain, instruct and inspire, although this is not their primary aim. In Long's view their primary aim has a more general and existential orientation: ". . . to recount events as they were thought to have occurred with a feeling for their meaning in the lives of people caught in the ambiguities of human, earthly existence."[22]

Our survey of the various descriptions of the literary genre most commonly called "historical narrative" shows that, while the terms use to designate the genre have varied somewhat, there is a consensus concerning what constitutes its literary characteristics, and its typical compositional circumstances. One aspect of this genre that receives less emphasis in later treatments is the conviction that this genre is marked by the author's fundamental concern to present an objective account of the events narrated. In the more recent treatments, greater emphasis is placed upon the role that the author's imagination has played in portraying events.[23] It seems that the earlier form critics were not adequately sensitive to distinguish stylistic realism from objective description. Distinguishing "objectivity" and "realism" is needed since it is clear that even pure fiction can be styled realistically in order to create the impression that actual events are being reported. While historically accurate descriptions tend toward realism, realistic style does not guarantee historical accuracy, or even indicate that this was the concern of the author.[24] In the case of the genre under consideration, a quest for

---

[21] Ibid., 7.

[22] Ibid.

[23] Among the older works that explicitly deal with form-critical issues, only Bentzen seems to appreciate the control that imaginative and artistic concerns exert on works belonging to this genre.

[24] The failure of eighteenth and nineteenth century biblical scholars to come to terms with the realistic style of biblical narrative and the question of historical accuracy is discussed by Hans W. Frei, *The Eclipse of Biblical Narrative: A Study in Eighteenth and Nineteenth Century Hermeneutics* (New Haven: Yale University, 1974).

objectivity does not seem to have been the primary intention of the author. This is clearly indicated by the fact that something as fundamental as plot structure may be subordinated to artistic and imaginative interests. In addition, the overall presentation may be strongly informed by the biases of the author who has pushed aside a concern to provide an accurate report. But aside from this important correction concerning the intention of this genre, one finds widespread agreement over what constitutes the typical literary features and compositional circumstances of "historical narrative."

How does our text compare to these descriptions of this genre? It is clear that 2 Kings 9–11 manifests that blending of realistic description and imaginative construction that is typical of this genre. The realistic orientation is indicated by the fact that in the original story no mention is made of direct divine intervention. Yahweh is not even portrayed as a player in the drama.[25] In addition, the events are portrayed with convincing realism, and the leading characters are given a psychological depth that surpasses other forms of OT narratives.

But though the events are painted realistically, it is not difficult to see that imagination has played a major role in depicting the events. This is betrayed by the fact that no single individual could have witnessed all of the verbal exchanges ostensibly "reported" in the account. Who could have witnessed Elisha's private discussion with his prophetic disciple and the oracle privately delivered to Jehu, and yet be in a position to overhear Jehu's dialogue with his fellow commanders? And who could have heard the watchman's exchanges with Jehoram, and Jehu's words to Jehoram's messengers, and the final words spoken by Jehoram? Other conversations ostensibly reported include Jezebel's attempted seduction of Jehu, the correspondence between the elders of Samaria and Jehu, Jehu's orders to deposit the heads of the princes at the city gates, Jehu's speech to the Jezreelites, Jehu's proclamation to convene a sacrifice for Baal in Samaria, his orders to the wardrobe warden, and his secret instructions to the guards to ambush the servants of Baal. It is obvious that no one could have been in a position to have heard the words that the narrative ostensibly "reports."

The omniscience and the omnipresence of the narrator are further shown by the fact that he provides information that could have only come from a member of Jehoiada's inner circle, such as the verbatim report of Jehoiada's secret instructions to the guard, Athaliah's cry of protest, and the priest's order to see to Athaliah's execution. Such considerations show that although our narrative is styled realistically, it is obvious that the narrator

---

[25] Yahweh is only mentioned in connection with the anointing of Jehu (2 Kgs 9:3, 6, 12). The Dtr redactor, however, gives Yahweh a leading role in the account by means of his prophetic, history-directing word.

could not have witnessed all of the events reported. We are not dealing with an objective reporting of historical events, but with an account that is in fact an "imaginative reenactment" of the events it purports to describe.

Besides the fact that imagination has played a major role in the portrayal of events, we find that the narrative shares another characteristic typical of this literary genre—artistic sophistication. Many of the refined techniques of plot construction typical of this genre are encountered. The previous discussion of the structure of the story has shown that the plot is creatively fashioned to draw comparisons and contrasts between the northern and southern coups. Moreover, the plot moves according to the steps of "historical story" as outlined by Long. It begins with a description of the background and setting for the action (the battle with the Arameans), presents a problem (the presence of Omride rulers in Israel and Judah), builds tension (the series of murders of various Omrides), and concludes with a sense of rest (the termination of municipal upheaval following Joash's installation). Also, conforming to a feature typical of this genre is the presence of a complex plot structure. The principal theme of the narrative is developed in two major parts, within which are found a series of scenes, each containing its own dramatic tension and resolution. Some of these scenes contain the specific artistic techniques associated with this genre such as arousing the curiosity of the reader,[26] retarding the action to create suspense,[27] and employing verbal and thematic parallelism.

The manner by which characters are developed also conforms to the literary traits typical of this genre. The major characters are the "nationally prominent" figures such as the prophet, the army officers, the kings, the queen-mothers, the priest, and the princes. Often a scene contains more than two characters, and, as the exposition of the original narrative will illustrate, certain characters (Jehu, Jezebel and Jehoiada) are developed with much more psychological depth than one finds in saga or legend. The author is also concerned with revealing rather than stating motives. These are indirectly revealed through the artful use of dialogue and action, allowing the reader to make value judgments.

Our comparison of 2 Kings 9–11 with previous descriptions of "historical narrative" shows that this work belongs to this genre classification. However, the most common designation "historical narrative" does not in

---

[26] For example, in the scene of Jehu's murder of the servants of Baal, the motives behind Jehu's convening of a sacrifice to Baal would arouse curiosity since such an act is out of character given Jehu's hatred of "Jezebel's harlotries." But the reader by this time has also learned that Jehu is a master of deceit. The narrator is here inviting the reader to ponder Jehu's strange action.

[27] This is illustrated in the episodes that describe ruler's encounter with the conspirators.

my view adequately convey the artistic and imaginative qualities of this type of writing. For this reason, I prefer Coats's term "novella," since it provides an indication of the type of literary sophistication that is characteristic of this particular genre.

While the designation "novella" communicates something of the literary traits and compositional circumstances of the work, it does not cover all the essential ingredients of this narrative. The earlier discussion of the intention of the text led to the conclusion that its composition was motivated by political and apologetic concerns. Apparently disturbed by damaging comparisons to Jehu's coup, our author sought to exonerate Jehoiada by emphasizing the differences that distinguish his revolt from Jehu's. In order to communicate this essential feature of the story it seems appropriate to designate it more specifically as a "political novella."

D. Setting

The foregoing discussion of the genre to which our narrative belongs has to a certain degree anticipated our conclusions regarding the setting of this story. We have seen that there is widespread agreement that this type of literature is not forged in the process of oral tradition. Rather, it is the literary creation of an individual who belongs to the educated class of Israelite society. Court scribes have been identified as the particular social group responsible for this type of sophisticated literary product. In the case of this particular narrative, a setting in the royal court is supported by our conclusions concerning its specific apologetic intention. Since the text manifests a concern to justify Jehoiada's coup, it seems most natural to ascribe its composition to a scribe who was commissioned by Jehoiada to provide an account of the private doings that led to the establishment of a new administration. It may be surmised further that the text was written soon after the events it describes since it would be at this time that the need for an official account of the coup intended to legitimate Joash's reign would be most pressing.[28] It therefore seems reasonable to date our story to the early years of Joash's reign, perhaps even to his first year (837 B.C.E.).[29]

---

[28] Posener's conclusions concerning the "Prophecies of Neferti" are very similar to what we have deduced about the compositional circumstances of 2 King 9–11*. Concerning its author and his intention, Posener writes (60): "He is a clever propagandist who placed into the service of the founder of the dynasty the resources of literature and who worked under commission. The Prophecy of Neferti, urged by the king or his advisors, exploits the tastes, the memories, the fears and the hopes of the people of that time in order to enhance the early initiatives of Amenemhet I and to consolidate his still precarious authority."

[29] Treating 2 Kings 9–10 separately from 2 Kings 11, most critics date the former account to Jehu's reign (Kittel, 228; Šanda, 123–24; Montgomery, 399; Miller, 309; Steck, 32; Würthwein, 339–40). Schmitt (30) and Jepsen (*Nabi*, 74), however, think that it fits better in the reigns

K. Whitelam has recently underscored the need to attempt to identify the intended audience and the means of dissemination when dealing with OT literature that manifests a propagandistic purpose. Stressing the restricted literacy of monarchic Israel, Whitelam concluded that the "Defense of David" was primarily written for the "urban elite" since they were a part of the population ". . . *which were a threat or potential threat to his ambitions.*"[31] The apologetic intention of our narrative suggests that one should seek the intended audience in a group that that held political influence in ancient Israel. While there is no warrant to exclude the possibility that a general readership was in view,[32] one specific group within Israel and Judah that exerted considerable influence on the king was that of the elders.

With roots reaching back to Israel's pre-monarchic days, the office of elder continued to exert considerable political influence throughout the period of the monarchy.[33] Before the founding of the monarchy, it was the prerogative of the elders to make a person the leader of their people in exchange for delivering them from a threatening foe.[34] This privilege is reflected in the roles that the elders of Israel and Judah play in establishing David as king. Addressing the elders of Israel, Abner exhorted them as follows: "In times past you were seeking for David to be king over you. Now then, do this" (2 Sam 3:17-18). Similarly, it was the elders of Judah who installed David as their king (2 Sam 5:1-3).

Although the election of a king meant loss of some of their political authority, the elders continued to play an important role in the leadership

of one of Jehu's descendants. As for 2 Kings 11, few have attempted to give it a precise dating. The so-called "priestly source" is thought by most to be older and more reliable than the "secular source." Montgomery, Šanda and Levin are more specific, suggesting that it was written by an eye-witness shortly after the events it describes.

[30] Whitelam, *Defense*, 61-62.

[31] His emphasis.

[32] Weinfeld (164) notes that in Israel and Assyria it was customary for kings ". . . to publish and to teach new law through royal officers, who were sent out to every town and hamlet. . . ." A similar practice may have been used to disseminate the type of political material contained in our narrative.

[33] C. U. Wolf, "Traces of Primitive Democracy in Ancient Israel," *JNES* 6 (1947) 98-108; J. L. McKenzie, "The Elders in the Old Testament," *Bib* 40 (1959) 522-40; A. Malamat, "Kingship and Council in Israel and Sumer: A Parallel," *JNES* 22 (1963) 247-53; J. van der Ploeg, "Les Anciens dans l'Ancien Testament," *Lex Tua Veritas* (ed. Heinrich Gross and Franz Mussner; Trier: Paulinus, 1961) 175-91; G. Bornkamm, "*presbys*," *TDNT* 6 (1968) 651-83; J. Conrad and G. Johannes Botterweck, "*zaqen*," *TDOT* 4 (1980) 122-31; T. N. D. Mettinger, *King and Messiah. The Civil and sacral Legitimation of the Israelite Kings* (Lund: Gleerup, 1976) 111-23; H. Tadmor, "Traditional Institutions and the Monarchy: Social and Political Tensions in the Time of David and Solomon" *Studies in the Period of David and Solomon and Other Essays* (ed. T. Ishida; Winona Lake: Eisenbrauns, 1982) 239-57.

[34] According to Judg 11:1-11; 1 Sam 11:1-15.

of the nation. According to 2 Sam 17:15, Hushai's counsel was not directed at the king alone, but also at the elders of Israel. Their continuing political power is also seen in 2 Samuel 19, where the elders are seen exercising their right to re-install David as king following Absalom's rebellion. Also, according to 1 Kgs 20:7-8, Ahab sought their advice when faced with Ben-Hadad's unreasonable and conflict-provoking demands.

Our own text provides additional testimony to the political power of the elders. 2 Kgs 10:1-7 is striking in that it illustrates that it was the prerogative of the elders of Samaria to assume the leadership of the nation following the death of Jehoram. The formal tone of Jehu's challenge to them reveals that Jehu is aware of their leadership status, and the content of the challenge indirectly reveals that the elders were not only presently in command of the army, but also that it was their duty to select a new king to meet the challenge. As the present leaders of the nation, it was they who formally surrendered to avoid a conflict with Jehu.

Since the elders constituted a political body that could exert considerable political influence even over the king, it seems reasonable to assume that the king must also try to influence them favorably to achieve a unified and stable regime. And if it was customary for the elders to sanction royal investitures as T. N. D. Mettinger has maintained,[35] then there would be a great need to convince them of the legitimacy of Joash's reign in light of the fact that this group had no part in placing Joash on the throne. The dynamics of the political relationship between king and elders therefore seems to constitute the political matrix that generated the type of material that is found in 2 Kings 9–11.[36] Its earnest apologetic purpose suggests that it sought to convince the elders of Judah that Jehoiada's coup, *unlike Jehu's,* was a heroic and righteous act of loyalty to the Davidic dynasty. Furthermore, the narrator informs his audience that within Jerusalem, Joash's rule remains uncontested. The narrative thus seems aimed at the elders of Judah, intended to cause them to reject the unfavorable comparisons being made with Jehu's coup in the hope that they will support the new king and consolidate relations with his administration.

E. Conclusions

With the examination of the form-critical issues completed, we may now summarize our main conclusions. The original account contained in

[35] Mettinger, 111-24.

[36] The "Apology of Hattusilis," intended to justify Hattusilis's overthrow of his nephew, King Urhi-Teshub, was written for the *pankus* who wielded political authority similar to that of the elders in Israel and Judah. See E. H. Sturtevant and George Bechtel, *A Hittite Chrestomathy* (Philadelphia: University of Pennsylvania, 1935) 84; O. R. Gurney, *The Hittites* (Melbourne: Penguin, 1952) 68-69, 175-77.

2 Kings 9–11 consists of two major parts, both of which contain four corresponding sections. This parallel arranging of the material has been informed by the apologetic intention of the narrative. By drawing comparisons and contrasts between the northern and southern coups, the author hoped to justify Jehoiada's overthrow of Athaliah by contrasting it with a negative portrayal of Jehu's seizure of the throne. The narrative has therefore been classified as a "political novella" that served as propaganda for the newly inaugurated reign of Joash in Jerusalem. The elders of Judah were probably the intended audience. The narrative solicits their political support by ardently rejecting the damaging charge that Jehoiada was motivated by the same self-serving goals that seven years earlier had driven Jehu when he seized the throne of Israel through deception and violence.

III

AN EXPOSITORY READING
OF THE ORIGINAL NARRATIVE

Our form-critical investigations have indicated that the original edition of this work was probably written shortly after the events described in chapter eleven (ca. 837 B.C.E.) by a court scribe who was commissioned by Jehoiada to present an account of the events that would justify his overthrow of Athaliah. As news of the coup spread throughout Judah, voices of criticism arose that negatively compared his actions to the bloody takeover that Jehu had perpetrated in the north seven years earlier. To answer these criticisms, the scribe constructed an account that compared and contrasted Jehu's coup with Jehoiada's with the intent of showing that while Jehu was a violent and deceitful man, Jehoiada was a great hero, a man driven by the deepest piety and patriotism. The scribe portrayed characters and events to show that unlike Jehu and his coup, which involved treachery, deceit and the most extreme displays of violence, Jehoiada's removal of the queen was carried out as a sacred task. Special emphasis is placed on showing that the queen alone was killed, and that the anticipated counter-revolution failed to materialize either during or following the installation of the new king.

In this chapter, we shall offer additional support for these conclusions by offering a close reading of the individual episodes that comprise the narrative. Special attention will be given to characterization and plot development in order to show how both contribute to the apologetic intention of this work.

A. Part One: The Establishment of Jehu's Reign through the Eradication of the Omride Rule in Israel

As noted previously, the first half of this narrative describes how Jehu came to seize the throne of Israel through a series of violent actions directed at various members of the Omride royalty. Jehu's coup is introduced by a brief description of the dire circumstances that Israel faced before Hazael's aggression at Ramoth Gilead. The story then tells of Elisha's successful attempt to move Jehu against his lord, and how Jehu subsequently killed

Jehoram, Jezebel, and the seventy princes of Samaria. Part one concludes with a presentation of how Jehu consolidated his reign by destroying all the "servants of Baal" through a cleverly conceived and ruthlessly executed massacre.

1. The Setting for the Coup (2 Kgs 9:14b–15a).

This brief introduction serves two main purposes: to describe the setting for subsequent events and to introduce the audience to three characters — Hazael king of Aram, Jehoram king of Israel, and Jehu the commanding officer of the Israelite defense at Ramoth Gilead. Although the narrator does not develop Hazael's character, the mention of his presence at Ramoth Gilead serves as a significant element of the scenery. On the other hand, Jehoram and Jehu are developed in the course of narrative, the latter being given the most attention since Jehu is the central character in the first part of this account. When the story opens, the reader finds Israel locked in a military crisis.

> Now Jehu[1] and all Israel were defending Ramoth Gilead against Hazael, king of Aram. And Jehoram the king had returned[2] to Jezreel to recover from the wounds the Arameans had inflicted[3] on him while battling Hazael, the king of Aram.

These introductory lines set the scene with a terse description of Hazael's assault on Ramoth Gilead. This ambitious usurper has confronted Jehoram hoping to extend his border southward by seizing the Israelite territory that lies beyond Israel's border fortress.[4] The severity of this situation is concisely communicated by the statement that "all Israel" was needed to stay Hazael's aggression.[5] The tone of crisis is further heightened by the

---

[1] Gratz's suggestion to read *yēhû'* for *yôrām* has been adopted by several commentators (Burney, 298; Gressmann, 306; Snaith, 233; Gray, 544; Schmitt, 226–27). Since *yĕhôrām* occurs in v 15a, the mention of *yôrām* in 14b is suspect. Furthermore, v 15a includes Jehoram's official title, *hammelek,* giving it the appearance of an introductory reference. The change from the original *yēhû'* to *yôrām* can be explained as a late attempt to harmonize 9:14a with 2 Kgs 8:28.

[2] The context indicates that this action took place in the past prior to the action described in the preceding clause. I have therefore translated it as a pluperfect. The juxtaposition of these two statements indicates a causal relationship between them — Jehu was given command of the troops as a result of Jehoram's injury.

[3] Reading *hikkuhû* with 2 Chr 22:6 instead of *yakkuhû.*

[4] 1 Kings 22 seems to indicate that Ramoth Gilead became the possession of Aram following Ahab's defeat there. But our story opens with Israel in possession of this border town. E. Kraeling (*Aram and Israel* [New York: Columbia University, 1918]) thinks that Jehoram exploited the death of Adad-idri (Ben Hadad I?) by seizing Ramoth Gilead. So also M. F. Unger, *Israel and the Arameans of Damascus* (Grand Rapids: Zondervan, 1957).

[5] As Šanda observes (95), the reference should not be taken literally since 10:2 indicates

ominous note that the king Jehoram, the commander of the army, had been wounded in action and forced from the battlefield. Israel finds itself in the position of facing a serious threat to its border, a situation made worse by the fact that the Israelite king was wounded and no longer leads the defense. Jehu is introduced as the officer left in charge to face this grim predicament.

The state of emergency described by the introduction cannot be fully appreciated without some attempt to understand what the readers would have associated with the mention of Hazael. An examination of both biblical and non-biblical sources reveals that two characteristics of this Aramean king are prominent: he was a notorious usurper and a fierce warrior.

The fact that Hazael came to the Aramean throne through force appears to have been widely known. Even the distant and powerful Assyrian king Shalmaneser III knew that Hazael was a usurper without royal pedigree. In the following Assyrian text, Shalmaneser notes Hadadezer's death and disdainfully refers to Hazael's seizure of the throne:

> Hadadezer (himself) perished.[6] Hazael, a commoner (lit: son of nobody), seized the throne, called up a numerous army and rose against me. I fought with him and defeated him, taking the chariots of his camp. He disappeared to save his life. I marched as far as Damascus, his royal residence [and cut down his] gardens.[7]

Another text describes the same campaign but provides more detail. It not only tells of Hazael's valiant and successful efforts to defend his kingdom, but also sets his decision to fight Assyria in contrast to Jehu who chose to pay tribute:

> In the eighteenth year[8] of my rule I crossed the Euphrates for the sixteenth time. Hazael of Damascus put his trust upon his numerous army and called up his troops in great number, making the mountain of Senir, a mountain, facing the Lebanon, to [?] his fortress. I fought with him and inflicted a defeat upon him, killing with the sword 16,000 of his experienced soldiers. I took away from him 1,121 chariots, 470 riding horses as well as his camp. He disappeared to save his life (but) I followed him and besieged him in Damascus, his royal residence. (There) I cut down his gardens (outside of the city, and departed). I marched as far as the mountains of Hauran, destroying, tearing down and burning innumerable towns, carrying booty away from them which was beyond counting. I (also) marched as far as the mountains of Ba'li-ra'si which is a promontory (lit:

that Samaria was host to a sizeable number of military personnel. Still, a large army must have been involved since we later learn that several troop commanders are present in Ramoth (9:5). Our narrator clearly intends to create a mood of crisis.

  [6] Unger sees here a reference to Hadadezer's assassination (75).
  [7] *ANET*, 280.
  [8] 842 B.C.E. according to Kraeling (79); 841 B.C.E. according to Unger (77).

at the side of the sea) and erected there a stela with my image as king. At that time I received the tribute of the inhabitants of Tyre, Sidon and of Jehu, son of Omri.[9]

Given the fact that Hazael was practically alone in his opposition to Shalmaneser's advance, it is all the more impressive that Shalmaneser was not able to take Damascus, but had to be content with the devastation he wreaked in Hazael's kingdom. M. Unger rightly attributes this impressive feat to Hazael's valor and military prowess:

> It was unquestioningly Hazael's valorous and stubborn stand that frustrated Assyria's attempt to reduce Central Syria. His success in thwarting such a formidable danger practically single-handed not only evidences his military prowess, but also his indomitable spirit and boded ill for those who like Israel had dared to conciliate the foe and had refused to aid him in his hour of desperate need.[10]

In Israelite tradition, Hazael is likewise remembered as a notorious usurper and as an aggressive enemy. That he was a known usurper is seen from two biblical traditions. In 1 Kgs 19:15–18 he is associated with Jehu, who like him was motivated by Elisha to conspire against his king. A variation of the same tradition is found in 2 Kgs 8:7–15, according to which Hazael is cleverly induced by Elisha to seize the throne of Aram. The fact that these traditions about Elisha included an account of Hazael's usurpation indicates that it was common knowledge that Hazael had usurped the throne of Aram.

Several biblical texts reflect the aggressive side of Hazael's rule. 2 Kgs 9:14b and 2 Kgs 8:28–29 report that Hazael fought Jehoram in an attempt to conquer Ramoth Gilead, and 2 Kgs 10:32–33 relates that he was finally successful in taking land from Israel. Hazael was even able to press his assault to the walls of Jerusalem and was turned away only by Jehoash's tribute (2 Kgs 12:17–18). In the course of his campaigns Hazael left Israel devastated. In some traditions these events were interpreted as Yahweh's punitive actions. 1 Kgs 19:17 credits his military success to Yahweh, who had chosen Hazael to lead a death-dealing assault on the worshipers of Baal. But Amos disassociates Yahweh's involvement in Hazael's conquests. For the prophet, Hazael's ruthlessness could earn only Yahweh's wrath.

This is what Yahweh says:

---

[9] Ibid. Kraeling, followed by Unger, suggests that Jehu's choice to submit to Shalmaneser rather than back Hazael had serious repercussions for Israel. The latter writes: "It was a decision of far-reaching consequences for subsequent history, and bred an implacable hatred for Israel which was later to spur Hazael on to commit terrible atrocities when he was relieved of the Assyrian menace and able to wreak his vengeance on Israel."

[10] Unger, 78.

> For three sins of Damascus, for four I will not hold back my wrath. Because it threshed Gilead with sledges having iron teeth.

> I will send fire upon the house of Hazael that will consume the fortresses of Ben-Hadad. I will break down the gate of Damascus (Amos 1:3-4).

An even more graphic description of the misery spread by Hazael is found in 2 Kgs 8:11-12. Here Elisha receives a vision that moves him to weep. When asked by Hazael to explain this display of grief Elisha answers,

> Because I know the calamity that you will bring upon the sons of Israel: their strongholds you will set on fire, and their young men you will kill with the sword, and their little ones you will dash in pieces, and their pregnant women you will rip open.

These traditions show that Hazael was remembered as a vicious enemy. The mention of him in the introduction to our account was clearly intended to heighten the gravity of the situation. The threatening presence of Hazael at Israel's threshold provides an important but easily forgotten piece of background information for the events that are subsequently narrated. Indeed, it places Jehu's coup in a negative light from the start.[11]

The second character mentioned in the introduction is Jehoram, king of Israel. The fact that he was an Omride, and related to the hated Athaliah, no doubt evoked some negative feelings toward this character. Yet the account of his death seems intended to evoke neither jubilation nor sympathy. When the story opens, Jehoram's situation is described in a somewhat detached manner. We are told that he has been separated from his troops due to a wound that he received while defending Israel's border. When he next appears, he plays the role of an unsuspecting victim. Anxious to receive news of the battle at Ramoth Gilead, he fatefully leaves the protection of the palace when he learns that Jehu, his trusted officer, is approaching the city. Acting exactly as Jehu had hoped he would, the king met his death as the victim of a conspiracy. Through all this the author shows no interest in developing Jehoram's character. He simply serves as the target of Jehu's clever ambush.

Additional information about Jehoram must be obtained from other texts. From these we learn that Jehoram was an Omride, a family that was allied with the Judean royalty by means of Athaliah's marriage to the Judean king Joram. Because most of the major characters in 2 Kings 9-11 were

---

[11] The fact that Hazael eventually penetrated and conquered Israelite territory casts a negative light on both Elisha's and Jehu's deeds. This was correctly perceived by G. W. Ahlström, "King Jehu: A Prophet's Mistake" (*Scripture in History and Theology: Essays in Honor of J. Coert Rylaarsdam* [ed. Arthur L. Merrill and Thomas W. Overholt; Pittsburgh: Pickwick, 1977] 47-69). Our narrator probably wishes to imply that Jehu's abandonment of his post in the face of the advances of such a dangerous enemy was inexcusable.

related, the relationships created by the marriage between a Judean king and a member of the Israelite royal family are important for our understanding of 2 Kings 9–11 . The following chart illustrates the intricate web of family relationships presupposed by the story:

A dash (−) indicates a blood relationship:
A plus sign (+) indicates a marriage relationship:
An asterisk (*) indicates characters mentioned in 2 Kings 9–11:[12]

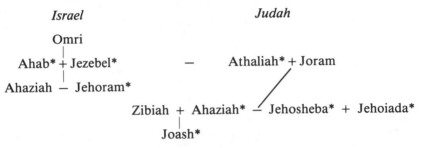

2 Kings 9–11 describes the killing of four individuals who were closely related. The cousins Jehoram and Ahaziah were the first to die. Both deaths are handled rather dispassionately, with no attempt on the part of the author to emphasize the wickedness of these two kings. By contrast, the descriptions of the deaths of the sisters Jezebel and Athaliah reveal a more engaged perspective. In their cases, the author expends effort to move the reader to approve of the demise of these Omride women. Jezebel is portrayed as a seductive opportunist, an ambitious woman prepared to give herself and her shallow loyalty to the strongest party. Athaliah is portrayed as a ruthless murderer, willing to kill members of her own family to seize the throne of Judah. Jehoram's gravest fault seems to lie in his relationship to these wicked women.

Even the Dtr historian does not heartily condemn Jehoram as he does most of the other kings of Israel. We are told that he relaxed the militant Baalism that characterized his father's reign. The Dtr historian gave him a qualified condemnation:

> And he did what was evil in Yahweh's sight, though not like his father and mother; for he removed the sacred pillar of Baal which his father had made (2 Kgs 3:2).

This verdict appears to agree with the portrayal of Jehoram that we find in 2 Kgs 3:4–14. In this story, Israel and Judah are faced with the crisis of

[12] For the sake of clarity, I have used the long form of the names for the Israelite kings, and the short form for the Judean kings.

Moab's rebellion. Feeling the need to consult a prophet of Yahweh, Jehoshaphat, with Jehoram's approval, summons Elisha. Upon his arrival, Elisha treats Jehoram with great contempt. But Jehoram responds with a great show of humility toward Elisha, appearing to be desperate for the prophet's counsel. At one point in the exchange, Elisha scornfully refuses to aid him and angrily instructs him to seek the advice of his own prophets, the prophets of Baal. But Jehoram, with a surprising show of faith in Yahweh, answers, "No, for *Yahweh* has called these three kings together to give them into the hand of Moab." Jehoram is here portrayed as accepting Yahweh's supremacy when faced with a crisis, and indicates that he was not the Baal zealot that his parents were. This independent tradition lends support to the Dtr historian's statement that he made concessions to Yahwism.

But it is also clear that Jehoram, for the most part, accepted the state religion of Baalism. Elisha's disdainful instructions that he should seek the counsel of the prophets of his father and mother suggests that this was Jehoram's usual practice. Another clear indication that Baalism thrived during his reign is the fact that according to 2 Kings 10:18-25, a temple to Baal existed in Samaria, and that a large number of the "servants of Baal" attended Jehu's royal "sacrifice." Moreover, Jehu's retort to Jehoram's greeting in 2 Kgs 9:22 confirms that Baalism was the dominant religion in Israel during Jehoram's reign. According to Jehu, this was Israel's chief problem, a problem that was the result of his mother's zealous patronizing of Baalism: "How can there be peace so long as the seductions and sorceries of your mother Jezebel are so great!" (2 Kgs 9:22).

The overall impression conveyed about Jehoram is that he did maintain his family's traditional patronage of Baalism, and for this he died at the hands of Jehu. But he is also pictured as one who understands Yahwism as the traditional religion of Israel, and the Dtr historian's evaluation of him indicates that he made some concession to Yahwism in contrast to the intolerant Baalism of his parents.[13] Jehoram thus emerges from tradition as a "moderate" supporter of Baalism who had the unfortunate fate of encountering the forces of militant Yahwism.

Jehu, the third character mentioned in the opening verses, later reenters the story as the protagonist of the northern coup. He is described as military "leader" (*śar*), a rank that he shared with others stationed at Ramoth Gilead (9:5). Elisha's reference to the other leaders as Jehu's "brothers" (*'ah*), and the relaxed relationship that he had with them also indicate this. Jehu, however, seems to be in charge temporarily, since he is named as the one who

---

[13] In this connection it is noteworthy that in 2 Kgs 9:22, Jezebel rather than Jehoram is blamed for the prevalence of Baalism within Israel. Similarly, in 2 Kgs 10:18 Jehu ascribes militant Baalism to Ahab, Jehoram's father, rather than to Jehoram himself.

was given the responsibility of defending Ramoth Gilead (9:14b). Another indication of his slightly superior rank is indicated by the fact that he speaks for the entire group of officers when the young prophet approaches (9:5).

Jehu possesses those attributes that we would expect to find in a seasoned, high-ranking soldier. He has gained a reputation as an aggressive charioteer (9:20), and his skill as an archer is demonstrated by his deadly aim (9:24). As an officer, he also knows the importance of assessing the possibility of victory before engaging the enemy. Apparently uncertain that he can muster the forces to dethrone Jehoram, Jehu commits himself to the overthrow of the Omrides only after he is convinced of his comrades' support (9:11–13, 15b). Similarly, from Jehu's letter to the elders of Samaria, it is clear that Jehu had assessed the enemy's military resources before he issued his challenge (10:2–3).

This experienced soldier is adept at the techniques of subterfuge. He instinctively discerns that his chances of slaying Jehoram will be greatly increased if he can maintain the element of surprise. Immediately after resolving to attack the Omride establishment, he orders that Ramoth be sealed up lest the news of the conspiracy precede him to Jezreel and thus thwart his plans to maneuver Jehoram into a defenseless position (9:15b).

Jehu's method of luring Jehoram to him also speaks of his military shrewdness. By detaining the king's messengers from returning to Jezreel, and by depending on the king's trust in his commanding officer, Jehu was able to draw Jehoram from the protection of Jezreel and to kill him without difficulty. Throughout this episode, we feel the strength and confidence of a warrior who knows how to set a trap, and who is confident in the use of his martial tactics.

Jehu's confidence and experience again emerge in his dealings with Samaria. Having exposed his intention to overthrow the present regime, he knew that he had to deal with Samaria in a more direct manner. He therefore challenged the city to a contest of strength, calling upon the rulers of Samaria to send their best man against him in battle. But the episode indicates that Jehu had anticipated their surrender. Indeed, the challenge to battle was the first phase of a greater strategy—the execution of the princes in a way that would conceal his responsibility. Here again Jehu's confidence and cleverness are set before the reader.

The final scene portrays the same characteristics. Having entered Samaria as the new king of Israel, he realized that his rule would be secure only when those who had been loyal to the previous dynasty were exposed and killed. To do this, he presented himself as a king whose patronage of Baal would far outstrip that of Ahab. This statement of policy was undoubtedly intended to quiet any doubts that the servants of Baal had about this new ruler. By preying on these fears, Jehu successfully sent these potential dissidents to an unsuspected death.

When Jehu's speech is examined, we see that he speaks with the intimidating authority of a military commander. In fact, most of what he says consists of giving orders. He issues commands to his own men (9:15b, 9:27), to Jehoram's messengers (9:18, 19), to the queen's eunuchs (9:33), to the servants at the palace in Jezreel (9:35), to the leaders of Samaria (10:3, 6), to his own messenger (10:9), to the Baal functionaries (10:19, 20), to the wardrobe warden (10:22) and to the guard (10:25a). The absolute authority of his commands is shown by the fact that even when his orders called for an act of murder, they were carried out without any vacilation (9:27, 33; 10:6, 25a).

But Jehu's prominent characteristic is his unrelenting and unrestrained violence. He himself initiated the bloodshed with the murder of Jehoram (9:24) and was directly responsible for the deaths of Ahaziah (9:27), Jezebel (9:33), the seventy princes of Samaria (10:6) and the servants of Baal (10:25a). Jehu's ruthlessness is graphically depicted in the dramatic scene in which he encounters the formidable Jezebel. After Jezebel's fatal fall from her palace window, Jehu vents his animosity toward the despicable queen-mother by trampling her splattered body. Then, as if unaffected by this gory act of brutality, he enters his victim's palace and feasts on the royal cuisine. This unsavory aspect of Jehu's personality appears again when he demands the delivery of the decapitated heads of the seventy princes of Samaria, and when he engineers the wholesale slaughter of the servants of Baal.

In addition to the violent side of Jehu's character, this ambitious officer was politically shrewd, skilled at manipulating public opinion. After he had seen to the death of the princes of Samaria, Jehu set out to convince the Jezreelites of his innocence in the affair. Our narrator portrays his craftiness by having Jehu admit his treachery toward his king in order to cover up his responsibility for the death of the princes, and at the same time to convince the Jezreelites that he has the support of the Samaria's aristocracy (10:9). But the narrator allows the reader to see through Jehu's deceit by revealing that Jehu had in fact forced the Samaria's rulers to carry out the heinous crime. Jehu is presented as a man who was prepared to use any means to achieve power, as long as he could justify his actions in the arena of public opinion. Jehu's military experience, burning ambition, unrestrained violence and political shrewdness enabled him to seize and to maintain Israel's throne without opposition.

2. The Instigation of the Coup (2 Kgs 9:1-6, 10b, 11-13, 15b-16).

With the scene set and some of the major characters introduced, the narration of the events that led to the fall of the house of Omri begins. In this first episode, a new character is introduced, Elisha the prophet, whose actions set in motion a series of events that shook the foundations of both Israel's and Judah's political structures. The portrayal of Elisha in 2 Kings 9–11, with its remarkable realism, sets it apart from his appearance in prophetic legends. This is not the Elisha who beckons supernatural powers to resolve problems. Elisha acts with political shrewdness, taking advantage of an opportune circumstance to incite a coup. He is aware of the danger to which his messenger will be exposed, and therefore provides him with practical instructions intended to minimize the risk of delivering a treasonous oracle. The same sort of ear-to-the-ground pragmatism is apparent in the fact that Elisha seems to have been monitoring anti-Omride feelings within the ranks of the army officers. His selection of Jehu appears to be based on the gamble that Jehu would take up the prophet's cause against the Omrides.[14]

The portrayal of Elisha as one who manipulates political forces to achieve his desired end is also found in the story of Elisha's fateful encounter with Hazael.[15] This account is of special interest since the prophet's actions are similar to those found in our narrative. Both share a central concern in portraying Elisha as the initiator of a political coup. The similarity in style and content of 2 Kgs 8:7–15*[16] and 2 Kgs 9:1–6 suggests that the Elisha-Hazael episode can serve as a source for our understanding of the character of Elisha as he appears in the Elisha-Jehu episode.

In 2 Kgs 8:7–9 Elisha appears on the scene as a "man of God" who is widely known for his prognostic abilities. When he enters Damascus, his presence is reported to the ailing Ben-Hadad who instructs Hazael to take "gifts" to the prophet and to find out whether he will recover from his illness.[17] Hazael, speaking for his master, approaches the prophet with humility, referring to the king of Damascus as Elisha's "son" (2 Kgs 8:9). Elisha's response to Hazael's request is noteworthy: "Go and tell him, 'You will surely live,' but Yahweh has shown me that he will surely die."

---

[14] Gunkel (*Die Revolution,* 295) describes the political motives behind the prophetic choice of Jehu as follows: "However, that the prophets of that time chose just this man as the instrument of their plans shows that even they were ruthless, realistic politicians; they selected him because, according to position and temperment, he was the man to execute the bloody deed that was laid upon him."

[15] 2 Kgs 8:7–15*. A similar realistic portrayal of the prophet is found in 2 Kgs 6:24–7:20* and 2 Kgs 13:14–17.

[16] Schmitt (82–89) in my view correctly sees 8:11b–13a as a later addition. These verses interrupt the flow of the narrative and reflect a redactor's effort to vindicate Elisha's part in bringing Hazael to the throne by portraying his deep sorrow over the miseries that this usurper will bring upon Israel.

[17] 1 Sam 9:7, 1 Kgs 14:3, and 2 Kgs 5:15 suggest that it was customary to give a gift for prophetic services.

Although this response portrays Elisha as instructing Hazael to lie to Ben-Hadad, commentators have been uncomfortable with drawing this conclusion. Yet it is difficult to avoid the impression that this is what was intended, especially in light of the parallel structure of the sentence in which *hāyōh tiḥyeh* is contrasted with *môt yāmût*. Elisha instructs Hazael to tell Ben-Hadad the exact opposite of what Yahweh had revealed.

In order to understand the message of this episode, we must ask why it was that Elisha *informed Hazael* that the answer he was to give to Ben-Hadad was in fact a lie? Elisha (and the reader) must have realized that Hazael, out of loyalty to his king, may decide to expose the prophet's deceit to his master. Anticipating this, Elisha introduces a powerful inducement to share in the fraud: "Then Elisha said, 'Yahweh has shown me that *you* will be king over Syria.'" The dramatic tension of the remainder of the episode turns on whether Hazael's desire to be king will cause him to share in Elisha's deceit. Verses 14–15 resolve this tension by stating that not only did Hazael lie to his master, but that he also killed Ben-Hadad on the following day and became king in his place.[18]

This episode presents Elisha as a prophet who used his office to bring about the death of Ben-Hadad. It appears that by indirectly suggesting by means of an oracle that Hazael should kill the Syrian king, Elisha shrewdly and successfully incited a political coup. Here we see the prophet employing the same strategy he used to remove Jehoram from power. In the case of Jehoram, as with Ben-Hadad, Elisha delivers an oracle to a trusted army officer who, upon hearing the message, was incited to move against his lord. In both stories, Elisha is depicted as manipulating political forces by means of his prophetic influence. The two traditions contain portraits of Elisha that are remarkably similar.

In addition to Elisha, the scene introduces a second character who is identified as one of the *běnê hannĕbî'îm*. Although he plays a minor role, his presence adds another ingredient into our story, showing that Elisha was actually the leader of a distinctive social group within Israelite society. That "the sons of the prophet" were a well-known social group found in ninth-century Israel is shown by Jehu's reference to their typical behavior and speech (2 Kgs 9:11). These followers of Elisha appear to be integrated with Israelite society, living in various cities such as Bethel (2 Kgs 2:3), Jericho (2 Kgs 2:5, 15), Gilgal (2 Kgs 4:38), and throughout the hill country of Ephraim (2 Kgs 5:22). That they were not isolated from mainstream society

---

[18] Gray (532) does not want to attribute Ben-Hadad's death to Hazael and prefers to interpret the singular subject of *wayyiqah* as "indefinite." This interpretation makes Ben-Hadad's death appear to be more an act of Yahweh rather than the result of Elisha's calculated "prediction." But this view does not account for the fact that Elisha instructs Hazael to lie to the king.

is shown by 2 Kgs 4:1-2 that presupposes that these disciples marry, have children, own property and incur debts.

As their title suggests, "the sons of the prophets" had a special relationship with their prophet "father." The disciples of Elisha regularly met together with him in a special place whenever he came to their town (2 Kgs 4:38; 6:1). They adopted a stance of complete submission to their prophetic "father," bowing before him (2 Kgs 2:15), and describing themselves as Elisha's "servants" (2 Kgs 2:15; 4:1; 6:3) and him as their "lord" (2 Kgs 6:5). Their veneration of his spirituality is reflected by their referring to him as a "man of God" (2 Kgs 4:40). They appear anxious to help Elisha, volunteering to search out the missing Elijah even though their master knew that the search would be futile (2 Kgs 2:15-17). Elisha, for his part, periodically meets with his disciples, encouraging them to remain loyal to traditional Yahwism (2 Kgs 4:1). He also miraculously helps them out of difficult situations by providing money for the widow of one of the disciples, by rendering a poisonous pot of stew harmless, by retrieving a borrowed ax head that had fallen into a river, and (according to Gehazi's account) by buying clothes for two of his disciples out of his own pocket. This sort of subordinate relationship to Elisha explains why the young disciple obediently carried out Elisha's instructions even though the act involved great personal risk (2 Kgs 9:1-6, 10b).

a. Covert Preparations (9:1-6, 10b, 11-12).

Having gained a more vivid impression of the two characters that appear in the first scene, we may now examine the first episode more closely. It describes the prophet's successful efforts to inspire a political coup. The first (vv 1-6, 10b) of two parts focuses on Elisha's covert preparations. It tells of the delivery of a seditious message that designates Jehu as the new king of Israel. The second (vv 11-13, 15b-16) describes how the message was received, first by Jehu and then by his fellow officers. The dramatic tension revolves around the question of whether Jehu will accept the designation since this entails that he betray his king and exterminate the royal family. This tension is resolved when Jehu, seeing that he has the support of the other officers, seals off Ramoth Gilead and sets out for Jezreel to murder Jehoram.

The first part of this episode, 9:1-6, 10b, has a simple structure, being comprised of two complementary parts: vv 1-3 contain Elisha's commission and vv 4-6, 10b record its execution.

The Commission:

Now Elisha the prophet summoned one of the prophetic disciples
and instructed him,

A   Tuck your cloak into your belt, take this vial of oil with you, and
     go to Ramoth Gilead.
B   When you get there, search out Jehu ben Nimshi.[19] And when you
     find him, draw him away from
     his fellow commanders and take him into a secluded room.
C   Then take the vial, pour the oil on his head and declare, "Thus says
     Yahweh, 'I anoint you king over Israel.'"
D   Then open the door and flee without delay!

The Execution:

A' So the young man[20] went to Ramoth Gilead.
B' When he entered and looked and there were army officers sitting
     together. He said to them, "Commander, I have a message for you."
     Jehu responded, "For which one of us?" "For you, Commander,"
     he answered. So Jehu arose and entered a house.
C' Then the young man poured oil on Jehu's head and said, "Yahweh
     says this: 'I anoint you king over Israel.'"
D' Then he opened the door and fled.

The noteworthy feature of this commission/execution is not the disciple's obedience to his prophetic father. This is what the reader would expect. What does generate interest is the mood of intrigue that permeates this episode. As already mentioned, the situation described in vv 14b-15a provides the key to understanding the motive behind Elisha's actions. Judging that these circumstances favored a successful coup, the prophet moved to rouse Jehu against the king. With Jehoram separated from his troops and Jehu in command of the army, Elisha perceived that the time was right to designate Jehu as Yahweh's appointed ruler over Israel, hoping that Jehu would also realize that this was the time to strike. He therefore instructed his disciple to carry out his instructions immediately so that the opportunity would not be lost.[21]

---

[19] The Syriac lacks the reference to Jehoshaphat and LXX[L] places it after *nimši*. Some (Šanda, 93; Kittel, 229) have explained this by supposing that Jehu's grandfather, Nimshi, was better known than his father, Jehoshaphat. But because 2 Kgs 9:20 and 1 Kgs 19:16 do not mention Jehoshaphat, it seems likely that his mention here is a late expansion.

[20] The MT has *wayyēlek hanna'ar hanna'ar hannābî'* ("Then the young man, the young man, the prophet went"). The LXX and S lack the first *hanna'ar*. Some (Burney, 297; Kittel, 229) suggest that the original *hanna'ar na'ar hannābî'* was corrupted by the inclusion of a definite article. Others (Benzinger, *Könige*, 150; Montgomery, 400-1; Šanda, 93; Eissfeldt, 556) add that the uncorrupted *na'ar hannābî'* was an expansion to specify the identity of the messenger.

[21] Elisha's command that the disciple "tuck his cloak into his belt" shows that Elisha wanted his message to Jehu dispatched quickly.

The tactical shrewdness of Elisha's timing is also seen in the concern for secrecy. Elisha chose not to deliver the message himself, but rather commissioned one of his disciples to execute the assignment. Although the story does not indicate how well Elisha was known for his "unpatriotic" attitudes, the decision to send a disciple to the army officers was probably intended to avert an inhospitable welcome that would frustrate the prophet's designs.

Even with this precaution, Elisha knew, as did the audience, that the designation was an act of treason. The disciple was therefore instructed to deliver it in a secluded room, safely away from the ears of the other commanders. Even then, the disciple would face the possibility that Jehu would reject his message and move against the traitor. Hence Elisha further instructed him to leave the area immediately after delivering the message. These details indicate that the episode was intended to highlight the sense of danger and intrigue arising from the treasonous nature of Elisha's designation.

b. Jehu is acclaimed King of Israel (9:13, 15b-16).

Once the messenger is safely away, attention is directed to Jehu's response.

> Then Jehu went out to the commanders, the servants of his lord,[22] and they asked,[23] "Is everything all right?[24] What did this madman[25] have to say?" Jehu replied, "You know the kind of things these people say." "Don't try to deceive us,"[26] they said. "Tell us what he said!" Jehu responded, "This is exactly what

[22] The reference to Jehoram as the "lord" occurs seven times in the original narrative (2 Kgs 9:11, 31; 10:2, 3, 3, 6, 9). Those explicitly named as Jehoram's servants include Jehu, his fellow officers, and the leaders of Samaria, all of whom broke loyalty to their king. By emphasizing this, the narrator registers a criticism of the events that took place in the north. In contrast to Jehoiada's coup, the author does not seem to accept the view that the conspirators were betraying their queen, although this is clearly Athaliah's perspective. Like the Dtr redactor, the narrator does not accept the legitimacy of Athaliah's reign. Removing her involved no breach of loyalty. On the contrary, loyalty to the legitimacy of the Davidic house "demanded" her removal.

[23] The MT has the singular *wayyōmer*. The often accepted plural reading *wayyōmerû* is supported by LXX, S, V and T.

[24] *haššālôm* is a conventional greeting, intended to ask about the welfare of a specific individual (Gen 29:26; 43: 27; 2 Kgs 4:26), or about things in general (2 Kgs 5:21; 9:11, 18, 19, 22, 31). The customary response — assuming that everything is all right — is "*šālôm.*" For more elaborate interpretations of the significance of this phrase see D. J. Wiseman, "Is it Peace? Covenant and Diplomacy," *VT* 32 (1982) 311-26; Olyan, 652-68.

[25] *hammēšuggāʿ*, the officers' designation for the young man, can mean one who is literally insane. It is used in this sense when David feigns madness before Achish (1 Sam 21:15-16). In an extended sense, it is applied to those 'driven mad' by a terrible experience (Deut 28:28, 34; Zech 12:4). In our passage it is used as a derogatory term applied to the eccentric behavior of the prophets. Hosea (Hos 9:7) and Jeremiah (Jer 29:7) were likewise insulted.

[26] Used as an absolute *šeqer* is an exclamation. In Jer 37:14 it is used to deny vehemently

he said:[27] 'Yahweh says this: "I anoint you king over Israel."'" Then each man quickly took his cloak and covered the landing (?) of the steps[28] before him,[29] blew a trumpet and shouted, "Jehu is king!"[30] So Jehu said, "If this is what you want,[31] let no one slip out of the city to go to Jezreel to report what has happened here." Then he mounted his chariot and rode toward Jezreel because Jehoram was recovering there. Now Ahaziah king of Judah had come down to see Jehoram.

The scene that now unfolds demonstrates the author's subtle yet effective skill at dramatic narration. With elegant conciseness, the scribe allows us to peer into the motives of Jehu and his compatriots. Here Jehu is the center of attention. He has just been told by the young prophet that Yahweh has anointed the new king of Israel. Jehu's response to this message now becomes the central issue in the narrative.

Jehu leaves the secluded room to return to the other officers to whom the author refers as "the servants of his lord" (v 11). Why does the narrator choose at this point in the story to apply this particular description to Jehu's consorts? It appears to be the author's intention to indicate what Jehu was wrestling with as he walked down the steps to return to his curious comrades. Jehu now finds himself in a difficult situation. He knows that he will be asked to give an account of what transpired in the secluded meeting with this "fanatic." How will "the servants of his lord" react to a message that calls for Jehu to kill their king? Once they know what was said, they may well wonder why Jehu had allowed this disloyal instigator to leave alive. Jehu decides he can do only one thing—evade their probing questions.

---

an allegation. Here the officers bluntly inform Jehu that they see through his feeble attempt to avoid addressing the clear intention of their question.

[27] The idiom *kāzō' t wĕkāzō' t* has two usages: (1) without introduction to direct discourse, it functions as a literary device that allows the narrator to forego the repetition of speech (2 Sam 17:15; 2 Kgs 5:4); (2) when preceding direct discourse, as in our passage, it indicates the accuracy of what is reported (Josh 7:20; 2 Kgs 9:12).

[28] *'el-gerem hamma'ălôt* is a difficult phrase. The word *gerem* literally means "bone," and based on an analogous use of the synonym *'esem* to mean "self," some have translated the phrase "on the steps themselves." But it seems strange to emphasize the fact that the cloaks were laid on the "bare steps." Gray's suggestion that we are dealing here with an obscure architectural term makes the better sense.

[29] Literally, *taḥtāyw* ("under him"). This indicates that as Jehu ascended the steps, the officers placed their cloaks before him.

[30] This cultic cry of royal acclamation, known from the so-called "Enthronement Psalms" (Pss 47:8; 93:1; 96:10; 99:1. Ps 47:5, which describe Yahweh's ascent to the throne, is similar to the ritual described here with its mention of ascending steps to a throne accompanied by shouts of joy and trumpet blowing: "God has ascended amid shouts of joy, Yahweh amid the sounding of trumpets."

[31] Cf. Gen 23:8; Jer 15:1.

When Jehu returns to the group, they ask the question Jehu had anticipated: "What did that madman have to say to you?" Jehu then delivers his
evasive response: "You already know the kinds of things these people say."
The subtext of this statement runs something like this: "You don't want to
be bored with the particulars of our encounter. This fellow said the type of
things that you have already heard from such people. Let's leave it at that."
But the officers immediately see through Jehu's evasiveness. They know that
he is aware that they will want a detailed account of what transpired behind
closed doors. When Jehu denies them this, they protest, letting him know
that they have seen through his feeble attempt to withhold the information
they desire.

Jehu now realizes that any further attempt to evade their query would
only increase their curiosity. In an effort to convince them that he regards
the whole matter is trivial, he provides them with a verbatim report of the
young man's words.

The officers' response to the message provides the dramatic crescendo
of the scene. To Jehu's surprise, rather than doubting Jehu's loyalty, they
erupt into a frenzied display of support for the "new king." Suddenly Jehu
finds himself with the manpower needed to place himself on the throne. He
therefore assumes command, ordering his new subjects to demonstrate their
support by sealing off the city.

An important interpretive question is raised here. Why does the author
develop the scene in this way? What message is being conveyed? In terms of
plot development, the scene shows that Elisha's attempt to incite a revolt
against the Omrides was successful. In the end, Jehu commits himself to
what Elisha had hoped he would — the eradication of Omride rule in Israel.
But the author stresses that this partnership was not the result of a friendly
cooperation between the prophet and the commanders. On the contrary, the
narrator emphasizes that the two parties were alienated from one another.[32]
So how did it happen that Jehu and his men became the agents of Elisha's
designs to destroy the Omrides? The author informs his readers that Elisha
actually manipulated these military men by suggesting to them the idea of
revolt at a time when Jehoram was separated from his troops. Elisha is
gambling that their ambition would awaken them to the possibility of
putting Jehu and themselves in power. In the end the prophet's gamble paid

---

[32] Gunkel (*Die Revolution*, 295) drew this conclusion from Jehu's derogatory remarks
about the messenger: "The narrator intentionally laid such disrespectful words in Jehu's mouth:
Jehu in no way acted as a follower of Elisha, and is presented as a fully secular personality.
Also the king certainly would have not entrusted him with such a high office if he had publicly
listened to prophetic opposition. In what follows he acted only, or at least primarily, on behalf
of himself and his ambition, just as politicians have always done (Napoleon I was a master of
this), using religion as an acceptable guise for his designs."

off. Jehu's initial reticence to give any credence to the designation finally gave way to a murderous resolve. The scene concludes with Jehu and his men setting out for Jezreel where their first targets presently reside.

3. The Extermination of the Old Regime (2 Kgs 9:17–10:17a*α).

This section is central to the account of Jehu's overthrow of Omride rule in the north. Elisha has successfully fanned the fires of political ambition among Jehu and his men, and now Jehu proceeds to launch three attacks against the Omride regime. He begins with Jehoram, who is recuperating from his wounds in Jezreel and awaiting news from the battle front.

a. The Murder of Jehoram and Ahaziah (9:17–21bα, 22–24, 27abα).

The scene that now unfolds again illustrates the literary skill of the narrator. By switching back and forth between the king's dialogue with the watchman in Jezreel, and Jehu's dialogue with the king's messengers, the reader is drawn into this step-by-step account of how Jehu's masterful ambush was executed.

In this scene the author uses a traditional literary device of Hebrew narrative in which repetition is employed to create and build suspense. The episode contains a three-fold structure, each part beginning with the watchman's report and concluding with Jehu's response to those who came to meet him. This literary device is found in 2 Sam 18:24–27 where we also find a tripartite arrangement of a text that likewise begins with the watchman's report and ends with the king's response. Just as the recognition of Jehu by the way he drives his chariot breaks the scene, so also the identification of Ahimaaz by the way he runs pauses the action momentarily:

> While David was sitting between the inner and outer gates, the watchman went up to the roof of the gateway by the wall. As he looked out, he saw a man running alone. The watchman called out to the king and reported it. The king said, "If he is alone, he must have good news."

> While the man approached the city, the watchman saw another man running, and he called down to the gatekeeper, "Look, another man running alone!" The king said, "He must be bringing good news also."

> Then the watchman said, "It seems to me that the first one runs like Ahimaaz ben Zadok." The king responded, "He is a good man. He comes with good news."

Here repetition serves to emphasize the king's empty hope that the messengers are bringing "good news." In our passage, it is used to build suspense and arouse curiosity as the reader gropes to understand Jehu's designs. Although the audience knows that Jehu will succeed in killing Jehoram and

Ahaziah, the logic of Jehu's actions does not appear until the climactic third encounter.

Another example of the scribe's artistic techniques is seen in the way later developments in the plot are anticipated in this episode. The earlier mention of Ahaziah's presence in Jezreel (9:16), and the recounting of his death in this scene (9:27) anticipate a development of the plot that is taken up only after the narration of Jehu's coup is completed. The role that the account of Ahaziah's death plays in the development of the story does not become apparent until it is subsequently revealed that it was Athaliah's knowledge of this event that moved her to seize the Judean throne (11:1-3).

In addition to preparing for the account of Athaliah's takeover, our narrator anticipates the dramatic scene that immediately follows. Jehu's angry reference to Jezebel's evil influence upon the kingdom of Israel sets the stage for his tense encounter with the nefarious queen mother. The malice that is here verbally expressed, is fully vented in the next scene where Jehu orders her execution and then tramples her corpse. Also, Jehu's specific reference to Jezebel's "seductions and sorceries" not only looks forward to Jezebel's attempt to seduce Jehu, but also draws a thematic link to the final episode of Jehu's coup in which he engineers the destruction of the worshipers of Baal, of those who have fallen victim to Jezebel's "charms."

This scene opens by placing the reader at the watch tower of Jezreel where the watchman looks to the east awaiting word from the battle front:

> The watchman who was standing on the tower in Jezreel saw Jehu's band as it approached and reported, "I see some troops[33] coming." Jehoram ordered, "Summon a rider and send him out to meet them, and have him ask, "Is all well?" Then the rider rode out to meet them. Arriving he said, "The king says this: 'Is all well?'" Jehu replied, "What do you care?[34] Fall in behind me!"
>
> Then the watchman reported, "The messenger met them but did not return." So Jehoram sent a second rider out to them. When he arrived he said, "The king says this, 'Is all well?'" Jehu replied, "What do you care? Fall in behind me!"
>
> The watchman reported, "He met them but did not return. But the way the leader drives his chariot is just how Jehu ben Nimshi drives his—like a madman."[35] Then Jehoram ordered, "Prepare my chariot!" And when it was

[33] Reading *šip'â* for *šip'at*. Others suggest that *'ănāšîm* originally followed the construct form *šip'at*.

[34] This rhetorical question (lit: "What to you and to peace?") is an idiom used to deny emphatically a relationship between the two terms introduced by *lě* (Cf. Judg 11:12; 2 Sam 16:10; 19:23; 1 Kgs 17:18; 2 Kgs 3:13). Jehu is not denying that the messenger has the right to represent the king. He is saying that the messenger, as an emissary of the king, cares nothing for the welfare (*haššālôm*) of the nation. The intention of this question is made clear later in the episode by Jehu's fuller response to Jehoram.

[35] This probably refers to Jehu's constant whipping of his chariot team. The reference here

prepared, Jehoram king of Israel and Ahaziah king of Judah both rode out, each in his own chariot, to meet Jehu. When Jehoram saw that it was Jehu he asked, "Is all well, Jehu?" He answered, "How can all be well[36] as long as the seductions and sorceries of your mother Jezebel are so many?"

Then Jehoram reared about and fled, calling out to Ahaziah, "It's an ambush, Ahaziah!" But Jehu took his bow and shot Jehoram in the back, and Jehoram slumped down dead in his chariot.

When Ahaziah realized what was happening, he fled on the road toward Beth Haggan, and Jehu pursued him and ordered, "Shoot him also!" And they shot him[37] in his chariot at the road to Gur near Ibleam.[38] Then Jehu rode into Jezreel.

Although the reader knows that it is Jehu who is racing toward Jezreel, his approaching party is not immediately recognized by the watchman. It first appears as a cloud of dust off in the distance. Upon seeing it, the watchman reports to the king, informing him that the group is still too distant to be identified. The king responds by ordering that a rider be sent out to it. This action apparently reflects his concern over the war at Ramoth Gilead by revealing his desire to receive the news from the battle front as quickly as possible.

The scene then shifts to the messenger's encounter with Jehu. Upon arriving, the royal messenger executes his orders, formally announcing that he represents the king and stands ready to receive Jehu's report. Jehu's response no doubt puzzled the messenger and the reader alike. Instead of reporting on the situation at Ramoth Gilead, Jehu expresses hostility toward the messenger and rudely detains him from returning to the king. We are then returned to the palace where Jehoram receives the report that the messenger failed to return. Hoping to receive an explanation for this strange turn of events, the king dispatches a second rider. But the rider receives the same hostile reception and is likewise detained. However, by this time the party has advanced close enough so that the watchman can identify the leader of the group by means of his characteristic manner of driving his chariot team. The king is informed that it is Jehu, the officer the king had left in command of the troops at Ramoth Gilead, who is racing toward the city.

---

to Jehu's "madness" (*šiggā'ôn*) not only connects Jehu with the "mad" prophet (*hammešuggā'*) that visited him, but also seems to be the way the narrator wanted to epitomize Jehu's character—as someone wildly and cruelly obsessed with carrying out his intentions.

[36] The MT has two interrogative particles: *māh haššalôm*. Because of this redundancy, it seems better to read with the Versions and the Targums *māh šalôm*.

[37] Reading with LXX and S. The MT omits *wayyakkuhû*.

[38] The place where Jehu caught Ahaziah is explicitly specified. He was shot south of Beth Haggan and north of Ibleam at the intersection of "the road to Gur."

Once the king becomes aware that one of his trusted officers is approaching, and that he no doubt carries urgent news meant only for his ears, he sees no reason to remain behind the protective walls of the city. Furthermore, the fact that Jehu himself chose to leave the battle to see the king personally indicated to him that Jehu bore important news about the war — either victory or defeat. So Jehoram ordered that his chariot be prepared. He then sets out with Ahaziah to meet Jehu. At this point the narrator retards the tempo of his narrative by naming the full title of the kings and explicitly stating that they rode forth, as if to underscore the significance of this action: "And when it was prepared, Jehoram king of Israel and Ahaziah king of Judah both rode out, each in his own chariot,[39] to meet Jehu" (9:21b). This was the crucial act, for by it Jehoram and Ahaziah sealed their fate.

Knowing that Jehu would eventually succeed in killing the two kings, a perceptive reader would now have enough information to deduce Jehu's plan. His ploy was to draw the king into a vulnerable position where he would become easy prey, away from the security of the palace within the city walls. The drama builds as the reader awaits a confirmation of these suspicions.

Upon reaching Jehu's troops, Jehoram learns that the watchman had correctly identified the leader of the group. Jehoram addresses Jehu by name, asking him to report on the situation. Jehu responds with the same contempt he had earlier directed toward the king's messengers, calling the queen mother a whore and a witch.[40] With this blatantly insubordinate answer to the king's query, the scene has reached its dramatic climax. Up to this point, the design of Jehu's plan remained concealed. But with this response, the king perceives Jehu's murderous intention. Suddenly he knows why his messengers were detained, and that he has been cleverly maneuvered into an ambush.

Next follows the brief report of the murder of the two unfortunate kings. The narrator makes no attempt to build dramatic tension by suggesting any real chance of escape. With mechanical conciseness he informs the reader that when the two kings realized their perilous situation, they did

---

[39] The note that they took separate chariots anticipates their separate attempts to flee from Jehu.

[40] Jehu is here accusing Jezebel of offering something to Israel through illicit activities comparable to the trades of the harlot and the witch. Her ardent sponsorship of Baalism is thus compared to the body-selling harlot and spell-dealing sorceress. In Nah 3:4 the same two words (zĕnûnîm and kĕšāpîm) are figuratively used to describe Assyria's practice of selling slave labor to make allies. Just what Jezebel offered Israel for their allegiance is not stated. We may surmise that Israel was "seduced" and "bewitched" by the material prosperity and national security that the Baal-worshipping Omrides brought to Israel.

attempt to escape—but in vain. A single shot from Jehu's skilled bow took care of Jehoram, and Ahaziah's death was expedited after a seven-mile pursuit. The scene concludes with Jehu traveling back toward Jezreel where he would find Jezebel waiting to welcome her "champion."

b. The Murder of Jezebel and her Aborted Burial (9:30b–34a, 34b–36*,37).

The scene now switches from Ibleam to the palace in Jezreel where we find the queen mother Jezebel preparing for Jehu's inevitable arrival. Perhaps more than any other woman, Jezebel came to be regarded as the great enemy of Yahwism. As the daughter of Ethbaal king of Sidon, she was given in marriage to Omri's son Ahab to consolidate a political alliance (1 Kgs 16:31). She bore two children, both of whom suffered an unnatural death. Her first son, Ahaziah, was mortally injured by a fall from an upper room (1 Kgs 1:2–17), and Jehoram died at the hands of Jehu.

Information from early traditions about Jezebel is found in 1 Kgs 18:1–46, 19:1–18, 21:1–29 and 2 Kgs 9:30b–34a. In the Elijah traditions, she is treated as the villainess of Israel due to her militant Baalism and oriental despotism. Her zeal for the god of Sidon was expressed in the building of a temple for Baal in Samaria (1 Kgs 16:31–32), in her patronage of the prophets of Asherah and Baal (1 Kgs 18:19), and in her persecutions of the prophets of Yahweh, especially Elijah (1 Kgs 18:4, 13; 19:1). Her despotism is graphically depicted in the affair of Naboth's vineyard. Disgusted with Ahab's failure to behave as a king, she steps forward to secure the desired vineyard. This she does without the slightest tinge of conscience by having Naboth falsely condemned and killed by the elders and nobles of Jezreel. Throughout the whole affair, Jezebel acts as if such acts were the prerogative of royalty. In the character of Jezebel, we see not only a woman who zealously sponsored the propagation of Baalism in Israel, but who is also remembered as an immoral and despotic foreigner who cared little for the traditions of the Israelite people.

The dramatic encounter between Jezebel and Jehu found in this episode recounts the second action that Jehu and his band took to exterminate Omride rule. Killing the king was only the first step of this difficult task. Jehu still had to exterminate all who could claim the throne, secure the support of the rulers of Samaria, and convince the Jezreelites that his attack on the Omrides had wider support beyond his own group. But before Jehu can proceed to this business, he must first deal with the most powerful living Omride—the queen mother Jezebel.

The episode that now unfolds contains two scenes. In the first we witness Jezebel's unsuccessful attempt to seduce Jehu, a failure that led to her being thrown to her death from the palace balcony. The second scene tells how

Jehu's own maliciousness frustrated his attempt to have Jezebel buried and how in the end he justified his brutal actions by announcing that she did not after all deserve the burial he had earlier ordered.

The first scene begins with a description of events that actually took place before Jehu entered the city. Sometime between the killing of Ahaziah and Jehu's entrance into Jezreel, Jezebel was informed that he had killed her son. She responds to this news by preparing herself for an encounter with her son's murderer.

> When Jezebel heard about it, she made up her eyes, arranged her hair and waited for Jehu at her window. When Jehu entered the city[41] she asked him "Is all well, my champion,[42] slayer of his lord?" Then he looked up and called out, "Who supports me? Who?" Some eunuchs looked down and Jehu said, "Throw her down!" So they threw here down and some of her blood splattered on the wall and on the horses. Then he trampled[43] her body, entered the palace and dined.

Until recently, the common interpretation of Jezebel's reception of Jehu was based on a particular understanding of Jezebel's words to Jehu as he entered the city, usually rendered as "Is all well, you Zimri who murdered his master?" According to this view, Jezebel is here alluding to Zimri, another officer who usurped the throne, but whose reign lasted only seven days (1 Kgs 16:9–15). It is commonly thought that Jezebel is addressing him sarcastically and implicitly calling for a similar fate to befall Jehu. On the basis of this understanding, Jezebel is portrayed positively. Her cosmetic preparations are seen as a mark of her fearlessness as she prepares to meet her death with dignity: "Jezebel has no illusions about her fate. She makes up her face carefully and dresses royally, not to seduce Jehu, but because she is determined to die like a queen."[44] But as S. Parker has recently argued, this interpretation of her words does not adequately account for the significance of Jezebel's actions. Drawing on both biblical and ancient Near Eastern texts, Parker convincingly argues that these show that both the painting of the eyes and the arranging of hair were customary preparations made by women in anticipation of love-making:

---

[41] Reading *bā'îr* with LXX. MT has *baššaʿar*. It is not likely that the palace was at the gate. Jehu entered the city and arrived at the royal residence to assume command of the city. It was here that Jezebel awaited his arrival.

[42] As discussed below, I follow S. Parker ("Jezebel's Reception of Jehu," *MAARAV* 1 [1978] 67-78) who derives the noun from *zmr* III* (See *HALAT* 1 [1967] 263). I differ, however, in understanding the final *yod* as a pronominal suffix. Parker thinks the *yod* is comparable with other nouns and adjectives ending in –*î*, such as *'akzarî* "cruel (one)," *tahtî* "lower," *hopšî* "free."

[43] Reading with the MT. Most commentators follow the LXX and read a plural form of the verb.

[44] Ellis, 200-1. So also Kittel, 233; Šanda, 100; Gressmann, 311-12; Landsdorfer, 171.

On the evidence of the two acts ascribed to Jezebel before her appearance at the window, and of the connotations of such acts and the role of women's hair and eyes in the various literatures, we are justified in concluding that Jezebel here intends to seduce Jehu.[45]

Parker then offers an interpretation of Jezebel's words that is consistent with her actions. His argument centers on a proposal concerning the meaning of *zimrî*. In contrast to the interpretation mentioned above in which *zimrî* is taken as a name, Parker understands it as a common noun meaning "hero or champion." This allows an interpretation that brings consistency to Jezebel's deed and words:

Far from being an expression of malevolence, the word is now recognizable as an expression of admiration. Jehu has just proved himself stronger than the late king. . . Jezebel is now seen to be pursuing the same course on which she initially embarked.[46]

This interpretation is supported by Jehu's earlier allusion in 9:23 to the sexual prowess of Jezebel where he compares Jezebel to a harlot. This earlier characterization is here dramatically illustrated.[47] This scene thus portrays Jezebel's unsuccessful attempt to seduce Jehu. Both her cosmetic preparations and flattering words were intended to let Jehu know that she appreciated a man of his accomplishments and that she desired to become a member of his new political order.

An examination of the structure of this short but forceful scene reveals that it contains a two-part structure, each part consisting of the words and deeds of the two main characters — Jezebel and Jehu. Jezebel's actions (v 30b) take the form of some cosmetic preparations made in anticipation of Jehu's imminent arrival. Her words (v 31) reveal her attempt to seduce the usurper upon his arrival at the royal residence. The second part of the scene shows the same type of arrangement, but reverses the order. It begins with Jehu's words, where he calls for a show of support and orders that Jezebel be thrown from the window. Then a description of his subsequent actions is given in which the narrator portrays Jehu applying his own brand of cosmetics! He tramples her corpse, enters the palace, and dines. Thus the structure of the episode may be represented as follows:

1. Jezebel's seduction (30b–31)
   A. Jezebel's deeds: Cosmetic preparations
   B. Jezebel's words: Seductive greeting

---

[45] Parker, 69.

[46] Ibid., p 72.

[47] The sexual implications of Jezebel's actions are also suggested by author's use of the common "woman in the window" motif. See W. F. Albright, "Some Canaanite-Phoenecian sources of Hebrew wisdom," VTSup 3 (1955) 1-15, esp. p. 10.

2. Jehu's response (32–34a)
   B′. Jehu's words: Order to kill Jezebel
   A′. Jehu's deeds: Trampling of the corpse

Out of this two-part structure, the narrative builds suspense by first revealing Jezebel's preparations to meet Jehu. Upon hearing that Jehu has killed her son, she paints her eyes and arranges her hair. The suspense builds when Jehu arrives at the palace and finds an admiring and alluring Jezebel awaiting him. Jehu is now faced with a critical decision. The narrative tension is strung across the question, "Will Jehu succumb to Jezebel's charms and accept her proposition?"

This tension is prolonged by Jehu's first response. Rather than answering Jezebel, he calls out to those inhabiting the royal residence, demanding that as a show of support they respond to his summons.[48] The significance of this action is not immediately apparent. Only with the next action does the reader learn what Jehu had in mind. The eunuchs were called for the specific purpose of killing the queen mother. Upon their arrival at the window, Jehu commands them to throw the woman from the window. Realizing that it was either her life or theirs, they comply without any hesitation. With the throwing of Jezebel from the window, the scene reaches its denouement. Through it Jehu is portrayed as completely impervious to Jezebel's charms. Indeed, Jezebel's seductive designs backfired. Instead of swaying him to join forces, she ignited the seething hatred that he had earlier expressed in his encounter with her son.

Had the narrator desired to portray Jehu only as a victor over Jezebel's temptation, he could have concluded the scene at this point with a summarizing statement such as "So Jezebel died." But the author's interest in portraying Jehu in a negative light moved him to continue the scene. We are told that when Jezebel hit the street, her blood splattered on the wall of the palace and on the horses, thereby informing the reader that Jezebel's corpse now lay near Jehu's chariot team. The scene then concludes with a terse description of Jehu's actions: "and he trampled her body, entered the palace and dined." It is not difficult to see that the author wishes to portray Jehu as one who is fanatically driven by his hatred toward Jezebel. Not content to show Jehu as merely the murderer of Jezebel, the narrator portrays Jehu as venting his vehemence by the gruesome act of abusing her corpse. In addition, Jehu's callousness is emphasize with the note that immediately after mutilating Jezebel's body he entered the palace and ate.

---

[48] Jehu's distrust of everyone is indicated in the story by the fact that on three different occasions Jehu demands a show of loyalty. His men were to show loyalty by sealing off Jezreel; the palace residents are to show it by answering his summons and following his orders; the elders of Samaria were to show their loyalty by sending Jehu the heads of the princes.

This last action lays the basis for the second scene of this episode. In it Jehu's unsuccessful attempt to see to Jezebel's burial is narrated:

> Then he said, "Take care of that accursed woman and bury her, for she was of royal blood." But when they went out to bury her, they found nothing except her skull, her feet and her hands. And they went back and told Jehu, who said, "Jezebel's body will be[49] like excrement on the field[50] so that no one will be able to say, 'This is Jezebel's corpse.'"

This short scene consists of the issuing of an order, the complications that arose when the servants attempted to bury Jezebel, and Jehu's final response:

    a.   Jehu orders Jezebel's burial (34b).
    b.   Complication (35–36*).
    c.   Jehu's response (37).

The action is located in the palace where Jehu sits feasting at the table formerly used by two of his royal victims. While dining, he issues a surprising order: Jezebel is to be buried. Yet Jehu's concern for Jezebel's burial is not motivated out of respect for this "accursed woman." According to Jehu, she is to receive a burial because of her royal lineage.

It is difficult to determine whether the narrator wished his readers to believe that Jehu's order was motivated by a genuine respect for the royal class, or whether Jehu's stated motive cloaked a desire on his part to remove from public inspection the evidence of his brutal treatment of Jezebel's corpse. In either case, Jehu's command eventually placed him in an embarrassing situation. When the servants attempted to carry out their task, they discovered that Jehu had so mangled Jezebel's corpse that only the distinctive parts of her body could be identified. When they reported this to Jehu, he responded in a way that contradicts his earlier concern for Jezebel's burial. He boldly announces that Jezebel does not in fact deserve to be buried and that her body parts should be left scattered on the ground like dung!

How Jehu's "reversal" is to be interpreted depends upon how one understands the motive that moved him to see to Jezebel's burial in the first place. If the author meant to represent Jehu as genuinely concerned that Jezebel be treated as royalty, then this scene seems to be intended to show that this concern was immediately displaced by his need to justify his unmitigated violence. As soon as Jehu realized that his own brutality had made Jezebel's burial impossible, he exonerates his actions by stating that Jezebel deserves no burial. But if Jehu's real purpose in having Jezebel buried was to remove

---

[49] The qere corrects the old Qal feminine form *hāyat* to read *hāyĕtâ*.

[50] LXX^L omitted the gloss *behĕleq yizrĕ'e'l*.

her mangled remains from the view of the public, then Jehu's reversal could be construed as the author's means of showing that Jehu never had any genuine concern for Jezebel's internment. Rather he was only concerned that her body be removed from the street. Accordingly, when Jehu learned that no evidence of his brutality remained, he revealed what he had thought from the start was a fitting fate for the corpse of this "accursed woman." Whether this scene is understood to depict Jehu as one who was quick to rationalize his brutality, or as one who sought to remove the evidence of it, it appears that the scene was constructed in order to register another criticism of Jehu's character.

c. The Murder of the Princes of Samaria (10:1-9, 17aα).

Jehu now mounts a third and final attack against Omride royalty that will secure for him the throne of Israel:

> Then Jehu wrote letters and sent them to Samaria, addressed to the leaders of the city,[51] to the elders, and to the royal guardians.[52] The first said, "Since you are with the king's sons and possess chariots and horses, fortified cities[53] and weapons,[54] as soon as this letter arrives, choose the best and most worthy from among your lord's sons and set him upon his father's throne. Then defend your lord's house!" But they were terrified and said among themselves, "Since two kings could not withstand him, how can we?" So the palace administrator and the city governor, the elders, and the royal guardians replied, "We are your servants and will do anything you say. We will not appoint anyone as king. You may do as you wish."[55]

> Then he wrote them a second[56] letter which said, "If you do indeed support me and will do what I command, then take the heads of the men of your lord's house[57] and deliver them to me in Jezreel by this time tomorrow." (Now the

---

[51] The MT has *yizrĕ'e'l*, but this is obviously a corruption since Jehu's letters originated from there. Its presence is probably a result of the corruption of *hā'îr wĕ'el*.

[52] The syntactical awkwardness of *'ahāb* raises doubts about its presence in the text. Furthermore, the fact that the text refers to Jehoram's sons ("sons of the king") rather than to Ahab's sons supports the conclusion that it is a gloss. It is likely that it was added by the Dtr redactor who has a special interest in the destruction of Ahab's house (cf. 2 Kgs 9:7-9).

[53] Reading the plural with some manuscripts and the versions since every other noun in this enumeration is plural.

[54] Ezek 39:9 enumerates what is meant by *hannāšeq*: "Then those who live in the towns of Israel will go out and use weapons (*nešeq*) for fuel and burn them up—the small and large shields, the bows and arrows, the war clubs and spears."

[55] The LXX has, "Whatever you say, we will do." But this seems redundant.

[56] The MT has *šēnît* which may be retained if it is taken as adverbial. But reading the adjective *šēnî* with several manuscripts and the LXX is less strained.

[57] Reading *bêt* for *bĕnê* which allows the retention of the otherwise redundant *'anšê*. The previous mention of their "lord's house" in v 3 is picked up here. Having refused to defend it, they are now to assault it on Jehu's behalf.

royal princes, all seventy of them, were under the care of the leading men of the city whose task it was to rear them.) When the letter arrived, these men took the princes and massacred every one of them. Then they put the heads in baskets and sent them to Jehu in Jezreel.

Then a messenger came to Jehu and told him, "They have brought the heads of the princes." Then Jehu ordered, "Put them in two piles at the entrance of the city[58] until morning." When morning arrived, Jehu went out and stood before all the people and said, "Judge for yourselves. I admit that I conspired against my lord and killed him. But who struck down all these people?"

This episode falls into two main sections, each of which contains two subsections:

I. The murder of the princes (10:1b–7)
   A. The first correspondence (1b–5)
      1. Challenge to battle (1b–3)
      2. Surrender (4–5)
   B. The second correspondence (6–7)
      1. Orders to massacre the princes (6)
      2. Execution of the orders (7)

II. Jehu's self-vindication (10:8–9)
   A. The order to display the heads (8)
   B. Jehu's speech to the Jezreelites (9)

The first section contains a report of a private communications between Jehu in Jezreel and the leadership of Samaria. In his first letter, Jehu boldly challenges the leaders to appoint a new king and meet him in battle to decide who is to rule Israel. The leaders are terrified by Jehu's previous actions and quickly surrender to his authority, thereby making him the new king of Israel. Jehu then sends a second letter intended to test their proclaimed loyalty. They are ordered to massacre the princes and to deliver their heads to him in Jezreel within twenty-four hours of the time they receive these instructions. The first part concludes with the leaders of Samaria sending to Jehu the heads of the princes.

The action of the second section takes place in Jezreel. It begins with Jehu receiving word that the heads have arrived from Samaria. The heads apparently arrived sometime during the night, for Jehu orders that they be piled up at the city entrance and left there until the next morning. When morning arrives Jehu goes to the city gate and addresses the people.

Although the first part of this episode contains the potential to build and resolve dramatic tension, the narrator chose not to exploit it. When Jehu

---

[58] Reading *petah hā'îr* with the LXX. The MT has *petah haššaʿar*.

issued his challenge to the Samaria's rulers, their surrender is immediately reported after a short discussion. No tension is created over the decision of whether to surrender or not. The same is true of the next scene. Instead of creating a dilemma over Jehu's order that they slaughter the princes who were in their care, the author has the leadership execute their orders without any delay. The central tension of this episode concerns the heads delivered to Jezreel. All that has preceded prepares for the denouement that occurs in the next scene.

The demand for the heads of the princes does not at first appear to be particularly significant. Jehu may have simply wanted proof that the guardians of the princes had carried out his demanding orders. But the next scene opens with a messenger informing Jehu that the baskets have arrived. From the reader's point of view, this piece of information is given to inspire curiosity. Why is attention suddenly focused upon the dismembered heads? Jehu's next action increases the interest. He orders that they be placed on public display at the city entrance, the one location that is visited by more people than any other. The action was intended to make the city aware of the pile of heads and so prepare for Jehu's explanation for their presence.

The dramatic climax now arrives. As the people buzz with conjecture among themselves, Jehu steps forward to account for the presence of the heads. He begins his explanation by expressing his confidence in their judgment, challenging them to draw their own conclusions. He then makes a clever concession: "I admit that I conspired against my lord and killed him. . . ." Jehu knows that there are some among the Jezreelites who are suspicious of the character of a man who betrays his king. He acknowledges that they are familiar with the brutal ambition that can drive usurpers to commit an extreme act of violence. But he goes on to argue that he is not to be classified as such. His defense is couched in the rhetorical question ". . . but who killed all these people?" Yes, he did kill his lord, but he is not responsible for the death of the seventy princes of Samaria. His defense rests on their knowledge that he had been with them in Jezreel since his arrival. Therefore, he could have had nothing to do with the death of the princes. Then how is the presence of the heads to be accounted for? Jehu wishes his audience to conclude that Jehu's betrayal of his king had the support of the leadership in Samaria. So he concedes that he betrayed and killed his lord, but not out of self-serving ambition. On the contrary, his actions had the backing of the leadership of the nation's capital. The offering of the heads of the princes bears witness to the enthusiastic support of Samaria's leaders.

Jehu's argument, intended to convince the Jezreelites of the virtues of his "representative actions," has precisely the opposite effect upon the reader. This is because the reader knows more about the affair than the Jezreelites, namely, that Jehu was indeed responsible for the deaths of the princes. The reader also knows that the leadership of Samaria was not motivated by deep-seated anti-Jehoram sentiments as Jehu implies. They were actually intimidated by the very characteristics that Jehu seeks to deny. By providing the reader with this additional information, the author skillfully places Jehu in the worst possible light. The Jezreelites may be duped by Jehu's deceit, but the reader is presented with a ruthless usurper and a cunning liar.[59]

The scene concludes with Jehu's leaving Jezreel and arriving at Samaria where he plans to take actions that will consolidate his rule over Israel.

4. The Consolidation of the New Regime (2 Kgs 10:18-22, 24-25a).

The episode that now unfolds is the final section of the account of Jehu's bloody coup. Having exterminated two kings, the queen-mother, and the seventy princes of Samaria, Jehu takes steps to consolidate his new regime:

> Then Jehu assembled all the people and told them, "Ahab's patronage of Baal was insignificant compared to the patronage that Jehu will show. Now let all of the prophets of Baal[60] and all of his priests be assembled before me. Let no one be absent, for I have a great sacrifice for Baal. Those who do not attend will forfeit their lives!" Then Jehu said [to the prophets and the priests], "Convene an assembly for Baal."[61] And they proclaimed it. So Jehu had it proclaimed throughout Israel, and all the servants of Baal came; no one was absent.

> Then they entered the temple of Baal and filled it from one end to the other, and Jehu told the keeper of the ritual garments, "Bring robes for all the servants of Baal," and he did so. Then they proceeded to make sacrifices and burnt offerings. Now Jehu had posted eighty men outside whom he had threatened saying, "The man who allows any of those whom I am delivering into your hands to escape will pay for it with his own life." So as soon as Jehu had completed making the burnt offering, he ordered the guards and officers: "Go in and kill them. Let no one escape!" So they went in and struck them down with their swords.

Two main sections comprise this scene. The first reports the steps Jehu took to convene a cultic assembly; the second describes the ritual events and the massacre that followed.

---

[59] The same sort of "inside information" is provided by the author of the Naboth affair to condemn Jezebel for the death of Naboth.

[60] The mention of "all his servants" is generally regarded as an addition, inspired by the mention of the "servants of Baal" in vv 22 and 23. The mention of the servants of Baal here thus confuses the narration of the events. As Burney notes (303–4), "Jehu summons the *prophets* and *priests* of Ba'al, who are commanded to proclaim a solemn assembly, to which the *worshipers in general* are summoned (v 20 f.)."

[61] Cf. A. Kuyt and W. Wesselius, "A Ugaritic Parallel for the Feast of Ba'al in 2 Kings x:18-28," *VT* 354 (1985) 109–11.

A. Jehu convenes a cultic assembly (10:18–20a)
1. Jehu summons the prophets and priests to appear before him.
2. Jehu orders them to proclaim cultic assembly.
3. The worshipers arrive at the temple.
B. The sacrifice and its outcome (10:20b–22, 24–25a)
1. The worshipers enter the temple.
2. The narrator's exposure of Jehu's plans.
3. Jehu orders the massacre of the worshipers.

The first part reports the steps that Jehu took to convene a cultic gathering. Upon his arrival in the capital, Jehu immediately proclaims his official policy toward the state's patronage of the cult of Baal. Addressing the people of Samaria, he announces that his royal sponsorship of Baal's cult will far outstrip that of Ahab. This boast is then followed by a summons to the priests and prophets of Baal. Failure to attend will be punished with death.

Some time later the religious functionaries appear before Jehu as commanded. Through them, he announces throughout Israel his intention to acknowledge Baal as the state god. As a result "all the servants of Baal" responded and gathered outside the temple precincts.

The second part opens with the throng's entering the temple for the sacrifice which it fills to capacity. Ritual garments are provided for the worshipers, and the sacrifices are offered. The narrator then interrupts the description of the events to inform the reader of the arrangements Jehu had made in preparation for the cultic gathering. He had instructed eighty men to station themselves at the perimeter of the temple and await his orders to kill those within. To insure that they will carry out his instructions, he had threatened to kill any soldier who allows a worshiper to escape the trap. Having informed the reader of Jehu's preparations, the author returns to a narration of the events. As soon as Jehu completed his sacrifices, he orders his men to carry out their instructions. The scene closes with the massacre of the worshipers of Baal.

The means by which the author builds the drama of this episode is similar to that employed in the scene that describes Jehu's ambush of the two kings. The reader, knowing that Jehu harbored a deep hatred toward Baalism that he had previously expressed through several acts of deceit and violence, would be suspicious at Jehu's boast to support ardently the cult of Baal. The suspense builds as Jehu sees to it that all of the worshipers of Baal are summoned to the temple and that they are provided with the proper ritual garments. The suspense is suddenly heightened with the narrator's exposing of Jehu's prior arrangements with the eighty men stationed outside the temple. By withholding this information from the reader until the last moment, it is as though the narrator wishes to have the readers share with the victims the sudden realization that a deadly trap had been set. The account then proceeds quickly to report that Jehu was again successful in laying a death-trap. The narrator concludes the scene with the image of the armed guards descending upon the helpless throng and slaughtering them.

It is not difficult to detect the message the author sought to convey about Jehu through this grisly episode. Once again Jehu is shown behaving with his characteristic cunning and violence. The author also wished to make it clear that Jehu's attack on the Baalists was not motivated by a devotion to Yahweh. He did this by telling his audience that Jehu called for the massacre of Baal's worshipers only after he had offered a sacrifice to Baal (v 25). By having Jehu perform an act that was deeply offensive to Yahwism, the narrator made the same point about Jehu's character that he made through Jehu's dialogue with his comrades following the visit from Elisha's disciple. Jehu was motivated not by a devotion to Yahwism, but by his own political ambitions.

Our analysis of the first part of this narrative has shown that the author was fundamentally concerned with depicting the negative aspects of Jehu's character by highlighting his self-serving political ambition, his deceitfulness, and most of all, his unrestrained propensity for violence. And although the narrator does not reflect a sympathetic attitude toward the Omrides or the Baalism they fostered, he is clearly critical of the means by which Jehu removed this regime and established his own in its place. In order to comprehend this unsympathetic treatment of the Omrides, and the critical portrayal of Jehu's coup, it is necessary to take into consideration the second part of the narrative.

Part Two: The Establishment of Joash's Reign through the Eradication of Omride Rule in Judah

The plot of part two follows the same course as part one. Beginning with a description of the circumstances that provided the motivation for Jehoiada's conspiracy, it next tells of Jehoiada's instigation of and preparations for the revolt. In the third section the Omride queen is arrested and executed, and the final section shows how Jehoiada consolidated Joash's new regime.

1. The Setting (2 Kgs 11:1–3).

We noted in chapter II that these introductory verses to the second part of the narrative not only provide a link with the events that transpired in the northern kingdom, but also set the scene for Jehoiada's overthrow of queen Athaliah in the south. Two principal actions are described: Athaliah's ruthless appropriation of the throne through the murder of the Judean princes, and Jehosheba's valiant rescue of the infant Joash.

> When Athaliah, the mother of Ahaziah, learned of the death of her son, she set out to exterminate the royal family. But Jehosheba, daughter of King Joram and sister of Ahaziah, took Joash, Ahaziah's son,[62] and stole him away from among the royal princes who were about to be murdered. She put[63] him in a bedroom with his nurse and hid[64] him from Athaliah so that he was not killed. For six years he remained hidden in Yahweh's temple while Athaliah maintained her rule over the land.

Athaliah's brutal actions gained her the distinction of being the only woman to sit on the throne of Judah. Like her father Omri,[65] and her sister Jezebel, she was prepared to take any action that would secure or advance her political powers. She obtained influence in Judah as a result of her father's practice of securing Israel's political strength by political marriages. Just as Omri had arranged the marriage between his son Ahab and Jezebel a princess of Sidon, so he also secured a political liaison with Judah by marrying his daughter Athaliah to the Judean king Joram. When that influence was threatened, Athaliah took drastic and immediate steps to defend her position of power.

Athaliah plays the role of the antagonist of Jehoiada, the hero of the account. Accordingly, she is presented in an extremely negative light. Not surprisingly, the Chronicler shares the same perspective. Her influence as queen-mother is tersely summed up with an evaluation of her son Ahaziah: "He too walked in the ways of the house of Ahab, for his mother encouraged him in doing wrong" (2 Chr 22:3). As for her six-year reign, the Chronicler indicates that she exhibited the same zealousness toward Baalism and disdain for Judah's traditional religion as her sister Jezebel: "Now the followers of that wicked woman Athaliah broke into the temple of God and used even its sacred objects for the Baals" (2 Chr 24:7).

Our account's portrayal of Athaliah begins with her receiving the news of the death of her son Ahaziah. Like Jezebel's reaction to the death of her son Jehoram, Athaliah showed no remorse at this news, but immediately

---

[62] The LXX is reading ben-'aḥîah "her brother's son."

[63] Supplying wattitten from 2 Chr 22:11.

[64] Reading with 2 Chr 22:11 and the LXX.

[65] 2 Kgs 8:26 and 2 Chr 22:2 state that she was the daughter of Omri, while 2 Kgs 8:18 and 2 Chr 21:6 describe her as the daughter of Ahab. Since her son Ahaziah was twenty-two years old when he became king in 842 (2 Kgs 8:26), Athaliah bore him in 864. Accordingly, supposing that she was about fifteen years old when she bore him, she herself would have been born ca. 879, three years before Omri became king of Israel (876–69). H. J. Katzenstein, "Who Were the Parents of Athaliah?" IEJ 5 (1955) 194–97, seeks to account for the epithet "daughter of Ahab" by suggesting that Athaliah grew up as a young orphan in the court of Ahab.

turned her attention to securing her own political power. In an act that reminds us of Jehu's gruesome method of dealing with the princes of Samaria, the ambitious queen-mother launched a program of mass murder by which she sought to eliminate every male that had a claim to the throne.[66] The fact that she was able to consolidate a six-year rule after such extreme actions testifies to her political resourcefulness.

Athaliah would have no doubt enjoyed a longer reign had it not been for the heroic actions of Jehosheba. We are told that she was the sister of Ahaziah although probably not the daughter of the woman she opposed. Apparently learning of Athaliah's plans through her connections with the court, she saved her brother's infant son by concealing the prince in the confines of the temple precincts. At first glance, the text seems to attribute this action to filial devotion. But the fact that she was the wife of Jehoiada[67] places her actions in a larger context. Like him, she was also concerned with preserving a legitimate heir to the throne. Together they secretly reared Joash, awaiting the opportunity to remove the usurper and replace her with the rightful heir to Judah's throne.

2. The Instigation of the Coup (2 Kgs 11:4-6, 8-9, 11-12).

That moment arrived six years later.[68] Jehoiada, the hero of the narrative, now enters the story with a plan to dethrone the queen and to reclaim the throne for Joash. When this narrative was composed, Jehoiada was well known among the readership as the high priest of Jerusalem who had removed Athaliah from the throne and placed the boy-king Joash in her place. In addition, it was probably common knowledge that as the king's uncle and regent, he was now virtual ruler of Judah.[69] But what the public lacked was an account of the events that put Joash (and Jehoiada) in power. This need was met by the narrative we have before us. In it Jehoiada is portrayed as a national hero who both planned and directed a coup that placed Judah's rightful heir upon the throne. Here the audience learns for the first time that six years earlier the bravery of Jehoiada's wife had prevented the death of the king's infant son, and that Jehoiada and his wife

---

[66] They would be the sons Ahaziah had sired through his many wives (like Joash), or possibly the descendants of Joram's six brothers whom Joram had killed when he consolidated his rule (2 Chr 21:4).

[67] This important piece of information is provided by 2 Chr 22:11. Its truthfulness is corroborated by the hiding place she chose for Joash. It was probably not stated in the account because this fact was well known at the time of writing. The same reason probably explains why Jehoiada's status of high priest is not mentioned until v 9.

[68] No explanation is given for the six-year delay. Perhaps it indicates that an age of seven years was the minimum age required to assume the royal office.

[69] The Dtr redactor notes that he "instructed" the king (2 Kgs 12:2).

had secretly reared the boy in the temple precincts. Here also they receive a detailed account of the events that led to the removal of the former regime and the establishment of the present political order.

The character of Jehoiada completely dominates the account. As both the political and religious leader of the coup, he instigates virtually every significant event that occurs. In addition to his clandestine rearing of the prince, he initiates the coup by summoning the captains of the guard, making them swear a solemn oath to secrecy before revealing to them that an heir to the throne had survived Athaliah's purge. He formulates a brilliant plan and oversees its execution, and he orders Athaliah's execution, and leads the victorious throng to the palace. Jehoiada thus stands at the center of this narrative as the political tactician whose intelligence brings about a highly efficient dethroning of the tyrant Athaliah and the enthroning of Judah's rightful heir.

But Jehoiada's role in these events extends beyond his shrewd leadership of the anti-Omride forces. He also performs several sacred acts that stand at the heart of Judah's religio-political life. Acting in his official capacity as the high priest, he places the royal insignia on Joash, pronounces him king, anoints him, and mediates a covenant between the king and his new subjects. The narrator has presented a picture of Jehoiada that portrays a man who combines political sagacity and religious piety, directing both toward the well-being of the nation.

Jehoiada and his wife Jehosheba are not the only ones in the account who are presented as national heroes. The coup could not have succeeded had it not been for the unquestioning loyalty of the commanders of the guard. Our narrator does not explain how it was that Johoiada could depend so heavily on their obedience. The author was primarily interested in showing that because they shared Jehoiada's patriotic conviction that Joash should occupy the throne of his father, they were willing to betray their queen and take on the responsibility of protecting Joash from the supporters of Athaliah. Their enthusiastic support of Joash is also depicted by the hand-clapping and shouts of acclamation they provide in response to Joash's coronation. In contrast to the calculating personal ambition of Jehu's support group, our author has portrayed Jehoiada's supporters as a group that was just as deeply committed to the same lofty cause that had inspired their leader.

Besides this sparkling presentation of the main characters of the story, the setting for the action also serves to foster the legitimacy of Jehoiada's deeds. Except for the final procession to the palace, all takes place within the sacred confines of the temple precincts. Here the endangered prince finds safety from Athaliah's murderous intentions and receives his nurturing. Even the planning of the coup takes place within Yahweh's abode where the commanders of the guard are sworn to secrecy by the sacredness of the place they occupy before Jehoiada will reveal the king to them.

The sacral aura that permeates the description thickens as the narrative approaches its climax. The narrator provides the reader with details that are intended to show that all was done according to traditional royal protocol. We are informed that Joash was made king on the Sabbath, that the ritual was performed in the temple, that he took his customary position by a pillar, and that the high priest placed on him the traditional royal insignia as well as proclaiming and anointing him king. We are also told that the people clapped and shouted his acclamation, that a covenant was made between king and people, and that the trumpets were sounded. All of these details are intended to convey the impression that Jehoiada's coup was an act dedicated to restoring Judah to its traditional and divinely sanctioned political order.

a. Covert Preparations (11:4–6, 8).

Similar to Jehu's coup, which was engineered by the prophet Elisha, Jehoiada enters the story with a carefully conceived plan to place Joash upon the throne. The plan required the help of the palace and temple guard, which Jehoiada received by making secret arrangements with their commanders:

> But in the seventh year, Jehoiada summoned the commanders of a hundred comprised of Karites[70] and the guards,[71] and brought them to Joash[72] in the temple of Yahweh. There he made a pact with them and put them under an oath, making them swear by Yahweh's temple,[73] and revealed the king's son to them. Then he gave them the following instructions: "This is what you shall do: one third of you, those who go duty on the Sabbath to keep guard at the palace, and two thirds[74] of you, those who go off duty [at the palace] on the Sabbath to keep

[70] Apart from the doubtful Ketib reading in 2 Sam 20:23 (the Q reads *hakkĕrētî* with 1 Sam 8:18 where they are also paired with *happĕlētî*), the term occurs only here and in 2 Kgs 11:19. A connection with the Carians who served as bodyguards in Egypt seems remote. All that can be said of them is that they were a special group who along with the *rāsîm* served as guards at both the palace and the temple. The term was obscure to the LXX translator, who transliterated it.

[71] These are the king's or (in this case) the queen's personal guard who have a special entrance to the palace (2 Kgs 11:6, 20). The commander of the *rāsîm* guards the palace door (1 Kgs 14:27) and his subordinates stand ready to execute the king's direct orders (1 Sam 22:17; 2 Kgs 10:25). 1 Kgs 1:5 mentions their involvement in Adonijah's coronation. In v 11 the term is used in a general sense that includes the *kārî*. This special attachment of the *rāsîm* to the palace suggests that the *kārî* had a corresponding responsibility for the temple.

[72] Lit: "to him." The pronoun may refer to Jehoiada, but it seems more natural to find its antecedent in v 3.

[73] Benzinger notes (*Könige*, 155) that a simple repetition of the location for these events would be superfluous. He therefore suggests that the second mention of the temple of Yahweh in the verse is to be understood as part of the oath Jehoiada made the commanders swear.

[74] For this use of *yād* see Gen 47:24; 2 Sam 19:44; Neh 11:1.

guard at the temple,[75] shall station yourselves around the king with drawn swords. Kill anyone who approaches your ranks[76] and remain with the king when he leaves [the temple] and when he enters [the palace].[77]

This section, intended to set the scene for what follows, is comprised of two subsections:

1. Jehoiada solicits the aid of the commanders of the guard (4).
2. Jehoiada instructs the commanders concerning the takeover (5-6, 8).

The episode begins a terse enumeration of the covert actions that Jehoiada took prior to the Sabbath to secure the cooperation of the guards in his holy cause. During the seventh year of Athaliah's reign, the priest springs into action by sending for the commanders of the guard. He then leads them to the temple where the prince has remained hidden for six years. Upon their arrival the priest makes a pact with them in common cause, places them under a solemn oath of secrecy, and finally reveals the prince to them.

Acting as their leader, Jehoiada next provides them with detailed directives concerning the execution of the coup. Here the narrator allows the reader to be privy to Jehoiada's carefully crafted plans. The morning of the Sabbath is chosen as the time to act. Jehoiada instructs the commanders to order their men to break their customary routine. Usually, the larger detachment, which is stationed in the palace during the week, exchanges duties with the smaller detachment stationed at the temple during the Sabbath celebration. But on the next Sabbath, Jehoiada instructs both detachments to abandon their duties and to assume a special formation in front of the temple. The Sabbath is chosen not merely because it is a holy day, but also because it will allow the unusual movements of the guard to go undetected. In addition, the plan is designed to strip the palace (where Athaliah resides) of the royal guard and to provide Joash with maximum security. The plan is well conceived and requires only that Jehoiada's instructions are carried out.

---

[75] The phrase 'el-hammelek, usually translated "for the king" seems out of place here and is therefore rejected by most commentators.

[76] Šanda (129) thinks haśśĕdĕrôt refers to a particular place at the palace where Athaliah was killed.

[77] The pairing of ys' and bw' is often used idiomatically and has therefore been interpreted to mean here "wherever he goes." But such a general directive seems less likely in this context. Jehoiada is giving detailed instructions to the guard, and so it would be more fitting to understand it with Gressmann (314), Skinner (339) and Kittel (217) as a reference to the expected procession of the king from the temple to the palace. Significantly, the anticipated armed resistance to Joash's enthronement never materializes. This emphasizes that Athaliah did not have dedicated followers. The execution of these instructions is described in v 19.

b. Joash is acclaimed King of Judah (11:9, 11–12).

The reader is then rapidly transferred to the Sabbath day on which the takeover was to occur:

> The commanders of the garrisons carried out the instructions of Jehoiada the priest. The commander of all those who went on duty on the Sabbath along with the commander of all those who went off duty on the Sabbath took their men and came to Jehoiada the priest. The guards, with their weapons drawn, stationed themselves on the right and left wing of the temple precincts, stretching from the altar to the temple in order to surround the king.[78] Then Jehoiada brought out the king's son and placed on him the crown[79] and the royal armband,[80] proclaimed him king, and anointed him.[81] Then they clapped their hands and shouted "Long live the king!"

This scene moves the account to its greatest dramatic tension. It first describes the actions of the troops and concludes with the joyful acclamation of Joash:

B. The Acclamation of the New King (11:9, 11–12)
1. The guards execute Jehoiada's instruction (9, 11).
2. Jehoiada invests Joash with royal authority and the king is acclaimed (12).

Here the narrator emphasizes that the commanders did indeed obey Jehoiada's directives. Besides explicitly stating that "the commanders of a hundred carried out all that Jehoiada the priest had commanded them," the

---

[78] Since Joash does not appear until verse nine, the phrase *'al-hammelek sābîb* should probably be taken as anticipatory although most commentators delete it.

[79] The etymology of the word *nēzer* suggests that this object symbolized the king's consecration to a sacred office. According to de Vaux (*Ancient Israel*, 465), it is to be identified as a "golden flower" (*sis*) like the one that was placed on the turban of the high priest (Exod 29:6, Lev 8:9). But the king's *nēzer* may have had a different appearance. Zech 9:16 mentions the jewels of the *nēzer*.

[80] Following Wellhausen's popular suggestion to read *hassĕ'ādôt* on the basis of 2 Sam 1:10. The emendation is supported by the fact that this object, like the *nēzer*, is part of the royal apparel. Others retain the traditional interpretation of seeing here written laws that define the king's relationship to Yahweh. The argument has been extended by G. von Rad ("The Royal Ritual in Judah," *The Problem of the Hexateuch and Other Essays* [New York: McGraw-Hill, 1966] 211–16) who compares it to Egyptian protocol. But the connection seems remote and the argument lacks the cogency of Wellhausen's suggestion. Finally, H. G. May, "A Key to the Interpretation of Zechariah's Vision," *JBL* 57 (1938) 173–84, compares it to the "tablets of destiny" that Marduk receives upon assuming kingship.

[81] Reading the singular with the LXX. The MT attributes the proclamation and anointing to the whole group, which seems unlikely, especially with regard to the act of anointing. According to 1 Kgs 1:34 Zadok the priest anoints Solomon.

narrator describes their actions in terms that correspond closely to Jehoiada's instructions.[82]

The description of the guard's actions provides the reader with additional information beyond that given in Jehoiada's instructions. Here the method by which the guard surrounded the king is described in detail. The temple porch and the altar provide immovable barriers on the east and west, while the armed guards on the north and south serve to enclose the area. This description is intended to heighten suspense by showing that Jehoiada was well-aware of the possibility that the supporters of Athaliah may appear at any moment to kill the young prince, and that he took the necessary precautions before exposing the king.

The scene climaxes with the crowning and acclamation of Joash. With the area protected from any possible encroachment, Jehoiada exposes the prince to public view for the first time.[83] Jehoiada, acting in his official capacity as high priest, then places the crown and the armband on Joash, proclaims him king, and anoints him. The assembly of guards and other temple personnel[84] respond with enthusiastic cheering, clapping their hands and shouting "Long live the king!" The public acclamation of a new king sets the stage for the inevitable conflict between the two parties that laid claim to the throne.

3. The Extermination of the Old Regime (2 Kgs 11:14–15a, 16).

The most striking contrasts our author draws between the northern and southern coups concerns the manner in which the old Omride regime was exterminated. In the presentation of Jehu's coup, much space is devoted to portraying the brutal means by which Jehu seized the throne of Israel. To do this Jehu had to kill Jehoram, Jezebel and the princes of Samaria. In recounting these deeds, the narrator fashioned his account to portray Jehu in an extremely negative light. In striking contrast to this presentation, the account of Jehoiada's coup is told in such a way as to emphasize the efficiency and ease with which Queen Athaliah was dethroned. Although Jehoiada twice took steps to prepare for opposition to the overthrow, it never materialized, either during or following the coup. Only Athaliah's blood was shed, and even this sole act of violence is portrayed as an orderly state execution.

---

[82] The correspondence between Jehoiada's instructions and their execution is illustrated in the diagram in chap. I, C 1 b.

[83] The text states that Jehoiada "brought out" Joash without specifying the prince's previous location. But since the guards were stationed to enclose the area between the temple and the altar, we may surmise that Joash was brought out of the temple onto the porch where he assumed the traditional position, "standing by the pillar according to custom" (v 13).

[84] Verse 13 mentions the singers and the trumpeters.

When Athaliah heard the noise made by the crowd,[85] she went to the temple of Yahweh where the crowd was gathered. She looked and there was the king standing by the pillar[86] in accordance with custom[87] while the singers[88] and the trumpeters beside the king sounded the trumpets. Athaliah tore her garment and cried out, "Treason! This is treason!'

Then Jehoiada the priest commanded the officers of the army:[89] "Escort[90] her out of the temple and kill anyone who follows her with the sword." So they arrested her. And when she had gone as far as the place where the horses enter the palace grounds, there she was killed.

This short but highly dramatic episode is composed of a two-part structure. The first part, which finds its thematic counterpart in 2 Kgs 9:17–21a, 22–23, recounts Athaliah's confrontation with the conspirators. Having been drawn to the temple by the clamor of the acclamation, she suddenly realizes that she has been overtaken by a revolt. The second part, paralleled by 2 Kgs 9:24, 27abα, reports that Jehoiada's order to take the queen out and execute her was carried out by a detachment of the guard. This episode thus shows the following structure:

A. The Death of Athaliah (11:14–15a, 16)
    1. Athaliah confronts the conspirators (14).
        a. Athaliah is drawn to the temple (14a)
        b. Athaliah's realization of the conspiracy (14b).

---

[85] Due to its ungrammatical position and its Aramaic form, *rāsîn* is regarded by most commentators as a gloss. Those who follow Stade's two-document hypothesis see its presence as an attempt to harmonize the two accounts. The LXX resolves the grammatical difficulty by inserting a *waw* between *rāsîn* and *hā'ām*. The word *'am* is not used here to refer to "the people" in general. As in 1 Kgs 1:39–40 (cf. Mettinger, 119–21), it designates the group who participate in the coup.

[86] Most commentators identify this as one of the two pillars at the temple entrance, but some think of it in terms of a raised platform. In either case, de Vaux (*Ancient Israel*, 103) is correct in concluding that ". . . a special place was reserved for the king in the Temple, just as there was a place for the Pharaoh in the Egyptian temples; the new king stood in this place during the ceremonies of consecration."

[87] Josiah also took up this position (2 Kgs 23:3).

[88] Reading with the LXX *šārîm* for *śārîm* since the latter is not a suitable subject for the verb *tq'*.

[89] The juxtaposition of two terms for the army officers, *śārê hammē'ôt* and *pĕqudê hahayil*, has led commentators to reject one or the other as a gloss. Since the former term is used elsewhere (v 9, 10, 19), most see its presence here as an attempt to harmonize the terminology. Num 31:14 shows that *pĕqudê hahayil* is fitting in this context since it is a general term that includes the *śārê hammē'ôt*.

[90] The phrase *'el-mibbêt laśśĕdērōt* is regarded as a gloss since according to v 8 the "ranks" were formed around the king within the temple precincts. But it makes good sense if it is taken to mean that Athaliah was flanked by a separate detachment of soldiers as she was taken to her execution.

2. Athaliah is executed (11:15a, 16).
   a. Jehoiada orders Athaliah's execution (15a).
   b. The guards carry out Jehoiada's order (16).

The previous scene, which climaxed with the acclamation of Joash, prepares for the denouement of the account. With the public appearance of Joash, and the revelation of a rival claimant to the throne, the inevitable conflict with Athaliah must soon follow. The reader now learns of the events that ultimately led to the establishment of the present regime.

Apparently in line with Jehoiada's expectations, Athaliah is drawn to the temple by the sound of the Joash's acclamation.[91] With her arrival at the temple, the author describes for the reader what captured her attention. Her eyes were drawn to the king who was standing in his traditional place on the temple porch; her ears were filled with the sound of trumpets announcing the acclamation of the new king.[92] This bombardment with the symbolic actions that signalled the rejection of her reign elicited from her the strongest reactions. Filled with rage at this "insolence," she tore her garment and condemned the whole affair as a despicable act of treason.

The narrator's portrayal of Athaliah's outrage is clearly intended to alienate the reader from her perspective. Having portrayed this woman as a ruthless despot who came to power through mass murder, the author now shows her evoking the moral standards of state loyalty to condemn the revolt. Such a display of hypocrisy would certainly invoke among the readership the strongest feelings of antipathy toward Athaliah. From the narrator's perspective, she is the actual traitor. In her perversion, she casts the heroes of the story in the role that she actually occupies.

The tension that Athaliah's appearance creates now moves to a speedy resolution. Jehoiada steps forward to deal with this criminal who has eluded justice for six years. Anticipating that her supporters may attempt to save her, the priest orders that she be escorted out of the temple and then executed. But the potential development of a conflict is not realized, and the narrative reaches its dramatic resolution with the guards' carrying out Jehoiada's instructions without incident. Jehoiada's plan to remove the old regime succeeded without involving widespread bloodshed.

4. The Consolidation of the New Regime (2 Kgs 11:17, 19–20a).

The final section of the narrative describes the actions that Jehoiada took to consolidate the regime that he had successfully brought to power.

[91] Compare 1 Kgs 1:41 where Adonijah was also alerted to the presence of a rival political power by the noise of Solomon's acclamation.

[92] 1 Kgs 1:34 suggests that the sounding of trumpets was done while the crowd clapped and shouted the acclamation.

Jehoiada continues to occupy the central role of the drama.

> Then Jehoiada mediated a covenant[93] between the king and the people.[94] And he took the commanders of a hundred with the Karites and the guards, and together they brought the king down from the temple of Yahweh and entered the palace by way of the Guard's gate.[95] Then they set him[96] on the royal throne,[97] and the city remained undisturbed.

With Queen Athaliah out of the way, the priest now moves to consolidate relations between the king and his newly acquired subjects. This takes place in two stages. Jehoiada first mediates a covenant between king and people, and then leads the procession to the palace for the enthronement ceremony.[98] The scene concludes with the enthronement of the new king and the statement that the expected resistance to the new reign failed to materialize:

A. Jehoiada prepares for the installation of Joash (11:17*).
B. Jehoiada leads Joash's enthronement procession to the palace (11:19).
C. Joash is enthroned and the city remains undisturbed (11:20a).

The special significance of this presentation emerges when it is contrasted with Jehu's attempts to consolidate his rule. Like Jehoiada, he assembled a ritual gathering ostensibly intended to consolidate his rule by announcing his royal patronage of the worship of Baal. This action corresponds to Jehoiada's mediation of a covenant between Joash and his new subjects. Jehu then saw that the worshipers were properly attired and led the throng into the temple of Baal. In a similar manner, Jehoiada led his throng to the temple in preparation for the enthronement ceremony. Jehu's concluding action is what distinguishes his attempt to consolidate his rule from the aftermath of Jehoiada's coup. Jehu's characteristic treachery and

---

[93] Weinfeld (88–90) suggests that the contents of this covenant may have been similar to the type of stipulations in the treaty of Esarhaddon in which the people are commanded to oppose all acts of rebellion and assassination attempts.

[94] The LXX and 2 Chr 23:14 omit the phrase *ûbên hammelek ûbên hā'ām*. Chronicles may have omitted it because it was irrelevant to the postexilic political situation. The LXX translator may have been guided by Chronicles or he may have reacted to the complexity of the text.

[95] 1 Kgs 14:27–28 provides the interesting detail that the king had a special guarded entrance by which he traveled to and from the temple. This detail highlights the precautions that Jehoiada took to secure the safety of the king.

[96] Reading with the LXX and 2 Chr 23:20. The MT has *wayyēseb*, "and he sat."

[97] The MT reads *hammĕlākîm*. But on the basis of 1 Kgs 1:46 and 2 Chr 23:20, *hammĕlûkâ* should be read.

[98] Weinfeld (86–87) notes that in Assyrian coronation ceremonies a procession from the temple to the palace was also the normal procedure.

violence are again displayed when he orders his men to move in and slaughter Baal's personnel. By contrast, it is explicitly stated that Jehoiada's coup came to a peaceful conclusion. The king was enthroned without incident, and the violent confrontation with Athaliah's supporters did not occur. In stark contrast to Jehu's means of consolidation, Jehoiada's method involved neither deceit nor violence. Herein lies the narrator's special emphasis in the presentation of Jehoiada's final actions. The treachery and bloodshed that permeated Jehu's coup from start to finish were virtually absent from Jehoiada's means of setting Joash's reign in place.

Although the removal of Athaliah defuses much of the tension generated in the narrative, the potential for future confrontations with forces resistant to the new king remains a possibility. The narrator alerts us to this possibility by means of Jehoiada's instructions to the guards when he commands that they draw their weapons and escort the king "when he leaves the temple and enters the palace" (v 8). When this order is executed without incident (v 19), the possibility remains that violence may still erupt after the enthronement. But the author assures the reader that no such event had occurred by concluding the account with the statement that "The city remained undisturbed." The fact that the final statement makes this point reveals that the author was intent on showing that Jehoiada's coup did not involve the rampant bloodshed that had characterized Jehu's overthrow.

C. Conclusions

Our analysis of this political novella has shown that its primary concern was to present an account of the events that led to the destruction of Omride rule in a way that draws a sharp contrast between coups led by Jehu of Israel and Jehoiada of Judah. Our inspection of the various episodes that recount Jehu's coup revealed that in each case some negative aspect of Jehu's character is placed before the reader. The scene that describes the instigation of the coup shows that Jehu's response to Elisha's anti-Omride oracle was not driven by his commitment to Yahwism. His decision to move against his king was conditioned solely upon a pragmatic consideration — the support of his fellow officers. The scene that records the murder of Jehoram and Ahaziah was intended to show how Jehu cunningly exploited the trust of Jehoram to secure the king's death. That this breach of loyalty was regarded negatively is shown by the fact that Jehu himself later attempted to justify it before the people of Jezreel. Jehu's murder of Jezebel, and his frustrated attempt to accord her the honor of a royal burial, graphically depict his callous brutality and his capacity to rationalize his deplorable actions. The episode that describes the means by which he secured and justified the massacre of the Samaria's princes offers another example of the deceit and violence that Jehu employed to achieve his political goals. The final scene, which likewise emphasizes these two aspects of Jehu's personality, reminds the reader that Jehu's attack on the worshipers of Baal was not driven by a concern to promote Yahwism. This was carried out in an attempt to consolidate his political rule by purging his kingdom of potential dissidents.

The substantial space that the narrator devoted to depicting the offensive aspects of Jehu's character arose from the literary concern to present Jehu as foil for Jehoiada. Although Jehoiada like his counterpart is cunning and resourceful, he does not exhibit those characteristics for which Jehu is severely criticized. In Jehoiada there is not any vacillation about leading a coup against Athaliah. His resolve to restore the throne to Joash is first exhibited by his secret rearing of the prince, and again when he took steps to marshal the necessary manpower to overthrow the queen. Jehoiada is also depicted as devoid of any self-serving political ambition. Although the success of the coup did place him in a position of considerable authority, the narrator is intent on showing that the priest did not seek to advance himself politically, but was motivated by a pious and nationalistic concern to see that Judah's throne was returned to its legitimate heir. By presenting Jehoiada as acting on behalf of Joash, the author credits him with an altruistic motive that stands in stark contrast to the political ambition that drove Jehu. But most of all, Jehoiada never exhibited the rampant violence and self-serving deceit to which Jehu often resorted. Jehoiada's great achievement was that he not only restored Joash to the throne, but also that he was able to dethrone Athaliah with a minimum of bloodshed, and as a result, he brought a lasting peace to the nation's capital.

IV

THE REDACTION OF 2 KINGS 9–11

Our endeavor to understand and to appreciate the original edition of the narrative contained in 2 Kings 9–11 required the removal of the textual accretions that in many ways obscure the original intention of this work.[1]

We shall now return to these accretions and attempt to understand their contribution to the interpretation of this earlier material. To gain an appreciation of the process of reinterpretation, we shall first discuss the various redactional layers according to their chronological sequence. Additions made by the Dtr historian will be treated first, followed by a discussion of post-Dtr expansions. Finally, we will examine the Chronicler's handling of 2 Kings 9–11.

A. Deuteronomistic Additions

The Dtr additions to 2 Kgs 9–11 vary in character. We find two examples of the brief historical notices that recur throughout the books of First and Second Kings: a report of a throne conspiracy (9:14a), and a concluding regnal résumé (10:34–36).[2] These dispassionate additions are primarily intended to provide strictly historical information concerning a king and his reign. In addition to them, we also encounter Dtr additions that reveal the redactor's theological interests. One theme, confined to expansions of the account of Jehu's coup, is that of dynastic duration. With typical Deuteronomic dualism, the Dtr historian explains the history of Israel's and Judah's kings by teaching that a king's obedience to Yahweh brings about an enduring "house," while disobedience sentences it to destruction. Both sides of the dualism are illustrated in the Dtr redaction of 2 Kings 9–10. The destruction of Ahab's dynasty is seen as a result of the king's failure to obey Deuteronomic law, while the perpetuation of Jehu's dynasty is interpreted as the outcome of Jehu's obedience to Yahweh's commission.

---

[1] See Chapter I.

[2] A corresponding résumé is not given for Athaliah, probably because the Dtr redactor did not regard her reign as legitimate.

A second theological theme centers on another well-known concern of Deuteronomism: the exclusive worship of Yahweh at his chosen sanctuary. The Dtr redactor used both 2 Kings 9–10 and 2 Kings 11 to show that Jehu and Jehoiada were cult reformers, both of whom showed their zeal for Deuteronomic cult law by destroying the Baal's sacred objects and his temple. For the Dtr redactor, the final achievement of the coups of Jehu and Jehoiada was that they eradicated the worship of Baal that had been introduced by Ahab.

In what follows, we shall first deal with the historical notices that the Dtr redactor inserted into the account of Jehu's coup. We shall then consider his contributions to the account of Jehu's coup, giving special attention to how the themes of dynastic duration and cult reform are developed. Finally, the Dtr historian's embellishments of the account of Jehoiada's coup will be considered. Here we shall analyze the redactor's presentation of Jehoiada's cult reform and his special interests in depicting the role that the "the people of the land" played in the establishment of Joash's rule.

1. Historical Notices

So Jehu ben Nimshi conspired against Joram (2 Kgs 9:14a).

The Dtr historian manifests a special interest in informing his readers of the circumstances of a king's accession by frequently noting the conspiracies that occurred within Israel and Judah. Eight such conspiracies took place in the north while only three occurred in the south. All of these notices, couched in typical Dtr phraseology, are found in a variety of literary contexts. The most common formulation is that of "The Report of a Throne Conspiracy" which, as Long has observed, usually contains four elements: (1) a conspiracy against the crown is noted (the verb *qāšar*); (2) the king is "struck down" (the verb Hiphil *nākâ*); (3) the murder is reported (the verb Hiphil *mût*); (4) the conspirator assumes the throne (often expressed with a phrase very similar to the regnal résumé Succession Formula: "and X reigned in his stead").[3] Besides its occurrence in this formula, *qāšar* occurs twice in the conclusion of the regnal résumé: "Now the rest of the acts of X and his conspiracy. . . ."[4] In one instance, the Dtr historian makes his own formulation of the contents of report that was spread abroad following Zimri's conspiracy: "And the people who were camped heard it said, 'Zimri has conspired (*qāšar*) and has also struck down (*nākâ*) the king.'"[5] Finally, in our passage the Dtr redactor showed the same sort of freedom by adding 2 Kgs

[3] Long, *1 Kings*, 168. Examples: 1 Kgs 15:14; 16:9; 2 Kgs 12:20; 15:10, 14, 25, 30; 21:23.
[4] 1 Kgs 16:20; 2 Kgs 15:15.
[5] 1 Kgs 16:16.

9:14a to what he considered to be the conclusion of the events that led to Jehu's conspiracy.

It is striking that, whereas many of the northern conspiracies were led by high-ranking officers of Israel's army (Zimri, Omri, Jehu and Pekah), in the south the conspiracies appear to have been perpetrated by parties close to the palace. In the conspiracies directed against Joash and Amon, the conspirators are called the king's "servants," which may indicate that they were charged with some duty specifically connected to the king.[6] It appears that these conspiracies shared the same sort of internal intrigue we see at work in Jehoiada's coup, and may best be described as "palace conspiracies." But the northern conspiracies partake of a different character. They usually took the form of overt military conflict, as though a demonstration of superiority was a necessary means of establishing the victor's right to rule.[7] In the south there seems not to have been any need to legitimate a rule through the demonstration of military superiority.[8]

The Dtr redactor does appears neither to condemn nor condone the conspiracies he reports. Although he sometimes attributes them to the outpouring of Yahweh's wrath upon an apostate king, he also notes dispassionately that the "good" kings, Joash and Amaziah, were also victims of conspiracies. No interest is shown in making a moral judgment on the legitimacy of a coup in and of itself. Conspiracies are either simply reported or retrospectively attributed to Yahweh's sovereign plans.

At the conclusion of the account of Jehu's coup we find the familiar concluding regnal résumé:

> As for the other events of Jehu's reign, all he did, and all his achievements, are they not written in the book of the annals of the kings of Israel? Jehu died and was buried in Samaria, and Jehoahaz his son succeeded him as king. Jehu reigned over Israel from Samaria for twenty-eight years (2 Kgs 10:34–36).

---

[6] The group responsible for Amaziah's death is left indefinite.

[7] That the "right to rule" could be legitimately settled by battle is clearly shown by Jehu's challenge to the leaders of Samaria. The same mentality is seen in Jezebel's address to Jehu when she attempted to seduce him by praising him for "slaying his lord."

[8] A. Alt ("The Monarchy in Israel and Judah," *Essays on Old Testament History and Religion* [Garden City: Doubleday, 1967] 312–35) perceived this difference between Israel and Judah and attempted to account for it by his well-known thesis that in Israel the old pre-monarchic notion of "charismatic kingship" survived, while in Judah a theory of hereditary succession prevailed. The thesis has been most forcefully challenged by T. Ishida (*The Royal Dynasties in Ancient Israel* [BZAW 142; Berlin: Gruyter, 1977]). To account for the instability of the northern kingdom, Ishida suggests four causes: (1) the reigning dynasty's failure in military affairs; (2) the rivalry between northern tribes; (3) the antagonism between the ruling dynasty and the people; (4) the failure of the northern kings to produce a royal-dynastic ideology.

This résumé contains four elements, the first three of which are often found in the summary of a king's regime: (1) a citation formula; (2) a death and burial formula; (3) a succession formula; (4) a statement of the length and place of the reign.[9] The context of the fourth element in our passage is unusual since it is typically found in the introductory regnal résumé. Its atypical position seems to have been determined by editorial considerations. As in the case of Jeroboam,[10] the use of a narrative source made it difficult to interject the usual introductory formula. Accordingly, this crucial piece of information concerning the length and place of Jehu's reign was included in the concluding résumé.

2. The Dtr Interpretation of Jehu's Coup

A look at the Dtr characterization of Ahab's reign reveals the significance of the Dtr insertions to the account of Jehu's coup. Ahab's wickedness is described as two-fold:

> Now Ahab the son of Omri did what was evil in the sight of Yahweh, more than all who were before him. As though it had been a trivial thing for him to walk in the sins of Jeroboam ben Nebat, he even married Jezebel the daughter of Ethbaal king of the Sidonians, and served Baal and worshiped him. So he erected an altar for Baal in a temple that he built in Samaria. And Ahab also made the '*ăšerâ*. Ahab did more to provoke Yahweh, the God of Israel than all the kings of Israel who were before him (1 Kgs 16:30-33).

Ahab is here condemned along with former Israelite kings for "walking in the sins of Jeroboam." Like them, he refused to acknowledge the Jerusalem temple as the only legitimate sanctuary for the worship of Yahweh. What sets him apart from his evil predecessors is the fact that he married Jezebel, who influenced him to adopt Baalism as the state religion and to erect a temple to Baal in Samaria. For this the Dtr redactor castigates him as doing "more evil than all who were before him." In order to show that Yahweh punished Ahab for both sins, the Dtr historian edited 2 Kings 9–10 to present Jehu as prophetically commissioned to destroy Ahab's dynasty and to purge Israel of the Baalism that had been introduced into Israel. We shall first investigate the theme of dynastic duration and then examine the Dtr's presentation of Jehu's cult reform.

---

[9] Cf. 1 Kgs 14:19-20; 16:5-6, 27-28; 22:39-40; 2 Kgs 13:8-9; 13:12-13 = 14:15-16; 14:28-29; 15:21-22. In several cases, when a king met his death at the hands of a conspirator, only the citation formula is found: 1 Kgs 15:31; 16:14, 20; 2 Kgs 15:11, 26, 31.

[10] See 1 Kgs 14:19-20.

a. Dynastic Duration

The Dtr redactor has much to say about the fate of Israel's dynasties. To appreciate this major Dtr concern, several closely related passages that deal with the destruction of Israel's dynasties will be examined. In most cases, the fate of a dynasty is explained by means of a prophetic oracle that predicts the destruction of the apostate dynasty. After providing a description of the downfall of the dynasty, the Dtr redactor often inserts a "fulfillment notice" to emphasize that Yahweh did indeed bring about what he had predicted.[11] To illustrate the Dtr historian's method of explaining the demise of Israel's dynasties, we shall survey the Dtr texts that concern the destruction of the dynasties of Jeroboam, Baasha, Zimri, Omri/Ahab.

i. The Destruction of the house of Jeroboam
(1 Kgs 14:7-11 and 1 Kgs 15:29-30)

In terms of the northern kings, the Dtr device of cross-referencing prophecies with fulfillment notices is first applied to Jeroboam I. 2 Kgs 14:1-18 contains an account in which Jeroboam instructs his wife to disguise herself and to go to Ahijah the prophet to find out the fate that awaits their ailing son. Before her arrival, Yahweh informs Ahijah of the identity of the visitor and instructs him to tell her that the boy will die when she returns to her home in Tirzah. When she does, the boy dies as predicted.

This story has been expanded by Dtr redactor to include a prophecy against the house of Jeroboam:

(7) Go and tell Jeroboam, "Thus says Yahweh, the God of Israel:

'Inasmuch as I exalted you from the midst of the people and made you leader over my people Israel, (8) and tore the kingdom from the house of David and gave it to you,

but you have not been like my servant David who kept my commandments and who followed me with all his heart, by doing only what was right in my eyes, (9) but instead you did more evil than any who were before you by making for yourself images of other gods to provoke my anger, and have not followed me,[12]

(10) therefore I am about to bring disaster on the house of Jeroboam. Thus I will cut off Jeroboam's male descendants in Israel, both child and adult.[13] (11) I

---

[11] G. von Rad, "The Deuteronomic Theology of History in I and II Kings," *The Problem of the Hexateuch and Other Essays* (New York: McGraw-Hill, 1966) 205-21.

[12] Lit: "and have cast me behind your back." This clause stands in antithesis to David's actions, of whom Yahweh states that he "followed after me with all his heart."

[13] The meaning of the phrase *'asûr we'āzûb* is obscure (See Gray, 337-38). Since members of the royal family are in view, the suggestion that it refers to those under parental care *'asûr*, and those who have achieved independent adult status *'āzûb* best fits the context.

will completely sweep away the house of Jeroboam just as one sweeps away dung until it is all removed. The descendants of Jeroboam who die in the city the dogs will eat; those who die in the field the vultures will eat[14]

For Yahweh has spoken'" (1 Kgs 14:7–11).

This passage has been classified as a "prophecy of punishment."[15] The prophecy itself is introduced with a messenger's commission and begins with the messenger formula, "Thus says Yahweh, the God of Israel" (7aα). The body of the prophecy is comprised of two parts: an accusation (7aβ–9), and a declaration of judgment (10–11). The accusation is based upon a comparison between David and Jeroboam. Like David, Jeroboam was raised up by Yahweh from obscurity to become the leader (*nāgîd*) over his people Israel. The same thing is said of David:

> Thus says Yahweh of hosts, "I took you from the pasture where you tended sheep to become the leader (*nāgîd*) of my people Israel" (2 Sam 7:8).

In addition, Yahweh exhibited his favor toward Jeroboam by granting him rulership over ten of David's former tribes. But there the similarities end. While David was wholly obedient to Yahweh, Jeroboam responded to Yahweh's graciousness by disregarding his commandments. The deeper significance of this text becomes apparent when it is read in light of an earlier Dtr passage in which Jeroboam is given the same opportunity that had been offered to David. In Ahijah's oracle to Jeroboam, the Dtr redactor has Yahweh make the following promise:

> "Then it will come to pass that if you listen to all that I command you and walk in my ways, and do what is right in my eyes by observing my statutes and my commandments as my servant David did, then I will be with you and I will build you an enduring dynasty just as I did for David. And I will give Israel to you (1 Kgs 11:38).

According to this text, the divine privileges that David and his dynasty enjoyed were also offered to Jeroboam. Had Jeroboam obeyed Yahweh's law, he too would have been granted an enduring dynasty. But Jeroboam failed where David succeeded. Because of this, Yahweh's punishment would bring about the opposite result of what obedience would have won. Instead of the assuring of an enduring dynasty, Jeroboam's apostasy earned a punishment that would take the form of the destruction of his house.

---

[14] The prediction that the scavengers will ravage the corpses of Jeroboam's descendants is reminiscent of some of the curses contained in Esharhaddon's Vassal Treaty (*ANET* 534–41): "let dogs and pigs eat your flesh, and may your spirit have no one to take care and pour libations to him"; "May Palil, lord of first rank, let eagles and vultures eat your flesh."

[15] Long, *1 Kings*, 156.

The Deuteronomist's graphic description of the fate of Jeroboam's descendants reflects his bitter animosity toward Israel's first king. He begins with the general statement that calamity will befall his descendants and emphasizes that *every* male member of his family will be murdered. But even this horrible specter does not fully vent the redactor's outrage at Israel's apostate king. He further predicts that Yahweh will see to it that the members of Jeroboam's dynasty will receive no burial. Their bodies will be removed from Israel as one removes dung. Scavengers will serve as the instruments of the removal. The corpses of those that die in the city will be eaten by dogs; those that fall outside of the city will become food for the vultures. According to the perspective of the Dtr redactor, such is the just fate of the descendants of a king who, after being given the same opportunity as David, disregarded Yahweh's demands they as expressed in Deuteronomic law.

It was because of historical hindsight that the Dtr redactor could place such an oracle of disaster in the mouth of Ahijah the prophet. His sources informed him that Jeroboam's dynasty did come to a violent end. A certain Baasha, an officer in King Nadab's army, struck down his lord while Nadab was laying siege to the Philistine-occupied city of Gibbethon (1 Kgs 15:27–28). The Dtr historian attributed this event to the outworkings of Yahweh's justice. To make this theological point, he expanded Ahijah's prophecy to predict the event. When reporting the fulfillment of the prediction, a reference to the previous prophecy is provided:

> (29) And it happened that as soon as he was king, he struck down all the house of Jeroboam. He did not leave anyone of Jeroboam's family alive, destroying them all in accord with what Yahweh had spoken through his servant Ahijah the Shilonite. (30) This occurred because of the sins which he committed and because he made Israel sin, thereby provoking the anger of Yahweh (1 Kgs 15:29–30).

Although the Dtr historian does not explicitly state that the corpses of Jeroboam's descendants became prey for the scavengers, it can be reasonably concluded that he wished his readers to assume that the gruesome details of Yahweh's prediction were indeed fulfilled. In any case, the Dtr redactor attributed the usurper's destruction of Jeroboam's dynasty to the divine wrath that the king's apostasy had incurred.

ii. The Destruction of the house of Baasha
(1 Kgs 16:1–4 and 1 Kgs 16:11–13)

The Dtr redactor used the same method to explain the destruction of Baasha's dynasty. In this case, however, he did not expand an oracle contained in an underlying source as he did in the case of Jeroboam. With

Baasha, the redactor simply provided his own introduction, stating that the prophet Jehu ben Hanani received an oracle from Yahweh:

(1) Now the word of Yahweh came to Jehu ben Hanani against Baasha:

(2) "Inasmuch as I exalted you from the dust and made you leader (*nāgîd*) over my people Israel, and you have behaved like Jeroboam and made my people Israel commit sin, thereby provoking me to anger on account of their sins, (3) I am going to sweep away Baasha and his dynasty. I will make your dynasty like the dynasty of Jeroboam ben Nebat. (4) The one who dies in the city dogs shall eat; the one who dies in the field the vultures will eat" (1 Kgs 16:1–4).

The oracle's structure reproduces the one directed against Jeroboam. It begins with an accusation (v 2), and concludes with a prediction of disaster (vv 3–4). Like the accusation that was directed against Jeroboam, the one directed against Baasha contains two parts. Baasha is first implicitly compared to David and Jeroboam, who like him were raised from obscurity to become leaders of Yahweh's people. Then Baasha is explicitly compared to Jeroboam for his disobedience and implicitly contrasted with the obedient David. Instead of following David's example, Baasha chose to repeat Jeroboam's apostasy, and thus provoked the same punishment that Jeroboam had.[16] Yahweh would "make Baasha's house like that of Jeroboam." Scavengers would feed on the corpses of Baasha just as they had on those of Jeroboam's descendants.

Again, the Dtr historian based the contents of this oracle against Baasha on historical information provided by his sources: Baasha's son Elah was overthrown through a conspiracy. The Dtr historian informs us that while Elah was feasting at the home of Arza, an army commander by the name of Zimri murdered his king and took the throne. This event was seen as the fulfillment of the prophecy that was earlier introduced:

(11) And it happened that as soon as he was king and sat upon the throne, he smote the whole house of Baasha. He did not leave alive any male, neither family nor relative. (12) Thus Zimri destroyed the whole house of Baasha according to the word of Yahweh that he spoke through Jehu the prophet. (13) This occurred on account of all the sins that both Baasha and Elah his son committed. By their vain worship they made Israel sin, thereby provoking the anger of Yahweh, the God of Israel (1 Kgs 16:11–13).

These Dtr texts illustrate the means by which historical events were provided with theological interpretations. The rise and fall of the dynasties of Jeroboam and Baasha are explained in terms of Deuteronomic principles. By

---

[16] From Jeroboam's oracle we know that this refers to the worship of other gods and the images Jeroboam cast of them.

inserting these prophecies and fulfillment notices, the redactor taught that the hand of Yahweh had determined the fate of these dynasties. Yahweh predicted their destruction because the founders of Israel's first two dynasties dared to defy his Deuteronomic cult law.

iii. The Destruction of the house of Zimri (1 Kgs 16:18–19)

With his seizure of the throne, Zimri became the founder of Israel's third dynasty. One would expect that the Dtr historian would repeat the pattern he had established to explain the termination of the two dynasties that preceded Zimri. But apparently because of Zimri's extremely short reign (seven days) which left him no time to build a dynasty, the historian abbreviated his theological explanation of Zimri's demise. Unlike his treatment of Jeroboam I and Baasha, the Dtr redactor does not have a prophet appear to predict the disaster of the house of Zimri. But Zimri's death was nonetheless related to the theological scheme that our redactor had constructed. He does this by relating the cause of Zimri's death to the same cause that effected the fall of the houses of Jeroboam and Baasha. After describing Omri's attack against Tirzeh where Zimri was residing, the Dtr historian describes the circumstances of Zimri's death:

> (18) And it happened that when Zimri saw that the city was taken, he went into the citadel of the palace and set fire to it and killed himself. (19) This occurred because of the sins he committed, doing what was wicked in Yahweh's sight. He did as Jeroboam did and committed the same sin that Jeroboam had, and made Israel commit sin (1 Kgs 16:18–19).

Even if Zimri had desired to effect cult reforms, his extremely short reign would have not provided him with the opportunity to do so. The Dtr historian nonetheless faulted him for following Jeroboam's wicked precedent, and this accusation formed the grounds upon which Zimri's quick demise was explained theologically: Zimri's destruction, like that of the house of Jeroboam and Baasha, was in fact another historical manifestation of the outworking of Yahweh's retribution for cultic apostasy.

iv. The Destruction of the house of Omri/Ahab
(1 Kgs 16:25–26, 21:20b–22, 24 and 2 Kgs 9:7–9*, 21b, 25–26, 10:10–11, 17b, 12–14)

Omri was the founder of Israel's fourth dynasty. Surprisingly, the Dtr treatment of the founder of Israel's strongest dynasty is minimal. Apart from the typical information given in the Dtr framework, the reader is only told of the circumstance that won him the kingship from his rival Tibni, and that he purchased Samaria and made it the capital. The pattern established by the Dtr historian would lead us to expect him to introduce a prophetic prediction

of the destruction of Omri's dynasty. But such is not the case, even though
Omri received the typical Dtr condemnation, with the additional note that
his wickedness was unprecedented:

> (25) Now Omri did what was wicked in Yahweh's sight, and acted more wickedly
> than all who were before him. (26) For he behaved completely like Jeroboam
> ben Nebat and committed the sins which made Israel commit sin, thereby pro-
> voking the anger of Yahweh the God of Israel by his idolatry (1 Kgs 16:25–26).

The Dtr historian's decision to give Omri, the founder of the dynasty,
a cursory treatment seems to be motivated by his greater interest to portray
his son Ahab as the real villain who caused its downfall. Accordingly, the
Dtr redactor does not refer to this dynasty as "the house of Omri." Instead,
he prefers to call it "the house of Ahab."[17] The treatment of the demise of
Ahab's reign returns to the same pattern employed to describe the downfall
of the dynasties of Jeroboam and Baasha.

As noted above, Ahab was regarded as particularly wicked because of
his marriage to Jezebel and for his royal patronage of Baalism. To show that
the downfall of Ahab's house was the result of Yahweh's retribution, the Dtr
redactor spliced an oracle into an older story concerning Naboth the
Jezreelite. The older account reports that after Ahab and Jezebel had conspired to seize the property of Naboth, Elijah the prophet was commissioned
by Yahweh to announce that the dogs will lick his blood in the very place that
they had lapped up Naboth's blood. But according to the text as we have it,
Elijah does not deliver the oracle that he was told to utter. It has been
replaced by another oracle similar to those that had earlier predicted the
downfall of the dynasties of Jeroboam and Baasha. When Ahab disdainfully
asks, "Have you found me, my enemy?" The Dtr historian answers for Elijah
as follows:

> (20b) I have found you because you sold yourself to do what was evil in
> Yahweh's sight. (21) I am about to bring calamity upon you. I will utterly sweep
> you away. I will exterminate all of Ahab's male descendants, child and adult.
> (22) I will make your house like the house of Jeroboam ben Nebat, and like the
> house of Baasha ben Ahijah, because of what you did to provoke me to anger,
> by making Israel commit sin. (24) Anyone of Ahab's descendants who dies in
> the city the dogs shall eat; anyone who dies in the field the birds shall eat (1 Kgs
> 21:20b–24).

This third prophetic oracle, this time delivered by Elijah, shows some
interesting variations from the other two. Although it was inserted into an
underlying source as in the case of Jeroboam, the oracle lacks the statement

---

[17] 2 Kgs 9:7, 8, 9; 10:30. Cf. 1 Kgs 21:22, 29.

that Ahab arose from obscurity to become the leader of Israel. The fact that Ahab inherited the throne from his father Omri made such a statement inappropriate. Another variation concerns the structure of the oracle. The accusation not only uses a different Dtr cliché ("he sold himself to do what was evil in Yahweh's sight"), but another accusatory statement occurs within the context of the prediction of disaster (22b).[18] Still, it is clear that this prophetic oracle performs the same function as those delivered by prophets Ahijah and Jehu. The description of the destruction of Ahab's house uses the same formulae found in the oracles against Jeroboam and Baasha, and the reason for this dreadful judgment is similarly related to the transgression of Deuteronomic cultic law.[19] What is most distinctive about this treatment of the fate of Ahab's house is that the Dtr redactor used 2 Kings 9-10 to illustrate how this prophecy was fulfilled. In doing so, he radically altered the original narrative's portrayal of Jehu.

The Dtr redactor did not simply offer a terse description of the overthrow of Ahab's house as he did in the cases of Jeroboam and Baasha. In 2 Kings 9-10 he had at his disposal a narrative that could be altered to suit his purposes. To do this, he began by altering Elisha's commission to his prophetic disciple by expanding it with the addition of 2 Kgs 9:7-9*:

> (7) You are to destroy[20] the house of Ahab your lord. Thus I will avenge the blood of my servants the prophets that was shed (8) by the hand of the whole house of Ahab. I will destroy every male in Israel related to Ahab, both child and adult. (9) I will destroy the house of Ahab just as I destroyed the house of Jeroboam ben Nebat, and the house of Baasha ben Ahijah (2 Kgs 9:7-9*).

In terms of form, the passage is not an oracle but a prophetic commission. It therefore does not contain an explicit accusation or a prediction of punishment such as was found in the other oracles against the dynasties of Jeroboam, Baasha and Ahab. Nevertheless, an accusation is implicit. As we have seen, the Dtr redactor had introduced Ahab's reign by condemning him for cultic apostasy and his sponsorship of Baalism. Here he adds a related crime: the deaths of Yahweh's prophets at the hands of Ahab and his sons. Although the murder of Yahweh's prophets by either Ahab or his sons is

---

[18] The prediction of disaster contains an oracle against Jezreel that begins with a second messenger formula. It also seems to break the connection between v 22 and v 24 which leads to the natural conclusion that it has been inserted into the oracle. This holds implications for our understanding of 2 Kgs 9:10 and 2 Kgs 9:36 which will be discussed below.

[19] Stated in 1 Kgs 16:30-33. In addition, the insertion of the oracle in its present context relates Ahab's wickedness to his crime against Naboth.

[20] The MT reads *wehikkitâ,* but the LXX presupposes *wehikrattâ,* which is supported by 2 Chr 22:7.

nowhere explicitly recounted, the redactor was probably thinking of Elijah's references to Israel's killing of Yahweh's prophets.[21]

In spite of these differences, the terminology used in the commission is found in the previous predictions of disaster. Every male descendant would be killed just as the descendants of Jeroboam and Baasha were. But Jehu is portrayed in a different light than Baasha and Zimri who also served as the means by which an apostate dynasty was punished. Unlike them, Jehu is explicitly commissioned to carry out this task, while Baasha and Zimri are presented as passive agents of Yahweh's retribution. This distinction is important, for by making Jehu a willing agent of Yahweh's judgment on Ahab's house, the historian found a basis to explain the fact that Jehu's dynasty lasted four generations. The redaction of 2 Kings 9–10 therefore served two purposes. It was used to show not only that Elisha's prediction of the destruction of Ahab's house for his wickedness was fulfilled, but also that the longevity of Jehu's dynasty was Yahweh's reward for executing the Dtr commission.[22] An examination of several of the Dtr expansions will show that they are intended to emphasize that Jehu *consciously* acted in accordance with both the Dtr commission and the prophecies that had been directed against Ahab's house. As a result, the Dtr redactor could explain the longevity of Jehu's dynasty, even though Jehu did not depart from "the sins of Jeroboam."

Jehu's obedience to his commission is first emphasized in the expansion to the episode recounting Jehoram's death. When Jehoram came out to meet Jehu, the Dtr redactor states that the two happened to encounter one another "at the property of Naboth the Jezreelite." After Jehu kills his king, he issues the following instructions along with an explanation:

> (25) Then he said to Bidkar his officer, "Pick him up and throw him onto the field that belonged to Naboth the Jezreelite. For I recall that when you and I were riding[23] behind Ahab his father, Yahweh pronounced this oracle against him: (26) 'As surely as I have seen yesterday the blood of Naboth and the blood of his sons,' says Yahweh, 'I will repay you in this property,' says Yahweh. So take his body and throw it on that plot in accordance with the word of Yahweh" (2 Kgs 9:25–26).

As discussed in chapter I, the Dtr redactor took up an older oracle (v 26a) and applied it to the original account by means of the narrative

---

[21] See 1 Kgs 19:10, 14.

[22] The Dtr historian's teaching leads us to deduce that had Jehu acknowledged the sole legitimacy of the Jerusalem cult, he could have succeeded where Jeroboam had failed. Like David, he could have founded an eternal dynasty.

[23] The MT has *kî zĕkòr 'anî wā'attâ 'ĕt rōkĕbîm*, which is clearly corrupt. The LXX presupposes *zōker* and lacks *'ĕt*, and LXX[L] and S presuppose *'anî kî*. The text may thus be tentatively restored to read, *kî zōker 'ănî kî 'ănî wa'attâ rōkĕbîm*.

introduction found in vv 22b and 25. Although we cannot be certain, it seems that this older oracle belonged to the underlying narrative found in 1 Kgs 21:1-20a, 27-29. According to it, Elijah predicted that "In the place where the dogs licked up the blood of Naboth the dogs shall lick up your blood also" (1 Kgs 21:19). But because Ahab humbled himself, Yahweh told Elijah that Ahab's son, rather than Ahab himself, would suffer the punishment for the violence done against Naboth.[24] The account thus anticipates a scene in which Jehoram is killed and his blood is licked up by the dogs. But no account of the fulfillment of this prediction has survived. Apparently, the Dtr replaced the conclusion to the story begun in 1 Kings 21 with that of Jehu's overthrow of Jehoram, using only the fragment in 2 Kgs 9:26a. The fragment is informative in what it implies about the source from which it was extracted. Read independently of its present context, it presupposes that the following events took place: (1) like his father, Jehoram resisted the claim of Naboth's family to the disputed property; (2) the conflict resulted in Jehoram having Naboth's sons killed; (3) on the day following the massacre, a prophet appeared to Jehoram at the property and pronounced the oracle now found in 9:26a; 4) Jehoram was killed sometime later at the site and the dogs licked up his blood as predicted. Although an account of none of these events has survived, it is likely that the Dtr historian had it before him since in 9:26a he quotes from it. But because the account of Jehu's overthrow of Jehoram was more suited to his purposes, the narrative was set aside. Only the oracle found in 9:26a was utilized. But employing this oracle demanded that it be given a new context. This resulted in the Dtr redactor attributing the utterance to a prophet who spoke not against Jehoram (as the oracle itself implies), but against his father Ahab some twenty years earlier. In this way, the Dtr oracle in 1 Kgs 21:21-24 is portrayed as being fulfilled by Jehu, whom the Dtr historian has just commissioned to carry out the extermination of the house of Ahab. To show that Jehu was conscious of his sacred duty to carry out Yahweh's vengeance against the house of Ahab, the redactor has Jehu order Bidkar to cast Jehoram's corpse on the property of Naboth "in accordance with the word of Yahweh."

The redactor's strategy in utilizing the account of Jehu's coup to portray his obedience to the prophetic commission has also informed the inclusion of 2 Kgs 10:10-11. According to the original narrative, Jehu devised a deceitful scheme to secure the deaths of the princes of Samaria in order to convince

---

[24] However, the Dtr redactor went against his source and attempted to state that Ahab did suffer the punishment predicted by Elijah. In 1 Kgs 22:38 he informs the reader: "And they washed the chariot by the pool of Samaria and the dogs licked up his blood, according to the word of Yahweh which he spoke." But the redactor overlooked the fact the Elijah's original prophecy located both crime and its punishment at Naboth's property in Jezreel.

the Jezreelites that his revolt against Jehoram had the support of the rulers of Samaria. But the Dtr redactor altered the conclusion of the final scene to emphasize that Jehu's part in the massacre of the princes was carried out in accordance with Yahweh's will. Here the Dtr redactor has Jehu proclaim to the Jezreelites that the death of the princes fulfilled Yahweh's prophetic word:[25]

> Know then, that nothing of what Yahweh has spoken about the house of Ahab has failed to come to pass. Yahweh has done what he spoke through his servant Elijah (2 Kgs 10:10).

This insertion performs the same function as 2 Kgs 9:25–26. The account of the death of the princes of Samaria is altered to show that Jehu acted in accordance with Elijah's oracle (1 Kgs 21:21–24), and that Jehu's part in seeing to the death of the princes was actually motivated by his desire to execute faithfully the Dtr commission.

Verses 11 and 17b were also inserted with the same purpose in mind. According to both Elijah's oracle and Elisha's commission, Yahweh proclaimed that he would completely destroy Ahab's house. To show that Jehu's attack on the present regime was in keeping with Yahweh's desire, the redactor explicitly notes that the members of Ahab's house residing in both Jezreel and Samaria were exterminated by Jehu:

> Then Jehu smote all who remained of the house of Ahab in Jezreel — all his great men and his friends and his priests until he left him no survivor (2 Kgs 10:11).

> And he smote the rest of Ahab's descendants who were in Samaria so that all were destroyed according to the word that Yahweh had spoken to Elijah (2 Kgs 10:17b).

The Dtr redactor was not content to portray Jehu as limiting his destruction of the Omrides to those who lived in Israel. In order to demonstrate the completeness of his eradication of Omride rule, he utilized a fragment that told of Jehu's encounter with the forty-two princes of Judah:

> Then he left, traveling toward Samaria. (13) On the road at Beth Eked Haroim, Jehu met some relative of Ahaziah king of Judah and asked, "Who are you?" They answered, "We are relatives of Ahaziah, and we have come down to greet the family of the king and queen mother." (14) Then he said, "Take them alive." So they took them alive. And they slaughtered them by the well of Beth Eked, all forty-two, leaving no survivor (2 Kgs 10:10–12).

In chapter one, we noted that the abrupt turn that the story takes at the conclusion of the episode indicates a Dtr addition. After ascertaining the

---

[25] Similar proclamations about the effectiveness of Yahweh's predictions are made by Joshua (Josh 23:14) and Solomon (1 Kgs 8:56).

identity of the royal entourage, Jehu ordered his men to take them alive. But after his orders are carried out, we are suddenly told that the group was slaughtered on the spot. This suggested that v 14b comes from the hand of the Dtr redactor. It seems likely that it too was added to portray Jehu's deep commitment to carry out the destruction of anyone in any way related to the house of Omri. Since Athaliah's marriage to Joram had formed family ties with the Omrides, the redactor apparently felt that the massacre of these Judean princes fell within the province of Jehu's sacred task. Accordingly, this fragment was included and supplemented in order to provide another example of the thoroughness of Jehu's purge of Omride rule.

v. The Longevity of the house of Jehu (2 Kgs 10:30 and 2 Kgs 15:12)

The Dtr redactor's transformation of Jehu into the active agent of Yahweh's judgment on the house of Ahab culminates in an oracle in which Yahweh commends Jehu for his deeds and rewards him with a dynasty that will include four generations. Having shown that Jehu destroyed Ahab's dynasty and the worship of Baalism that Ahab had introduced, the Dtr redactor has Yahweh respond as follows:

> And Yahweh said to Jehu, "Inasmuch as you have done well in executing what is right in my sight, and have done to the house of Ahab according to all that I desired, your sons will occupy the throne of Israel to the fourth generation" (2 Kgs 10:30).

The insertion of a divine speech that is characteristically introduced by *ya'an* (*'ăšer*) is a common literary device of the Dtr school. It is used to explain major junctures in Israelite and Judean history by having Yahweh express either approval or disapproval toward the behavior of certain kings. We have already seen two instances in which an announcement of Yahweh's displeasure brought about the destruction of the dynasties of Jeroboam (1 Kgs 14:7) and Baasha (1 Kgs 16:2).[26] But as the promise made to Jehu illustrates, this device is not only used to express divine displeasure. In another Dtr passage, Solomon declares how Yahweh has indeed rewarded David's good intention to build a house for Yahweh by giving him a son who would accomplish the deed. Standing in the completed temple, Solomon refers back to Yahweh's promise to his father:

> (18) "Inasmuch as it was in your heart to build a house for my name you did well in desiring this. (19) Yet you will not build the house, but the son that you will sire, he shall build the house for my name" (1 Kgs 8:18-19).

---

[26] Other disapproving divine speeches introduced by *ya'an* (*'ăšer*) are: Judg 2:20-21; 1 Kgs 20:28; 2 Kgs 1:16, 21:11-15.

Another example of this use of a divine oracle to communicate Yahweh's favor is found in the account of Solomon's dream at Gibeon (1 Kgs 3:1-15). This Dtr oracle explains how Solomon obtained his legendary wisdom and came to enjoy in Israel unprecedented political and economic success:

> (11) "Inasmuch as you have asked for this thing and have not asked for yourself long life, nor riches for yourself, nor the death of your enemy, but have asked for yourself discernment to understand justice, (12) I will do what you ask. I will give you more wisdom and understanding than anyone has ever had or will ever have again. (13) I will also give you what you have not asked for: both riches and honor, so that there will not be any among the kings like you all your days" (1 Kgs 3:11-13).

The Dtr historian urges that Jehu had likewise earned Yahweh's pleasure and had been justly compensated. Jehu's dynasty, which continued longer than any other except for David's, was attributed to Yahweh's pleasure in response to Jehu's obedient eradication of the house of Ahab. Accordingly, when Shallum finally ends Jehu's dynasty by murdering Zechariah, the Dtr redactor related this event to Yahweh's promise to Jehu:

> "This [fulfilled] the word of Yahweh which he spoke to Jehu when he said, 'Your sons to the fourth generation shall sit on the throne of Israel.' And so it came about" (2 Kgs 15:12).

An examination of these texts show that the Dtr historian was deeply concerned with showing what were the divine conditions upon which a dynasty would continue, and how the responses of certain kings had determined the fate of their royal descendants. Through a series of cross-referencing texts, the Dtr historian sought to explain the perpetuity of David's dynasty as well as the termination of the dynasties of Saul,[27] Jeroboam I, Baasha, Zimri, Ahab and Jehu. The continuing line of David's successors was explained by the notion that David's obedience to Yahweh's commandments[28] had insured the perpetuity of his dynasty.[29] The failure of the northern kings to establish an eternal dynasty was correspondingly

---

[27] 2 Sam 7:15 refers back to 1 Samuel 15:23.

[28] Dtr texts expressing David's obedience are found throughout Kings: 1 Kgs 3:3, 14: 5:3; 9:4; 11:4, 6, 33, 38; 14:8, 15:3, 5, 11; 2 Kgs 14:3: 16:2; 18:3; 22:2.

[29] This notion is classically expressed in 2 Sam 7:11b-16. It is reinforced by the Dtr statements that say that Yahweh was committed to maintaining a "lamp" (i.e. a Davidic descendant) in Jerusalem even when the disobedience of David's descendants earned Yahweh's punishment (1 Kgs 11:36; 15:4; 2 Kgs 8:19). This view seems to clash with other Dtr statements that make the promise of dynastic perpetuity conditional upon the obedience of David's sons (1 Kgs 2:4; 8:25; 9:4-7). I am inclined to regard these as the additions of the exilic Dtr redactor who attempted to explain why the Davidic "lamp" was removed from Jerusalem.

explained by the indictment that none of Israel's kings followed David's pious example but chose instead to repeat Jeroboam's apostasy. The Dtr treatment of Jehu stands somewhat outside of this dualistic theory of dynastic duration, for although Jehu was not rewarded with a perpetual dynasty, his obedience to Yahweh's commission to destroy the house of Ahab earned him a dynasty that lasted four generations.

vi. A Qualification concerning Jehu's Dynasty (2 Kgs 10:31–32)

Although the Dtr treatment of Jehu was designed to explain the longevity of Jehu's dynasty, certain questions remained: If Jehu had earned Yahweh's favor, why was Jehu's dynasty eventually terminated? And why did Jehu suffer military defeat before Hazael's aggression? The Dtr redactor resolved these issues by charging Jehu with a failure of which every Israelite king was guilty — the refusal to acknowledge Jerusalem as the only place that Yahweh demanded to be worshiped:

> But Jehu did not depart from the sins of Jeroboam by which he made Israel commit sin (10:31*).

With this indictment, the historian not only explained why Jehu's dynasty eventually failed, but also why Israel suffered severe military defeats during his reign. Thus Hazael's conquest of Israelite territory is attributed to Yahweh:

> (32) At that time Yahweh began to reduce the size of Israel's territory. Hazael defeated Israel (33) in the area east of the Jordan — in both Gilead and Bashan (10:32–33*).[30]

The Dtr historian thus found a way to explain that, while Jehu was the founder of the longest lasting dynasty of any of Israel's kings, he did not engender an eternal dynasty as David had, nor did he experience the military success that obedience to Deuteronomic law had promised. The longevity of his dynasty was explained as Yahweh's reward for exterminating the house of Ahab, but the termination of his dynasty and the defeats that he suffered at the hands of Hazael were attributed to his failure to depart from the sins of Jeroboam.

b. Jehu's Cult Reform

Jehu's laudable deeds included not only the eradication of Omride rule from Israel, but also his purging of the Baalism that Ahab and Jezebel had

---

[30] A similar statement is made with respect to Jotham's failure to remove the high places: "In those day Yahweh began to send against Judah Rezin king of Aram and Pekah ben Remaliah" (2 Kgs 15:37).

introduced into Israel. This Dtr theme is represented most clearly in the Dtr appendage to the original narrative's final episode. However, the redactor's contributions to the text are not restricted to the appendage. The Dtr redactor found certain aspects of the portrayal of events that required some minor but significant alterations. Additions were therefore made that were intended to exonerate some of Jehu's questionable actions. Those Dtr additions that reflect an apologetic concern are found in 2 Kgs 10:15-16, 10:19 and 10:23.

The fragment that describes Jehu's killing of the Judean princes (2 Kgs 10:12-14) also contains an episode in which Jehu encounters Jehonadab ben Recab[31] as he traveled to Samaria (15-16):

> (15) After he left there, he came upon Jehonadab ben Recab who was on his way to meet him. Jehu greeted him and said, "Are you willing to support me as I have supported you? Jehonadab answered, "I am willing." Jehu said, "Then take my hand." And he did so and Jehu helped him up into his chariot. (16) "Come with me," he said, "and witness my zeal for Yahweh." So Jehonadab rode with him in his chariot (2 Kgs 10:15-16).

Why did the Dtr redactor include this scene in which Jehu and Jehonadab align themselves with one another? The answer no doubt lies in Jehonadab's reputation as a zealous Yahwist, and the admiration that Dtr circles had for him and his followers.[32] By inserting this scene into the original account, Jehu's commitment to Yahwism is placed beyond question by affiliating him with the legendary Jehonadab, the famous Yahwist zealot who was the founder of a group that expressed the purity of its Yahwism by abstaining from building houses, from farming, and from drinking wine (Jer 35:8-10). In this way the Dtr redactor assured his readers that Jehu's subsequent announcement that he would outstrip Ahab's patronage of Baal, and his participation in a sacrificial ceremony to Baal were only a ruse that in the end would demonstrate for Jehonadab and the readers that Jehu was a zealous devotee of Yahweh.

Although the redactor's use of the fragment is transparent, it is difficult to understand what the original intention of this scene and the previous one may have been. We do not know what preceded or followed these events in the source from which this fragment was taken. When its contents are

---

[31] Jehonadab was the founder of a reactionary group that rejected sedentary life and that continued to exist up until the time of Jeremiah. On this group see R. de Vaux, *Ancient Israel*, 1.14-15; M. H. Pope, "Rechab," *IDB* 4 (1962) 14-16. However, F. S. Frick, "The Rechabites Reconsidered," *JBL* 90 (1971) 279-87, identifies them as a guild of craftsmen perhaps involved in the manufacture of chariots and weaponry. See also his "Rechabites," *IDBSup* 726-28.

[32] That they were the objects of admiration is shown by Jeremiah 35, a chapter that must certainly be ascribed to the Dtr layer of the book. For the linguistic data see Weinfeld, who notes Dtr language in vv 7, 13, 14, 15, 17, 18, 19.

inspected, one notes that Jehu must have had a special reason for taking the Judean princes alive. It also presupposes that in a previous situation Jehu had supported Jehonadab in some way. Since Jehonadab was known as an ardent Yahwist who became a founder of a group that rejected sedentary life out of religious convictions, it may be that in the source from which this passage has been extracted, Jehu had earlier provided military support for some anti-Omride hostility that was headed by Jehonadab. This would explain why Jehonadab now comes seeking out Jehu, apparently wishing to return the favor of Jehu's earlier support. Jehu asks him if this is indeed the reason why he has sought him out, to which Jehonadab answers affirmatively. The two then ride off toward Samaria where Jehu plans to demonstrate his zeal for Yahweh in a way that required Jehonadab's support.

According to the present context, this demonstration came when Jehu ambushed the servants of Baal. But in the source from which this passage was extracted, it seems that this demonstration had something to do with the forty-two princes whom Jehu had captured and brought to Samaria. We may deduce that Jehu was planning to kill the captives in a way that required the help of Jehonadab and would at the same time demonstrate to Jehonadab his "zeal for Yahweh."[33]

This concern to distance Jehu from the charge that he flirted with Baalism surfaces again in a parenthetical statement following Jehu's announcement that he intends to support the worship of Baalism far more than Ahab had. To show the seriousness of his intention, Jehu orders that all of Baal's functionaries in Samaria are to appear before him with the threat that anyone who fails to do so will be punished with death. At this point the Dtr redactor felt compelled to inform his readers that Jehu was lying, and that he had a good reason for doing so:

> Now Jehu acted deceptively in order to destroy the servants of Baal (2 Kgs 10:19b).

The redactor's concern to defend Jehu's actions is indicated by an anxiety that moved the redactor to insert a parenthetical statement into the account that undercuts the element of surprise that the original narrative sought to create. By prematurely exposing Jehu's true motive, the Dtr redactor in effect emptied the episode's denouement of its dramatic power. Here we see that our redactor was not primarily interested in maintaining the artistic integrity

---

[33] The fact that we have another tradition that ascribes the death of the Judean princes to Athaliah rather than to Jehu raises questions. Does the existence of these conflicting traditions suggest that the source from which this fragment was taken was intended to exonerate Athaliah by attributing the death of the Judean princes to Jehu and Jehonadab?

of his source, but with fending off any suggestion that Jehu was the least bit serious about his promise to sanction Baalism as the state religion.

This following verse carries on the motif of Jehonadab's involvement and reflects the same concern to defend Jehu's actions. After seeing that the worshipers of Baal are ritually prepared for the royal sacrifice, the redactor inserts the following expansion:

> And Jehu went into the temple of Baal with Jehonadab ben Rechab. Then he said to the worshipers of Baal, "Search and see that there is none among you who are the servants of Yahweh, but only the servants of Baal" (2 Kgs 10:23).

This additional information exonerates Jehu in two ways. First of all, it reinforces Jehu's association with Jehonadab. Secondly, Jehu's actions are defended by the precaution he took to insure that none of the servants of Yahweh would fall victim to the impending slaughter. Even though it is extremely unlikely that a devoted servant of Yahweh would have responded to Jehu's demand that the servants of Baal attend the royal sacrifice, the redactor was anxious to assure the reader that Jehu took special care to avoid the very crime that the redactor had earlier accused Ahab's house of committing—the murder of Yahweh's servants.[34]

Related to the texts that were intended to emphasize the purity of Jehu's Yahwistic motives is the Dtr addition that portrays Jehu as a cult reformer. H. Hoffmann's study has shown that the Dtr redactor used 2 Kings 9–11 to present a third epoch in the cultic history of the monarchy, the age of "Revolution and Reform."[35] It brought to an end the Baalism that Ahab had introduced in the North and which had spread to the South through political ties with the Omrides. To show that Ahab's Baalism was terminated, the Dtr redactor took over a narrative that described two political conspiracies and inserted material to make the climax of the two revolts a cult reformation. The Dtr addition that describes Jehu's cult reform begins with the actions taken by Jehu's guard after they had massacred the servants of Baal:

> (25b) Then they cast them[36] out into the third court[37] and went into the

---

[34] 2 Kgs 9:7–8.

[35] Hoffmann, 97.

[36] Following Gray (558) who suggests *wayyašlîkûm* (MT: *wayyašlîkû*) since the transitive verb requires an object.

[37] The mention of *hārāsîm wehaššališîm* twice in v 25 has been suspected to be a corruption. Gray (558) notes that Klostermann suggested *wayyašlikû 'arsâ hā'ašērâ* ("They cast the Asherah to the ground), but Gray's own alternative, *hahasērâ haššālišît* ("the third court"), makes better sense since it is natural to expect a mention of the place where the bodies were deposited as the guard made way toward the inner shrine of the temple. Compare the expression *bištê hasrôt* in 2 Kgs 21:5.

innermost shrine[38] of the temple of Baal (26) and they brought out the sacred pillar[39] and burned it. (27) Then they tore down the altar of Baal,[40] and they tore down the temple of Baal and made it into a latrine which stands to this day. (28) Thus Jehu eradicated Baal from Israel (2 Kgs 25b-28).

As in 1 Kgs 18:17-40, which concludes with the massacre of Baal's prophets, the final episode in the original narrative concluded with v 25a. Taking this as a fitting place to insert material, the Dtr redactor included an expansion in which the guard, without any instruction from Jehu, become suddenly infused with zeal to reform Israel's cult by destroying both the sacred objects associated with Baal's sanctuary and the temple of Baal itself. The Dtr description has the guards first remove the bodies blocking their access to the innermost shrine of the temple. Once they are cleared away, the guards enter the temple, bring out the Asherah and burn it.[41] They then demolish the altar of Baal and finally the temple and desecrate it[42] by making it into a latrine.[43]

The redactor's purpose in presenting Jehu as a cult reformer complements his concern to picture Jehu as the means by which Yahweh poured out his wrath on the house of Ahab. According to the Dtr commission in 2 Kgs

---

[38] Gray (562) convincingly defends the MT's reading ʿîr.

[39] The MT reads maṣṣēbôt, but there is widespread agreement among commentators that the text should be emended: Stade, "Anmerkungen," 278; Gressmann, 310; Eissfeldt, Könige, 559; Skinner, 334; Burney, 306; Benzinger, Könige, 154; Kittel, 242; Šanda, 117; Landsdorfer, 176; Fricke, 136; Würthwein, 341. Several considerations have been offered to support reading ʾăšērâ. First, according to 2 Kgs 3:2, Jehoram had already put away the maṣṣēbâ. Second, a combustible object is in view, a characteristic that does not seem to apply to the maṣṣēbâ. Third, several Dtr texts mention the burning of the ʾăšērâ in the context of cultic reform (Deut 12:3; 1 Kgs 15:13; 2 Kgs 23:6, 15). And fourth, 1 Kgs 16:33 mentions that Ahab erected an ʾăšērâ in Samaria. But it must be acknowledged that this proposal does not solve all the difficulties since 2 Kgs 13:6 states that during the reign of Jehoahaz the Asherah remained standing in Samaria. But since this statement occurs within a post-Dtr insertion (4-6), 2 Kgs 10:26 may have already been corrupted.

[40] The MT reads maṣṣēbâ. Several commentators regard this reading as a corruption of mizbēaḥ: Stade, "Anmerkungen," 278-79; Eissfeldt, Könige, 559; Burney, 306; Gressmann, 310; Benzinger, Könige, 154; Kittel, 242; Šanda, 117; Fricke 136. This conclusion is supported by the fact that mizbēaḥ is often the object of nts in Dtr texts (Exod 34:13; Deut 7:5, 12:3; Judg 2:2, 6:28, 30, 31, 32), and by 1 Kgs 16:32 where it is stated that Ahab built a mizbēaḥ.

[41] The removal of cult objects from the temple for burning in a different location is paralleled in 1 Kgs 15:13 (ʾăšērâ), 2 Kgs 23:4 (hakkēlîm), 6 (ʾăšērâ).

[42] This indicates the thoroughness of Jehu's reform. The same point is made more emphatically with respect to Josiah who similarly defiled several illegitimate cult places (2 Kgs 23:10, 14-15, 16, 20).

[43] The Dtr redactor is fond of using strong, almost obscene language to describe the apostate and their fate in curses (Deut 28:25-68; 1 Kgs 14:10), in the formula concerning the unburied corpses (1 Kgs 14:11, 16:4; 21:21, 24; Jer 8:1 3; 16:4), and in the crude description of male descendants (1 Sam 25:22, 34; 1 Kgs 14:10; 16:11; 21:21; 2 Kgs 9:8).

9:7–9, the prophets of Yahweh had been killed by "the whole house of Ahab" because of Ahab's zeal to promote Baalism in Israel. Jehu is now presented as destroying those cult objects that Ahab's patronage of Baalism had introduced into Israel. A comparison with 1 Kgs 16:32–33 reveals that the Dtr description of Jehu's reform corresponds to the cultic innovations that Ahab introduced:

Ahab built:	Jehu destroyed:
ʾăšēâ	ʾăšēâ
mizbēaḥ	mizbēaḥ
bêt habbāʿal	bêt habbāʿal

In the Dtr conception, Jehu brought to an end the era of Baalism in Israel. Just as Ahab had "served Baal and worshiped him" (I Kgs 16:31), so Jehu is here credited with having "eradicated Baal from Israel" (2 Kgs 10:28). He therefore was not only the agent by which the house of Ahab was destroyed; he also served as the means by which Israel was purged of Ahab's corrupting influence, and therefore earned Yahweh's reward of dynastic longevity.

3. The Dtr Interpretation of Jehoiada's Coup

As with his embellishments to the account of Jehu's coup, the Dtr redactor used the account of Jehoiada's coup to portray the leader of the revolt as a cult reformer. He did not, however, explicitly relate the restoration of the throne to Joash to his teaching concerning David's "eternal dynasty." Instead, we find that his editorial activities reveal a special interest in portraying "the people of the land" as a part of Jehoiada's support group. "Cult reform" and "the people of the land" are the two central concerns that are reflected in his redaction of 2 Kings 11.

a. Jehoiada's Cult Reform

The theme of cult reform is not confined to the account of Jehu's coup since, according to the Dtr perspective, Ahab's Baalism did not remain confined to the north. Because of family ties with the Omrides, Baalism penetrated Judah to such an extent that a temple for Baal was built in Jerusalem. The Dtr redactor therefore correspondingly expanded the account of Jehoiada's coup to include an episode of cult reform. Together Jehu and Jehoiada are portrayed as cult reformers who put an end to the Baalism that was introduced into Israel and spread to Judah.

Just as the Dtr redactor made Jehu's cult reform the climax of his conspiracy, the account of Jehoiada's coup was expanded so that it too would culminate in the destruction of Baal's temple in Jerusalem. After Athaliah is led out of the temple and executed, and a covenant is made "to be the people of Yahweh," the redactor provides the following description of Jehoiada's cult reforms:

> Then all the people of the land entered the temple of Baal and tore it down. And[44] the altar[45] and its images they completely smashed, and they killed Mattan the priest of Baal in front of the altar[46] (2 Kgs 11:18a).

Although it is unlikely that a temple to Baal was built in Jerusalem, parallel themes in the original narrative led the Dtr redactor to cast Jehoiada in the role that corresponded to the one he had assigned to Jehu—that of cult reformer.[47] The Dtr historian never explicitly states who built this temple, or when it was built. However, the Dtr evaluation of King Joram implies that he brought Baalism to Judah by means of his marriage to Athaliah:

> And he [Joram] walked in the way of the kings of Israel, just as the house of Ahab had done, for the daughter of Ahab became his wife, and he did what was evil in the sight of Yahweh (2 Kgs 8:18).

Ahaziah, the son of Joram and Athaliah, is similarly condemned for the influence that the house of Ahab had upon him:

> And he [Ahaziah] walked in the way of the house of Ahab, and did what was evil in the sight of Yahweh, just like the house of Ahab, because he was the son-in-law of the house of Ahab (2 Kgs 8:27).

In these evaluations of father and son, the evil of which they are accused is explicitly related to the family ties Joram and Ahaziah had with the house of Ahab through Joram's marriage to Athaliah. The Dtr redactor apparently wished the reader to deduce that, just as Ahab had a temple for Baal constructed in Samaria for Jezebel, so Joram did the same for Athaliah in Jerusalem. Accordingly, the redactor charged that Baalism had made its way into Judah through Athaliah, and so it was only fitting that Jehoiada's usurpation of this Omride queen should also include the destruction of the temple that Joram had built for her.[48] The concern to draw a parallelism between

---

[44] Reading wĕ'et with LXX, T and Chronicles for the MT's 'et. The haplography is due to the final waw on the preceding word.

[45] Reading a singular form with Q for grammatical agreement with sĕlemāyw.

[46] Reading with S, T, and V for the MT's plural form.

[47] Hoffmann, 110-13.

[48] The mention of Mattan, the priest of Baal, is a detail that seems to be based on historical fact. Although it is unlikely that a temple for Baal was built in Jerusalem, it is conceivable that Athaliah had instigated the worship of Baal in the temple of Yahweh just as Manasseh later did (2 Kgs 21:4-5, 7).

Baalism in Israel and Judah accounts for the corresponding descriptions in 10:25b–27 and 11:18a of the actions Jehu and Jehoiada took to reform cult practices:

2 Kgs 10:25b–27:

    A And they went into the shrine of the temple of Baal.
      B And they brought out the sacred pillar from the temple of Baal and burned it.
        C And they demolished the altar of Baal.
        D And they tore down the temple of Baal.

2 Kgs 11:18a:

    A′ And the people of the land entered the temple of Baal
      D′ they tore it down.
      C′ And they smashed to bits its altar
    B′ and its images.

Jehoiada's reform is distinguished from Jehu's by the covenant ceremony that preceded the demolition of Baal's temple. The redactor expanded the original account of the covenant ceremony as follows (bold type indicates the Dtr expansion):

> And Jehoiada mediated a covenant between Yahweh and the king and the people, that they should be the people of Yahweh, and **between the king and the people** (2 Kgs 11:17).

The Dtr notion of Israel as Yahweh's chosen people involves the exclusive worship of Yahweh which demands that they destroy foreign cult objects (Deut 7:5–6). The Dtr redactor therefore expanded the account of Jehoiada's covenant mediation to prepare for the insertion that describes the destruction of the temple of Baal which immediately follows.

b. "The People of the Land"

Another difference between the two reforms concerns the agents who carried out the purge. In the treatment of Jehu's reform, the Dtr redactor simply extended the acts of the last named party so that the royal guard carries out the reform. But in Jehoiada's coup, the Dtr redactor has "the people of the land" suddenly appear as zealous reformers who enthusiastically proceed to carry out the destruction of Baal's temple and the murder of Baal's priest.

Besides making "the people of the land" the driving force of the reform, the redactor also portrays them as ardent supporters of Joash by having them rejoice over his acclamation and enthronement (vv 14, 19, 20a). His purpose in casting this group in this positive role shows that they were regarded by him as an especially important political and religious body.

The meaning of the phrase *'am hā'āreṣ* has commanded considerable scholarly attention, and yet to some extent its precise meaning remains a debated issue.[49] There is widespread agreement that the phrase is a technical term which in preexilic Israel referred to a group that included ". . . only the responsible male citizenry, the married men who live on their own land and have full rights and duties, including the duty of serving in the army and of participating in judicial proceedings and cult festivals."[50] But beyond this the ambiguity of the term makes it questionable whether the "people of the land" can be identified more specifically as an aristocratic group that "occupied the position just below that of the priests on the social ladder."[51] But de Vaux's examination of the data leads him to the conclusion that "Nowhere does the expression mean a party or a social class."[52] It is clear, however, that this group was sufficiently important to the Dtr redactor to cause him to make them active participants in Jehoiada's coup.

The redactor's interest in this particular group may be explained by the role that they played in bringing Josiah to the throne:

(23) Now the servants of Amon conspired against him and killed the king in his palace. (24) Then the people of the land killed all those who had conspired against King Amon, and the people of the land made Josiah his son king in his place (2 Kgs 21:23–24).

Here the people of the land are presented as the driving force behind Josiah's accession.[53] Writing at the time when this group was exerting its

---

[49] B. Oded offers a summary of the various interpretations of the phrase in his "Judah and the Exile," *Israelite and Judean History* (ed. John H. Hayes and J. Maxwell Miller; OTL; Philadelphia: Westminster, 1977) 435–89, esp. pp. 456–58.

[50] M. H. Pope, "'am ha'arez," *IDB* 1 (1962) 106–7, esp. p. 106.

[51] Ibid., 106. Similarly, Mettinger (129) describes Israelite social structure in terms of a four-tiered hierarchy: (1) the king; (2) the clergy and officials; (3) "the people of the land"; (4) women, slaves and sojourners.

[52] de Vaux, *Ancient Israel*, 1.70. E. W. Nicholson ("The Meaning of the Expression '*m-h'rs* in the Old Testament" *JJS* 10 [1965] 59–66) also thinks that scholars have over-interpreted the phrase.

[53] That they continued to support Josiah throughout his reign is indicated by 2 Kgs 23:30 where we are told that "the people of the land took Jehoahaz the son of Josiah and anointed him king in the place of his father." Jehoahaz's continued support of his father's policies is indicated by the fact that Necho dethroned him and replaced him with Jehoiakim, who then taxed the people of the land at Necho's command (2 Kgs 23:33–35).

political interest,[54] the Dtr historian voiced his approval of their support of Josiah by injecting them into the story of Jehoiada's overthrow of Athaliah and the installment of Joash, who likewise ascended to the throne through force. It may be that he sought to legitimate the actions of the people of the land in his own day by showing that this same group had earlier supported Jehoiada when he restored Judah's throne to a Davidic descendant.[55]

The Dtr redaction of Jehoiada's coup manifests two primary concerns. First of all, insertions were made to show that a covenant with Yahweh involved both the king and the people who were sworn to be "the people of Yahweh." This sacred pact was to be expressed by the eradication of all illicit worship from Judah. Secondly, "the people of the land" are portrayed as ardently supporting the overthrow of Athaliah and as rejoicing over Joash's coronation and installation. They are also presented as the primary agents of Jehoiada's cult reform. Both concerns appear to reflect important political and religious aspects of Josiah's reign. Parallels are drawn between the circumstances that brought both Joash and Josiah to power, and between the two regimes which enacted cult reforms as the necessary expression of Judah's covenant relationship with Yahweh.

B. Post-Deuteronomistic Additions

There are several additions that were either inserted within the context of the Dtr text or that reflect a priestly orientation. Because the post-Dtr additions to 2 King 9–10 are relatively brief and do not appear to manifest a consistent tendency, it is difficult to determine what may have motivated these additions, or even whether they should all be attributed to the same redactor.[56] Yet it is possible to detect something of the concerns that they reflect. A redaction-critical analysis of the post-Dtr material found in 2 Kings 11 is somewhat less difficult, for here one does detect that these additions manifest a certain consistency of character. Even so, the analysis of such a restricted scope of material does not permit us to arrive at definitive solutions as what may have motivated these insertions. The following results should therefore be regarded as suggestive.

---

[54] On the connection of the *'am-hā'āres* with Deuteronomy, see G. von Rad, *Studies in Deuteronomy* (STB 1/9; London: SCM, 1953) 60–69.

[55] The Dtr historian also anticipates Josiah's reign in 2 Kgs 11:17 by expanding the description of the covenant partners (Yahweh, king, and people) to parallel 2 Kgs 23:1–3. Likewise, the purpose of the covenant ("to be the people of Yahweh") expressed itself in cultic reform just as Josiah's reforms followed the making of the covenant. See Hoffmann, 110.

[56] For these reasons, I have not used the designation "Dtr²" since this would imply that I attribute all of these insertions to a single exilic redactor. I have therefore chosen to employ the more neutral designation "post-Dtr."

1. 2 Kgs 9:10 and 9:36

These two verses deal with prophetic oracles directed against Jezebel. The former verse is appended to the Dtr expansion of Elisha's commission to Jehu. The latter verse was inserted into the original narrative as Jehu's initial response when he found out that he had made Jezebel's burial impossible by trampling her corpse beyond recognition:

> As for Jezebel, dogs will devour her corpse at a place in Jezreel; no one will bury her (9:10).

> This fulfills the word of Yahweh that he spoke through his servant Elijah the Tishbite: "The dogs will devour Jezebel's flesh at a place in Jezreel" (9:36).

Both verses reflect a deep animosity for Jezebel in stating that she would be subject to the dreadful fate of being unburied so that her corpse would become food for the dogs that roamed the city streets as scavengers.[57] The psalmist, in a complaint to Yahweh, depicts the gruesome decimation of Jerusalem as follows:

> (2) They have given the dead bodies of your servants for food to the birds of the heavens and the flesh of your godly ones to the beasts of the earth. (3) They have poured out their blood like water around Jerusalem; and there was no one to bury them (Ps 79:2-3).

The prophet threatens sinful Judah with a similar image:

> "I shall appoint over them four kinds of doom," declares Yahweh. "The sword to slay, the dogs to drag off, the birds of the heavens to devour and the beasts of the earth to destroy" (Jer 15:3).

This special animosity toward Jezebel of a post-Dtr redactor probably arose from his reading of the Naboth incident. In the original narrative, only Ahab was explicitly singled out for judgment.[58] But because of Jezebel's prominent role in the murder of Naboth, a later redactor thought that a prophecy of judgment should be explicitly directed against her, and so added 1 Kgs 22:23 and 2 Kgs 9:10. Then, in order to show that Elijah's prophecy was fulfilled, this same redactor added the fulfillment notice in 2 Kgs 9:36.[59] The expansions of this redactor are driven by the concern to show that

---

[57] Cf. Ps 59:6, 14-15. Dogs were also known for licking up blood (1 Kgs 21: 19; 22:38; Ps 68:23).

[58] Most commentators hold that vv 1-20 contain an original narrative whose ending was supplanted by a Dtr expansion. For a summary of the source-critical conclusions regarding this chapter, see Long, *Kings*, 224.

[59] The expansion of 2 Kgs 9:7 conforms to this tendency where reference is made to Jezebel's murder of the "servants of Yahweh" who were not prophets. The redactor probably had Naboth in mind.

Jezebel's responsibility for the death of Naboth was finally avenged by Yahweh through Jehu.[60]

2. 2 Kgs 9:27bβ–28 and 2 Kgs 9:29

Two different concerns are reflected in these post-Dtr additions. The first seeks to show that the Judean king Ahaziah received a royal burial, while the second offers a synchronism concerning the reign of Ahaziah. The circumstances of Ahaziah's burial are described after Jehu's men carry out his order to "strike down" the fleeing Ahaziah:

> But he escaped to Megiddo and died there. Then his servants took him by chariot to Jerusalem and buried him with his fathers in his tomb in the city of David (2 Kgs 9:27bβ–28).

This addition leads the reader to believe that Ahaziah was not killed but only wounded at Ibleam,[61] and somehow managed in his wounded state to escape his pursuers. Yet it is hard to believe that Ahaziah could have outrun Jehu's men after they were close enough to injure him, or that these men would have abandoned the pursuit. Why then did the redactor wish to have Ahaziah die at Megiddo rather than at Ibleam? It seems that in his concern to inform his readers that every Judean king received a proper burial in Jerusalem — even those who did not die there — the redactor drew upon the Dtr historian's description of two other kings who were also transferred to Jerusalem for burial. Of Amaziah's burial we are told:

> And they conspired against him in Jerusalem, but he fled to Lachish. So they sent some men after him to Lachish and he was killed there. Then they brought him on horse and he was buried in Jerusalem with his fathers in the city of David (2 Kgs 14:19–20).

A similar report is made about Josiah's burial:

> In his days Pharaoh Necho king of Egypt went up to the king of Assyria to the river Euphrates. And King Josiah went to meet him, and when Necho saw him he killed him at Megiddo. And his servants brought him to Jerusalem and buried him in his own tomb (2 Kgs 23:29–30).

The report of Josiah's death seems to have served as the basis for the

---

[60] Note that the insertion of the fulfillment notice in v 36 subtly reinterprets the original narrative. In the original account, the finding of only the hands, feet and skull of Jezebel was a result of Jehu's brutal trampling of Jezebel's corpse. But the post-Dtr redactor interpreted this to mean that the dogs had meanwhile eaten Jezebel's "flesh."

[61] In the original narrative Jehu is said to have ordered his men to "strike down" Ahaziah just as he had done to Jehoram. The Dtr redactor exploited the ambiguity of *nākâ* to imply that he was only wounded. But Jehu certainly meant that his men were to kill Ahaziah.

details given for Ahaziah's burial. Noting that Megiddo is accessible by chariot from Ibleam, the redactor imitated the account of Josiah's death by having Ahaziah also die there, who was then transferred to Jerusalem by his servants.[62] By utilizing 2 Kgs 23:29-30, this redactor saw to it that Ahaziah, like every other Judean king, received a proper burial in Jerusalem.[63]

The following verse also comes from a post-Dtr redactor since, like the preceding one, it presupposes and (in this case) corrects information given by the Dtr historian:

> In the eleventh year of Joram son of Ahab, Ahaziah became king of Judah (2 Kgs 9:29).

According to the first edition of the Dtr History, Ahaziah began his reign in the twelfth year of Jehoram and reigned for one year (2 Kgs 8:25-26). But a subsequent editor reasoned that, since Ahaziah died one year after his accession, he must have begun his reign in the eleventh rather than the twelfth year of Jehoram's reign.

3. 2 Kgs 10:29

Like 2 Kgs 10:31, this verse offers a qualification concerning Jehu's success at eradicating Baal from Israel:

> However, he did not turn away from the sins of Jeroboam ben Nebat, who made Israel worship the golden calves at Bethel and Dan (2 Kgs 10:29).

The feature that distinguishes this verse from the usual condemnation of Israelite kings is the explicit mention of the worship of the golden calves to define what are the "the sins of Jeroboam."[64] Apart from the initial reference to these sins in 1 Kgs 12:28, 32, they are specifically named only once more in 1-2 Kings in a text that has been convincingly attributed to the exilic Dtr redactor.[65]

Although the explicit mention of the golden calves sets this verse apart from the other Dtr verdicts concerning Israelite kings, this is not its primary objective. Rather, its purpose is to qualify the Dtr redactor's statement that Jehu eradicated Baalism from Israel (v 28).[66] It seems that this subsequent

---

[62] The Chronicler also shows some editorial freedom in locating the place of Ahaziah's death which he places in Samaria.

[63] The Chronicler also made an adjustment to the text with respect to Ahaziah's burial by locating it in Samaria.

[64] The Dtr verdict formulae concerning the northern kings are found in 1 Kgs 15:26, 30, 34; 16:2 (cf. 16:7), 19, 26, 31; 22: 52; 2 Kgs 3:3; 10:31; 13:2 (cf. 13:6), 11, 14:24; 15:9, 18, 24, 28; 17: 21-22.

[65] Nelson, 55-63.

[66] The verse is introduced by the restrictive adverb *raq*. See Williams, *Syntax,* 65, par. 390.

redactor sought to play down Jehu's accomplishments by offsetting the preceding favorable statement with one that emphasized his failures. Apparently, he felt that the condemnation of the Dtr redactor found in v 31b was not sufficient, and that Jehu's disobedience should receive greater emphasis.

4. 2 Kgs 11:6, 10, 15b, 18b, 20b

An examination of the post-Dtr expansions in chapter eleven shows that they all reflect a concern over the sanctity of Yahweh's temple. Verse 6 expands Jehoiada's instructions to the guard:

> . . . and a third of you, those at the Horse Gate,[67] and a third of you, those at the Guard's Gate,[68] shall keep watch over the temple for defense.[69]

Because the details are obscure, it is difficult to determine precisely the meaning and intention of this addition. It is clear that two additional groups are added to those mentioned in the original text. What distinguishes these two groups from those named in the original is that, while the latter are described in general terms,[70] in v 6 they are identified according to the gate at which they were posted. This difference suggests that the redactor had specific knowledge about where the guard was located on the Sabbath and was concerned to show that Jehoiada provided his men with "proper" instructions by including these details about the location of the guard.

The next expansion recounts how Jehoiada provided the guard with special weaponry:

> Then the priest gave the commanders the spears[71] and shields that belonged to King David and were kept in the temple of Yahweh (v 10).

It is easier to recognize this verse as a gloss than it is to explain its presence. Nothing definite is known about the weapons of David that were kept in the temple. 2 Sam 8:7 notes that the booty that David took from Hadadezer included "the shields of gold which were carried by his servants," and

---

[67] Reading *sûs* for the MT's *sûr*. Chr 23:5 has *hayesôd*. The places named in this verse are obscure. I am guided by v 16 where Athaliah's death is located at the place where the horses enter the palace.

[68] Deleting *'aḥar* on the basis of v 19. Apparently two gates are in view. Both the Horse Gate and the Guard's Gate lead to the palace, but only the latter connects directly to the temple, providing the king special access to the temple. Athaliah seems to have been taken out of the temple by a different route and led to the Horse Gate where she was then executed.

[69] The meaning of *massāḥ* is obscure. It is most often rendered "for defense," which fits well with the context.

[70] In the original account, the two groups are described as those who guard the palace (*mišmeret bêt hammelek*) and those who guard the temple (*mišmeret bêt yhwh*).

[71] Reading a plural form with LXX, S, V and 2 Chr 23:9.

that these were brought to Jerusalem. We may surmise that the spears were also David's war booty which he had dedicated to Yahweh for giving him victory over his enemies, and that such weapons were utilized by the temple guard. But why did our redactor wish to emphasize that Jehoiada armed his men with these consecrated weapons? Perhaps this redactor knew that coronation ceremonies traditionally involved a ceremonial use of special weapons that were kept in the temple. To compensate for the omission of a detail of ceremonial protocol, this note was inserted to emphasize that Jehoiada carried out the ritual as dictated by tradition. This conclusion is supported by the observation that the same concern is apparent in the other post-Dtr expansions found in this chapter.

Another addition reflects an interest in showing the measures Jehoiada took to maintain the integrity of the temple. Here the reader is informed that Jehoiada took steps to protect Yahweh's temple from the potential reprisals of Athaliah's supporters:

And the priest stationed guards over the temple of Yahweh (v 18b).

The reason for this addition is not difficult to detect. According to the text that this redactor had before him, the destruction of the temple of Baal was followed by a procession from the temple to the palace. Our redactor was concerned that this would leave Yahweh's temple unguarded, and so added the note that the responsible Jehoiada appointed a guard before leading the throng to the palace. The redactor thus attempted to compensate for what could have been construed as carelessness on Jehoiada's part.

The two other post-Dtr expansions are complementary. The first explains the reasons Jehoiada had for commanding that Athaliah be led out of the temple precincts:

. . . for the priest had said "Let her not be killed in the temple of Yahweh" (v 15b).

Here again the redactor seeks to emphasize Jehoiada's priestly responsibilities. While the original story does not provide an explanation for Athaliah's execution at the Horse Gate,[72] this expansion provides the motive. Jehoiada was concerned for the sanctity of the temple and so ordered that she be executed elsewhere. That these orders were carried out is made explicit by the final post-Dtr expansion. At the conclusion of the narrative, we find this final piece of information:

. . . and they killed Athaliah with the sword at the palace (v 20b).

---

[72] Perhaps this was the customary location for executions.

The location of Athaliah's execution "at the palace" makes it clear that she was not executed in the temple in accordance with Jehoiada's previous instructions.

The post-Dtr additions that have been examined vary in content and yet reflect an interest in making certain minor adjustments to the text. To compensate for Jezebel's role in the Naboth incident, an additional prophecy (1 Kgs 21:23; 2 Kgs 9:10) and its corresponding fulfillment notice were inserted (2 Kgs 9:36). Similarly, the text was adjusted to account for Ahaziah's burial in Jerusalem (9:27b-28) and to correct the accession date for Jehoram (9:29). Certain alterations were also made to the Dtr redactor's conclusion to Jehu's coup. Verse 29 is quick to qualify Jehu's achievements in eradicating Baalism from Israel by noting that he still maintained the worship of the golden calves at Dan and Bethel. For this redactor, Jehu's commitment to Yahweh was lukewarm because he ignored covenant law.

The post-Dtr expansions to Jehoiada's coup are all intended to show that "the priest" conscientiously executed his duties as caretaker of Yahweh's temple. Jehoiada saw to it that the guards were stationed at the Horse Gate and Guard's Gate to defend the temple (v 6), and that they were given the ceremonial weaponry kept in the temple in anticipation of Joash's acclamation and enthronement (v 10). Jehoiada's scrupulous concern for temple protocol is again emphasized by the expansions which point out that he posted a guard at Yahweh's temple before leaving it (v 18b), and that the execution of Athaliah was carried out at the palace so that Yahweh's temple would not be defiled by her blood (vv 15b, 20b). The nature of the insertions made to the account of Jehoiada's coup indicate that they were added by someone who was very sensitive to matters of temple protocol, a concern that was projected onto Jehoiada the high priest.

C. The Chronicler's Treatment of 2 Kings 9–11 (2 Chr 22–23)

In the preceding discussion we relied on internal evidence to argue that 2 Kings 9–11 had been altered — sometimes radically — by later redactors. A comparison of the Chronicler's version with 2 Kings 9–11 provides additional evidence that a willingness to alter source material was a matter of course in Israelite literary tradition. By examining the Chronicler's redaction of 2 Kings 9–11, we shall see that he too made considerable alterations to the source he had before him, thereby continuing a process that had begun before this material came into his hands.

1. 2 Kings 9–10

The most striking aspect of the Chronicler's treatment of Jehu's coup is that he deals with it only insofar as it concerns Judah. This almost total disregard for the history of the northern kingdom reflects the Chronicler's extremely negative view toward a nation that was ". . . conceived in sin, born in iniquity and nurtured in adultery."[73] The Chronicler's treatment of 2 Kings 9-10 was therefore selective, dealing only with matters that relate to the death of the Judean king Ahaziah, and to Jehu's murder of the Judean princes. By contrast, he shows great interest in 2 Kings 11, virtually reproducing it. Furthermore, he introduces several alterations and expansions that reflect some of his characteristic concerns. As E. L. Curtis notes, "Nowhere else does the Chronicler's method of interpreting history and introducing notions of his own time as controlling factors in the earlier history more clearly appear."[74]

The Chronicler's treatment of 2 Kings 9-10 is assimilated into his introduction to the reign of Ahaziah. In 2 Chr 22:1-6, the Chronicler basically follows 2 Kgs 8:25-29. The most significant departure from his source is the emphasis on Ahaziah's wickedness resulting from following the counsel of his mother Athaliah (v 3) and of the house of Ahab (vv 4, 5).

In 2 Chr 22:7-9 the Chronicler's condenses Jehu's coup inasmuch as it relates to Judean royalty. After reporting that Ahaziah went down to visit the wounded Jehoram in Jezreel, a summary of some of the events recorded in 2 Kgs 9-10 is provided:

> (7) Now this turn of events,[75] when Ahaziah went to see Joram, was from God. After Ahaziah had arrived, he went out with Jehoram to Jehu ben Nimshi whom God had anointed to destroy the house of Ahab. (8) And it came about that when Jehu was executing judgment on the house of Ahab he found the leaders of Judah,[76] the brothers of Ahaziah, Ahaziah's servants, and he killed them. (9) And Jehu sought out Ahaziah and they captured him while he was hiding in Samaria. And they brought him to Jehu and killed and buried him. For they said, "He is the descendant of Jehoshaphat who sought Yahweh with all his heart." Now there was no one left of the house of Ahaziah to maintain power over the kingdom.

The Chronicler begins his résumé of Ahaziah's downfall with a theological interpretation. Having emphasized that Ahaziah's wickedness was a result of his liaison with the house of Ahab, he saw God's using this relationship to bring about Ahaziah's judgment. The timing of Ahaziah's visit was the crucial factor. God determined that Ahaziah would be visiting Jehoram just after Jehu had been anointed to destroy the house of Ahab.

[73] J. Myers, *I Chronicles*, AB 12 (Garden City: Doubleday, 1956) xxxiii.

[74] E. L. Curtis and A. A. Madsen, *The Books of Chronicles* ICC (New York: Charles Scribner's Sons, 1910) 423.

[75] Reading *něsibbat* instead of *těbûsat* on the basis of 2 Chr 10:15.

[76] Deleting *běnê* with the LXX and 2 Kgs 10:13.

It is clear that the Chronicler made some changes in the order of events described in 2 Kings 9–10. The statement that Ahaziah "went out with Jehoram to Jehu ben Nimshi" shows that he was reading 2 Kgs 9:17–26. But instead of next reporting Ahaziah's death, the Chronicler offers a generalization ("And it came about when Jehu was executing judgment of the house of Ahab"), and then jumps to 2 Kgs 10:12–14, which recounts the death of the forty-two Judean princes.[77] Only after reporting this episode does he return to Ahaziah, who is sought out by Jehu's men and captured in Samaria where he is executed and buried.

The purpose behind this manipulation of his source seems to center on the location of Ahaziah's burial. According to 2 Kgs 9:28, Ahaziah received a royal burial in Jerusalem. But according to the Chronicler, he was buried in Samaria. The Chronicler makes the additional point that even this was carried out reluctantly and was done only on the merits of his pious ancestor Jehoshaphat. It is as though the Chronicler thought that the wickedness of Ahaziah excluded him from receiving a royal burial in Jerusalem since he had betrayed the kingdom by aligning himself with the house of Ahab. It was therefore more fitting that he should be buried in Samaria, the object of his evil and misplaced loyalty.

2. 2 Kings 11

As noted above, the Chronicler's handling of the account of Jehoiada's coup reflects some of his characteristic concerns. The Chronicler does not add much to the description of the setting (2 Chr 22:10–12). The only important piece of information that goes beyond 2 Kings is that Jehosheba was the wife of Jehoiada the priest. Much more radical changes are made to the episode that describes Jehoiada's instigation of the coup (2 Chr 23:1–11). The first expansion is the naming of the five "captains of a hundred" summoned by Jehoiada. After entering into a covenant with them, the Chronicler reports that they "went throughout all Judah and gathered the Levites from all the cities of Judah, and the leaders of the clans of Israel."[78] These three groups, the captains, the Levites, and the clan leaders, comprise "the whole assembly" with whom Jehoiada enters into a covenant to restore Joash to the throne. The cooperation of these three groups is derived from the

---

[77] The Chronicler chose to mention this episode because he wanted to show that Jehu made it so that "there was no one to maintain power over the kingdom" (v 9), thus explaining why it was that Athaliah was able to seize the throne.

[78] According to v 8 this latter group actually represents "all Judah," and v 20 seems to equate them with "the nobles" and "the rulers of the people." An identification with "the people of the land" may also have been intended.

reforms that Jehoshaphat had earlier inaugurated. According to the Chronicler's account of Jehoshaphat's reforms, they were the king's primary agents of bringing spiritual leadership to the kingdom. Five "captains" accompany the priests and the Levites as they go throughout Judah teaching "the book of the law of Yahweh":

> In the third year of his reign he sent out the following captains to teach in the cities of Judah: Benhail, Obadiah, Zechariah, Nethanel, and Micaiah. They were accompanied by nine Levites and two priests: . . . . They took the book of the law of Yahweh and went through all the towns of Judah teaching it to the people (2 Chr 17:7-9).

"The leaders of the clans of Israel" also share with the priests and Levites the responsibility of administering justice:

> Also[79] in Jerusalem Jehoshaphat appointed some Levites and priests and some of the leaders of the clans of Israel to adjudicate sacral law and legal disputes between the inhabitants of the city (2 Chr 19:8).

It thus appears that the Chronicler's broadening of Jehoiada's support group was informed by his concept of the various parties Jehoshaphat employed to carry out his reforms.[80] For the Chronicler it was only fitting that these appointed officials should aid Jehoiada in restoring the Davidic throne to Joash.[81]

The Chronicler has also made some revealing alterations to Jehoiada's instructions to the Karites and the royal guard. They are here replaced by the priests and the Levites (the italicized material indicates the Chronicler's alterations):

> This is what you shall do: A third of you who enter on the Sabbath, *those who are priests and Levites, shall become gatekeepers*[82]*at the temple entrances,* a third shall be at the palace, and a third shall be at the *Foundation*[83] Gate. *And the rest of the people shall be in the courts of the temple of Yahweh. No one shall enter the temple of Yahweh except the priests and the ministering Levites.*

---

[79] This implies that the judges appointed by Jehoshaphat "in the fortified cities of Jerusalem" (vv 5-7) were also priests, Levites and clan leaders.

[80] The Chronicler's great respect for Jehoshaphat was earlier indicated in his version of Ahaziah's burial. The Chronicler explicitly states that the burial was performed out of respect for Jehoshaphat (2 Chr 22:9).

[81] The sanctity of the Davidic line is emphasized by the Chronicler's expansion in v 3, where after Jehoiada reveals Joash he solemnly proclaims, "This is the prince who shall rule just as Yahweh spoke concerning the sons of David."

[82] Reading *wĕlaśśô'ărîm lĕśōmĕrê*. Compare the Chronicler's expansion in v 19, where mention is made of the gatekeepers.

[83] 2 Kgs 11:6 has *sûr* which is probably a corruption of *sûs*.

They may enter because they are holy. But let the rest of the people keep
Yahweh's charge [and remain outside]. And the Levites shall surround the king,
each with his weapon in his hand. Whoever enters *the temple*[84] shall be killed
(2 Chr 23:4–7a).

These alterations show that the Chronicler was most concerned with the
temple and its sanctity. This issue was of such importance that he disregarded
the intention of Jehoiada's original instructions in order to underscore
matters of cultic law. For according to Jehoiada's original plan, no one —
except perhaps Jehoiada himself — had any reason to enter the temple.[85] The
Chronicler's concern with this matter moved him to emphasize that only the
priests and Levites may enter the temple, while the rest of the people must
remain in the temple courts. His seriousness about the issue is shown by his
statements that the people must keep "Yahweh's charge" and by the threat
that any who violate it will be killed.

The execution of Jehoiada's instructions are also altered to emphasize
matters of temple protocol. In v 8 the Chronicler replaces "the captains of
a hundred" with "the Levites and all Judah" as the groups "who did all that
Jehoiada the priest had commanded."[86] In addition, the expansion found in
v 8b seems intended to highlight Jehoiada's authority over duties of the
guard, stating that both the temple and the palace guard carried out his instructions because, ". . . Jehoiada the priest had not dismissed any of the
divisions." This note seems to imply that, at least in the Chronicler's view,
the guard and their rotations were under the direct authority of the high
priest.

The expansions of the scene describing Joash's acclamation again show
an interest in matters related to the cult. The Chronicler adds in v 11 that
Jehoiada's sons participated in Joash's anointing, while v 12 notes that the
people *were running* and praising the king. Cultic celebration is also
highlighted in v 13 which states that "the temple singers with their musical
instruments were leading in the celebration."

The Chronicler's editorial tendency to emphasize matters of cult is once
more apparent in his alterations to the episode of the reform of the Jerusalem
cult. In the covenant ceremony that precedes the destruction of Baal's
temple, a slight but significant alteration is made to the parties involved in
the covenant ceremony. According to 2 Kgs 11:17, Jehoiada the priest served

---

[84] 2 Kgs 11:8 has "the ranks," meaning the guard who surround the king.

[85] Assuming that Joash was waiting in the temple, and that Jehoiada brought him out
from there.

[86] The general distinction between "the Levites" and "all Judah" indicates that the
Chronicler was still thinking in terms of those who may enter the temple as opposed to those
who may not.

as the mediator of a covenant between Yahweh, the king and the people. But the Chronicler changed *ben yahweh* to read *benô* ("between himself") so that the pious Jehoiada is portrayed as placing himself under the obligations of the covenant. By making this change, the Chronicler emphasized that it was the high priest who led this national commitment "to be the people of Yahweh."

A sizable expansion is made to the steps that Jehoiada took to secure the temple precincts. 2 Kgs 11:18b has the brief statement, "And the priest appointed officers over the temple of Yahweh." But the Chronicler continues:

> . . . under the direction of the priests and the Levites.[87] And he re-established the duties of the priests and the Levites[88] whom David had organized to be in charge of the temple of Yahweh, to offer burnt offerings to Yahweh just as it is written in the law of Moses, with rejoicing and singing, according to the order of David. And he stationed the gatekeepers at the gate of Yahweh's temple so that none who were in any way unclean would enter (2 Chr 23:18-20).

This addition shows that the Chronicler thought that, under Athaliah's regime, David's organization of the cult personnel had been dismantled.[89] He therefore found it necessary to have Jehoiada re-establish the duties of the priests, Levites and the gatekeepers.[90]

Our examination of the Chronicler's handling of 2 Kings 11 makes it clear that he was deeply concerned with the holiness of the temple and with the consecrated personnel responsible for its proper maintenance. These concerns are illustrated by the fact that he cast the priests and Levites in that role originally played by the Karites and the royal guard. In addition, their exclusive right to enter the temple is emphatically noted, and their continuing duties within the temple precincts are portrayed as being re-established as a result of Jehoiada's reform. Among these duties, the Chronicler singled out for comment the gatekeepers' responsibility to keep the unclean out of the temple area. For the Chronicler, Jehoiada's coup was especially important because it restored a Davidic descendant to the throne of Judah and re-established the prescribed means by which the sanctity of Yahweh's temple was to be maintained.

D. Conclusions

The foregoing analysis illustrates how older traditions were taken up by subsequent redactors and altered to suit their particular purposes. The Dtr

---

[87] Reading with LXX, S, V. The MT has "Levitical priests."

[88] Reading with the LXX. The clause was deleted in the MT due to homoioteleuton.

[89] 2 Chr 24:7 states that ". . . the sons of the wicked Athaliah had broken into the temple of God and even used the holy things of the temple of Yahweh for the Baals."

[90] The Chronicler describes these in 1 Chronicles 23-26.

expansion of 2 Kings 9–11 is the most extensive and reveals several special interests. The Dtr handling of 2 Kings 9–10 manifests an attempt on the part of the redactor to account for the rise and fall of the dynasties of Jeroboam I, Baasha, Zimri, Omri-Ahab and Jehu. All of these dynasties — apart from Jehu's — were quickly destroyed by Yahweh because the kings who founded them transgressed Deuteronomic cult law. Jehu was also condemned for this sin, but this did not bring about a quick termination of his dynasty. Instead, in his case, the punishment for his apostasy came in the form of military defeat before Hazael's aggression. This special handling of Jehu was a result of the attempt to account for a dynasty that was perpetuated through four generations. The original account of Jehu's coup was expanded in order to show that his attack against Jehoram's regime was predicted by Elijah and commissioned by Elisha. For Jehu's willingness to eradicate the house of Ahab and the Baalism that this dynasty had fostered, Yahweh rewarded Jehu with dynastic longevity.

The cause-effect relationship drawn between obedience and dynastic duration suggests that had Jehu, or any of Israel's kings, been fully obedient to Yahweh, they would have engendered an eternal dynasty as David had. Through this principle, the Dtr historian was able to explain the instability of Israel's political vicissitudes and contrast it with the stability of Judah's Davidic dynasty. In his view, Yahweh had given the same opportunity to Israel's kings as he did to David. But rather than following David's example of obedience, they chose instead to "cling to the sins of Jeroboam."

The Dtr historian also found the account of Jehoiada's coup suited to his purposes. In Jehoiada's heroic act of restoring Judah's throne to the young king Joash, the Dtr historian found a historical precedent for the aggressive actions that "the people of the land" had taken to place the young Josiah on the throne. To drive home this correspondence, he introduced into the narrative "the people of the land," as enthusiastic supporters of Jehoiada's heroic coup and portrayed them as rejoicing over Joash's acclamation and enthronement. The role that "the people of the land" play in 2 Kings 11 corresponds to another controversial aspect of Josiah's reign. They are pictured as the primary means by which the covenant "to be Yahweh's people" was expressed in the enactment of radical cult reform.

Those expansions that have been labeled "post-Dtr" do not possess the broad vision evident in the Dtr redaction of 2 Kings 9–11. For the most part, they reflect a more modest attempt to add various nuances and corrections to the underlying material. In the post-Dtr additions to 2 Kings 9–10 are found expansions that emphasize that Jezebel received her just due, a statement concerning Ahaziah's burial in Jerusalem, a synchronism concerning

Ahaziah's reign, an emphasis on Jehu's failure, and a specification concerning the territory that Hazael conquered. The post-Dtr additions in 2 Kings 11 are not as varied; all focus upon the meticulousness with which Jehoiada carried out his duties as "the priest." These expansions emphasize that he insured that the guard took up their proper positions on the Sabbath, that the guard was outfitted with David's ceremonial weapons, that Yahweh's temple was properly protected, and that Athaliah was executed outside the temple precincts. This concern with detail leaves one with the impression that the alterations were inserted by a later priest or Levite who was deeply concerned with the high priest's duty to maintain temple protocol. Those aspects of the story that might impugn Jehoiada's character as the high priest were anticipated and answered by this scrupulous and devoted redactor.

The Chronicler's version of 2 Kings 9–11 reflects some of his characteristic interests. His selective treatment of 2 Kings 9–10 reflects his low estimation of the northern kingdom, moving him to deal with only those aspects that concern Judah. The introduction to Ahaziah's reign emphasizes that the king's wickedness was a result of his connections with the house of Ahab through his mother Athaliah. Ironically, it was this unholy liaison that God used to bring about Ahaziah's destruction. The reader is told that God commissioned Jehu to destroy the house of Ahab just when Ahaziah was visiting Jehoram. Altering the circumstances of Ahaziah's burial also functions to emphasize his wickedness. He was not honored with a royal burial in Jerusalem. Instead, Jehu's men reluctantly buried him in Samaria out of respect for his righteous grandfather Jehoshaphat.

The treatment of 2 Kings 11 in many ways reflects a further development of the tendencies seen in the post-Dtr additions to this account. In addition to naming the five captains, the Chronicler included among Jehoiada's supporters the clan leaders of Israel, and the priests and the Levites. Here the writer was guided by his account of Jehoshaphat's reform in which the same three groups served as the agents of Jehoshaphat's reforms. Of these three groups, the priests and the Levites receive special attention. Because the action took place in the temple area, the role that was originally played by the Karites and the guard was assigned to these sacred functionaries. Furthermore, the Chronicler's interest in sacred personnel is manifested in his more detailed description of the activities of the temple singers and of the gatekeepers. Finally, this version of the story strongly emphasizes that Jehoiada was concerned to maintain temple protocol according to "the instruction of Yahweh" which had been mediated through the Law of Moses and through the prescriptions of David. For the Chronicler, Jehoiada's coup not only brought about the enthronement of David's heir and the eradication of Baalism; it also re-established the activities of the sacred personnel who were divinely appointed to maintain the holiness of Yahweh's temple.[91]

---

[91] A discussion of the date of the Chronicler's work would take us beyond the scope of the present work (For a review of the various positions, see McKenzie, 17–32). But it is clear that the dating of this work must take into account the Chronicler's deep interest in the temple service. D. N. Freedman, "The Chronicler's Purpose," *CBQ* 23 (1961) 432–42, has argued that the original edition of Chronicles was written in connection with the restoration of the second temple. Such a setting would account for the interests we see reflected in the Chronicler's treatment of 2 Kings 11. Alternatively, Myer dates Chronicles to ca. 400 B.C.E., and if the low date for Ezra's mission (398 B.C.E.) is adopted, then this dating would also explain the Chronicler's handling of 2 Kings 11, who may have written in support of Ezra's reforms.

CONCLUSIONS

In our endeavor to elucidate 2 Kings 9–11, we have sought to answer a number of fundamental interpretive questions. To accomplish this task, several exegetical methods designed to deal with the complexity of OT narrative were brought to bear on this ancient text. Beginning with an analysis of the narrative's composition, we concluded that those theories that see a connection of 2 Kings 9–10 and 2 Kings 11 with a larger pre-Dtr literary context, or that attempt to sever the ostensive connection between chapters 9–10 and chapter 11, are not convincing. Having established that the original narrative is to be found in 2 Kings 9–11, we next turned our attention to defining the original narrative by isolating those passages that reflect the activities of subsequent redactors. Here we discovered that the original version of the account has been expanded by the Dtr historian, and that there are also indications that this material has been subjected to post-Dtr alterations.

The removal of the accretions to the original narrative allowed this work to be investigated from a form-critical perspective. An analysis of the literary architecture of the text revealed that the account was arranged in a way that would encourage a comparative reading of Jehu's and Jehoiada's coups, in order to convince the reader that, although the revolts shared some general characteristics, the motivation of the two leaders, and the means by which they established new regimes, were vastly different. The author offered a critical portrayal of Jehu and his coup in order to emphasize the virtues of Jehoiada's revolt. The uncovering of the narrator's literary strategy led us to the conclusion that the work was driven by an apologetic intention, aimed at answering the charge that Jehoiada had been infected with the same self-serving ambition that drove Jehu to commit the most offensive acts of bloodshed.

Our attempt to define the literary genre of the original work demonstrated that it manifests those literary qualities that have led several form critics to classify it as "historical narrative." But finding that this traditional designation reflects a view that overly emphasizes the author's alleged quest for historical accuracy, we preferred the designation "political novella." The designation is more suitable because it not only indicates the intention of the work, but also better communicates the substantial role that imagination has played in the creation of the narrative.

We further discovered that this genre of literature is typically the product of royal scribes who were commissioned to use their literary skills to defend a regime that had come to power through the use of violence. With regard to the specific compositional circumstances of 2 Kings 9–11*, we found likely that this work was composed shortly after Jehoiada's coup in order to serve the new regime's need to consolidate relations with the influential elders of Judah.

Following the form-critical analysis of the original narrative, a detailed exposition of the composition was offered in order to vindicate our claims concerning the literary quality of the work, and to support our arguments concerning the author's attitudes toward Jehu's and Jehoiada's coups. The analysis of the various scenes has shown that the author constructed them in a way that would contribute to his primary concern: to highlight the deceit and savagery of Jehu in order to contrast it with the pure motives and virtually non-violent means by which Jehoiada placed Joash in power.

Our discussion of the redaction of 2 Kings 9–11 revealed that this material was subjected to revision by the Dtr historian, by a post-Dtr redactor, and by the Chronicler. The earliest redaction reveals the Dtr redactor's attempt to account both for the political instability of Israel, and for the political stability of Judah, by attributing the cause to contrasting religious commitments of David and Jeroboam. The stability of the south was explained as the result of David's obedience. Because he pleased Yahweh, he was rewarded with an eternal dynasty. Jeroboam, however, chose to disobey, and for this Yahweh punished him with the destruction of his dynasty. The Dtr historian extended this theological explanation of historical events to account also for the demise of Israelite dynasties that succeeded Jeroboam. In the view of this theologically minded historian, these dynasties were likewise terminated because their founders imitated Jeroboam's refusal to acknowledge that Yahweh had chosen Jerusalem as his only legitimate sanctuary. Jehu's dynasty received special treatment, for even though Jehu had also "clung to the sins of Jeroboam," he engendered a dynasty that lasted close to a century. To account for this anomaly, the Dtr historian altered the account of Jehu's coup to portray Jehu as a willing servant of Yahweh, who went forth to fulfill Elijah's prediction against the house of Ahab in response to Elisha's prophetic commission. The length of Jehu's dynasty was explained as Yahweh's reward to Jehu for eradicating the house of Ahab and for purging the Baalism that Ahab had introduced into Israel.

The Dtr historian also found it necessary to explain some of the negative aspects of Jehu's reign. Jehu did not found an eternal dynasty; nor did he enjoy the military success that Deuteronomic theology had promised. To account for these historical facts, the Dtr historian qualified Jehu's positive relationship with Yahweh by means of the stereotyped accusation that Jehu did not depart from the sins of Jeroboam.

The Dtr handling of Jehoiada's coup was more concerned with apologetics than with historical explanation. The Dtr redactor's expansions to the account of Jehoiada's revolt reflect two primary concerns. "The people of the land" were introduced into the story as the enthusiastic supporters of Joash's investiture and as the spear-head of Jehoiada's cult reform. These additions reflect the Dtr historian's attempt to justify the role that "the people of land" had played in Josiah's accession. Perceiving a parallel between the coup that placed the young Joash on the throne and the counter-conspiracy that brought the young Josiah to power, the Dtr historian sought to legitimate the actions of "the people of the land," who had forcibly placed Josiah on the throne, by introducing this group into the account of Jehoiada's coup. Other expansions reflect the Dtr historian's attempt to justify Josiah's commitment to cultic reform by making the account of Jehoiada's coup climax with a renewal of the king and the people to the stipulations of Deuteronomic cult law.

The investigation of the post-Dtr expansions to 2 Kings 9–11 revealed that they do not reflect the broad historical and theological perspective of the Dtr historian. These additions deal with a variety of topics and, for the most part, reflect a concern to make certain minor adjustments to the Dtr version of this material. The post-Dtr expansion to 2 Kings 11, however, do not exhibit a diversity of interests. All are concerned with emphasizing Jehoiada's commitment to his responsibility as the caretaker of Yahweh's sacred precincts.

Our analysis of the Chronicler's version of the story exposed some of his typical perspectives and concerns. The Chronicler's low estimation of the northern kingdom is reflected by his selective treatment of 2 Kings 9–10, in which he chose to include only material that related to the kingdom of Judah. This historian was especially concerned to show that both Ahaziah's wickedness and his untimely demise were the result of the political and family relations that linked him to the Omrides of the north. By stating that God had synchronized Elisha's commissioning of Jehu with Ahaziah's visit to Jehoram, the Chronicler portrayed Ahaziah's death and his burial in Samaria as the means by which Ahaziah received a just punishment for his corrupting relationship to the Omrides.

The Chronicler's version of Jehoiada's coup was expanded in several places to show that Jehoiada's coup was motivated by a concern to reclaim the throne for a Davidic descendant, and to re-establish the cultic prescriptions laid down by Moses and David. Accordingly, special emphasis was given to the duties of the temple personnel—the priests and Levites, the temple singers, and the gatekeepers. The Chronicler was also especially interested in emphasizing the regulations that stipulate who may gain access to the sacred precincts of Yahweh's temple. Such concerns seem to reflect the Chronicler's attempts to support Ezra's efforts to re-establish the temple as the center of post-exilic Judaism.

The foregoing investigation has attempted to address several of the fundamental interpretive issues raised by the final form of the story contained in 2 Kings 9–11. We have seen that the conceptual integrity and literary qualities of the original work have been obscured by the accretions that have been introduced into the narrative by subsequent redactors. The removal of later expansions allowed us not only to deepen our understanding of the contributions of later redactors, but also to appreciate the literary achievements of the original author, and the nature of the message that he sought to convey to his readers. The original narrative, marked by a high degree of literary sophistication and by an earnest apologetic intention, places it within a literary tradition that produced some of the most artful and complex examples of Hebrew narrative. Similar to our narrative, politically motivated works such as the Yahwist's Epic,[1] the Succession Narrative,[2] the History of David's Rise,[3] show that kings of Judah were well aware of the

---

[1] W. Wolff, "The Kerygma of the Yahwist," *Int* 20 (1966) 131–58; R. E. Clements, *Abraham and David. Genesis XV and its Meaning for Israelite Tradition* (SBT 2/5; Naperville: Allenson, 1967); W. Brueggemann, "David and his Theologian," *CBQ* 30 (1968) 156–81; *idem*, "From Dust to Kingship," *ZAW* 84 (1972) 1–18; *idem*, "The Yahwist," *IDBSup*, 971–74; P. Ellis, *The Yahwist, the Bible's First Theologian* (Notre Dame: Fides, 1968); W. Wifall, "Bone of my Bones and Flesh of my Flesh—The Politics of the Yahwist," *CurTM* 10 (1983) 176–83.

[2] Rost, *The Succession to the Throne of David* (Sheffield: Almond, 1982); T.C.G. Thornton, "Solomonic Apologetic in Samuel and Kings, *CQR* 169 (1968) 159–66; R.N. Whybray, *The Succession Narrative. A Study of II Samuel 9–20; I Kings 1 and 2* (SBT 2/9; Naperville: Allenson, 1968); L. Delekat, "Tendenz und Theologie der David-Salomo-Erzählung," *Das nahe und ferne Wort* (BZAW 105; Berlin: Töpelmann, 1967) 22–36; E. Würthwein, *Die Erzählung von der Thronfolge Davids—theologische oder politische Geschichtsschreibung?* (ThSt (B) 115; Zurich: Theologischer Verlag, 1974); J. W. Flanagan, "Court History or Succession Document? A Study of 2 Samuel 9–20 and 1 Kgs 1–2," *JBL* 91 (1972) 172–81; F. Langlemat, "Pour ou contra Salomon? La redaction prosalomonienne de 1 Rois, I-II," *RB* 83 (1976) 321–79, 481–529; ; P. K. McCarter, "Plots, True or False. The Succession Narrative as Court Apologetic," *Int* 35 (1981) 355–67; K. W. Whitelam, *The Just King: Monarchic Juridical Authority in Ancient Israel* (JSOTSup 12; Sheffield: JSOT, 1979).

[3] Mettinger, 33–57; T. Ishida, *The royal Dynasties*, 55–63; Wolf, 118–178; P. K. McCarter, "The Apology of David," *JBL* 99 (1980) 489–04; K. W. Whitelam, "Defense," 61–87.

power of the word, and that the royal scribes of the Judean court stood ready to devote their mastery of rhetoric to the interests of the state.[4]

[4] G. A. Herion ("The Role of Historical Narrative in Biblical Thought: The Tendencies Underlying Old Testament Historiography," *JSOT* 21 [1982] 25–57, esp. pp. 29–33) discusses some of the characteristics of those OT narratives that reflect what he calls "The Official Tendency." Other attempts to locate Israelite thought within a continuum of sociological polarities are W. Brueggemann, "Trajectories in OT Literature and the Sociology of Ancient Israel," *JBL* 98 (1979) 161–85; P. Hanson, *The Dawn of Apocalyptic* (Philadelphia: Fortress, 1975).

SELECTED BIBLIOGRAPHY

Ackroyd, P. R. "The Succession Narrative (so-called)." *Int* 35 (1981) 383–96.

Ahlström, G. W. "King Jehu: A Prophet's Mistake." In *Scripture in History and Theology: Essays in Honor of J. Coert Rylaarsdam.* Ed. Arthur L. Merrill and Thomas W. Overholt. Pittsburgh: Pickwick, 1977, 47–69.

Albright, W. F. "Some Canaanite-Phonecian sources of Hebrew wisdom." VTSup 3 (1955) 1–15.

Alt, Albrecht. "Der Stadtstaat Samaria." In *Kleine Schriften zur Geschichte des Volkes Israel.* Band III. Ed. Martin Noth. Munich: C. H. Beck'sche Verlagsbuchhandlung, 1959, 258–302.

———. "The Formation of the Israelite State in Palestine." In *Essays on Old Testament History and Religion.* Garden City: Doubleday, 1967, 223–309.

———. "The Monarchy in the Kingdoms of Israel and Judah." In *Essays on Old Testament History and Religion.* Garden City: Doubleday, 1967, 312–35.

Alter, Robert. *The Art of Biblical Narrative.* New York: Basic, 1981.

Astour, M. C. "841 BC: The First Assyrian Invasion of Israel." *JAOS* 91 (1971) 383–89.

Baumgartner, W. *Hebräisches und Aramäisches Lexikon zum Alten Testament.* Lieferungen I, II, III. Leiden: Brill, 1967, 1974, 1983.

Bentzen, A. *Introduction to the Old Testament.* Vol. I. Copenhagen: Gad, 1958.

Benzinger, I. *Die Bücher der Chronik.* KHC. Leipzig: Mohr (Siebeck), 1901.

———. *Die Bücher der Könige.* KHC. Leipzig: Mohr (Siebeck), 1899.

———. *Jahwist und Elohist in den Königsbüchern.* BWANT NF 2. Berlin: W. Kohlhammer, 1921.

Bleek F. and Wellhausen J. *Einleitung in das Alte Testament,* 4th ed. Berlin: Reimer, 1878.

Bohlen, R. *Der Fall Nabot: Form, Hintergrund und Werdegang einer alttestamentlichen Erzählung (I Kön 21).* Trier: Paulinus, 1978.

Bornkamm, G. *"presbys." TDNT* 6 (1968) 651–83.

Brown, F., Driver, S. R., and Briggs, C. A. *A Hebrew and English Lexicon of the Old Testament.* Oxford: Clarendon, 1907.

Brueggemann, W. "David and his Theologian." *CBQ* (1968) 156–81.

——. "From Dust to Kingship." *ZAW* 84 (1972) 1–18.

——. "Trajectories in OT Literature and the Sociology of Ancient Israel." *JBL* 98 (1979) 161–85.

——. "The Yahwist." *IDBSup,* 971–75.

Bright, J. *A History of Israel.* 2d ed. Philadelphia: Westminster, 1972.

Burney, C. *Notes on the Hebrew Text of the Book of Kings.* Oxford: Clarendon, 1903.

Carlson, R. A. "Elisée — le successeur d'ēlie." *VT* 20 (1970) 385–405.

Clements, R. E. *Abraham and David. Genesis XV and its Meaning for Israelite Tradition.* SBT 2/5. Naperville: Allenson, 1967.

Coats, G. *Genesis, with an Introduction to Narrative Literature.* FOTL 1. Grand Rapids: Eerdmanns, 1983.

Cohen, M. A. "In All Fairness to Ahab: A Socio-Political Consideration of the Ahab-Elijah Conflict." *Eretz Israel* 12 (1975) 87–94.

Conrad J. and G. J. Botterweck, "*zāqēn.*" *TDOT* 4 (1980) 122–31.

Conroy, Charles. *1–2 Samuel, 1–2 Kings.* Old Testament Message, Wilmington: Glazier, 1983.

Cross, F. M. *Canaanite Myth and Hebrew Epic.* Cambridge: Harvard University, 1973.

Cully, R. C. "Structural Analysis: Is it Done with Mirrors?" *Int* 28 (1974) 165–81.

——. *Studies in the Structure of Hebrew Narrative.* Philadelphia: Fortress, 1976.

Curtis, E. L. and Madsen, A. A. *A Critical and Exegetical Commentary on The Book of Chronicles.* ICC. New York: Scribner's, 1910.

Daiches, S. "The Meaning of am ha-aretz in the Old Testament." *JTS* 30 (1929) 245–49.

Delekat, L. "Tendenz und Theologie der David-Salomo-Erzählung." In *Das nahe und ferne Wort.* BZAW 105. Berlin: Töpelmann, 1967, 22–36.

Denton, R. C. *The First and Second Book of Kings: The First and Second Book of Chronicles.* The Layman's Bible Commentary, 7. Richmond: John Knox, 1964.

de Vaux, R. *Ancient Israel.* New York: McGraw-Hill, 1961.

——. *Les Livres des Rois.* JB. Paris: Cerf, 1958.

Dietrich, W. *Prophetie und Geschichte: Eine redaktions- geschichtliche Untersuchung zum deuteronomistischen Geschichtswerk.* FRLANT 108. Göttingen: Vandenhoeck & Ruprecht, 1972.

Donner, H. "The Separate States of Israel and Judah." In *Israelite and Judean History.* Ed. John H. Hayes and J. Maxwell Miller. OTL. Philadephia: Westminster, 1977, 381–434.

Eissfeldt, O. "Die Bücher der Könige." *HSAT*, I/1. Tübingen: Mohr (Siebeck), 1922.

———. "Die Komposition von I Reg 16:29–II Reg 13:25." In *Das Ferne und Nahe Wort*. Berlin: Töpelmann, 1967, 49–58.

———. *The Old Testament. An Introduction*. New York: Harper & Row, 1965.

Ellis, P. "1–2 Kings." *JBC* 11.

Ellul J. *The Politics of God and the Politics of Man*. Grand Rapids: Eerdmans, 1972.

Elmslie, W. A. L. "The First and Second Books of Chronicles." In *IDB* 3.339–548.

Finkelstein, J. "Early Mesopotamia, 2500–1000 B.C." In *Propaganda and Communication in World History*, Vol I. Ed. Harrold D. Lasswell, Daniel Lerner and Hans Speier. Honolulu: University, 1979, 50–110.

Flanagan, W. "Court History or Succession Document? A Study of II Samuel 9–20 and I Kings 1–2." *JBL* 91 (1972) 172–81.

Fohrer, G. "Der Vertrag zwischen König und Volk in Israel." *ZAW* 71 (1959) 1–22.

Freedman, D. N. "The Chronicler's Purpose." *CBQ* 23 (1961) 432–42.

———. "Pentateuch." *IDB* 3.711–27.

Frei, Hans W. *The Eclipse of Biblical Narrative: A Study of Eighteenth and Nineteenth Century Hermeneutics*. New Haven: Yale University, 1974.

Frick, F. S. "Rechabites." *IDBSup*, 726–28.

———. "The Rechabites Reconsidered." *JBL* 90 (1971) 279–87.

Fricke, K. *Das Zweite Buch von den Königen*. BAT, 12/11. Stuttgart: Calwer, 1972.

Friedman, R. D. *The Exile and Biblical Narrative: The Formation of Deuteronomistic and Priestly Works*. HSM 22. Chico: Scholars, 1981.

Frost, S. B. "Judgment on Jezebel, or a Woman Wronged." *TToday* 20 (1963) 503–17.

Gardiner, A. "The Coronation of King Haremheb." *JEA* 39 (1952) 13–31.

Gillischewski, E. "Der Ausdruck '*m-h'rs* im A.T." *ZAW* 40 (1922) 137–42.

Gordis, R. "Sectional Rivalry in the Kingdom of Judah." *JQR* 2 (1934–1935) 237–59.

Gray, J. *I & II Kings: A Commentary*. OTL. Philadelphia: Westminster, 1977.

Gressmann, H. *Die älteste Geschichtsschreibung und Prophetie Israels*. SAT, 11/1. 2d ed. Göttingen: Vandenhoeck & Ruprecht, 1921.

Gunkel, H. *Die israelitische Literatur*. Darmstadt: Wissenschaftliche Buchgesellschaft, 1963.

———. "Die Revolution des Jehu." *Deutsche Rundschau* 40 (1913) 289–308.

————. *The Legends of Genesis*. New York: Schoken, 1964.

Gurney, O. R. *The Hittites*. Melbourne: Penguin, 1952.

Hagan, H. "Deception as Motif and Theme in 2 Sm 9–20; 1 Kgs 1–2." *Bib* 60 (1979) 301–26.

Hanson, P. *The Dawn of Apocalyptic*. Philadelphia: Fortress, 1975.

Harrelson, W. *Interpreting the Old Testament*. New York: Holt Rinehart and Winston, 1964.

Herion, G. A. "The Role of Historical Narrative in Biblical Thought: The Tendencies Underlying Old Testament Historiography." *JSOT* 21 (1982) 25–57.

Hirsch, E. D. *Validity in Interpretation*. New Haven: Yale University, 1967.

Hölscher, G. "Das Buch der Könige, seine Quellen und seine Redaktion." In *Eucharisterion*. FRLANT 36. Göttingen: Vandenhoeck & Ruprecht, 1923, 158–213.

————. *Geschichtsschreibung in Israel: Untersuchungen zum Jahvisten und Elohisten*. Lund: Gleerup, 1952.

Hoffmann, H. *Reform und Reformen: Untersuchungen zu einem Grundthema der deuteronomistischen Geschichtsschreibung*. ATANT 66. Zurich: Theologischer, 1980.

Hoffner, H. "Propaganda and Political Justification in Hittite Historiography." In *Unity and Diversity: Essays in the History, Literature and Religion of the Ancient Near East*. Ed. Hans Goedicke and J. J. M. Roberts. Baltimore: Johns Hopkins University, 1975, 49–62.

Ishida. T. "The House of Ahab." *IEJ* 25 (1975) 135–37.

————. *The Royal Dynasties in Ancient Israel: A Study on the Formation and Development of Royal Dynastic Ideology*. BZAW 142. Berlin: de Gruyter, 1977.

————. "Solomon's Succession to the Throne of David — A Political Analysis." In *Studies in the Period of David and Solomon and Other Essays*. Ed. Tomoo Ishida. Winona Lake: Eisenbrauns, 1982, 175–87.

Jepsen, A. *Die Quellen des Königsbuches*. Halle: Niemeyer, 1956.

————. *Nabi. Soziologische Studien zur alttestamentlischen Literatur und Religionsgeschichte*. Munich: C. H. Beck'sche Verlagsbuchhandlung, 1934.

Katzenstein, H. J. "Who Were the Parents of Athaliah?" *IEJ* 5 (1955) 194–97.

Kautzsch, E. *Gesenius' Hebrew Grammar*. 2d Ed. A. E. Cowley. Oxford: Clarendon, 1910.

Keil, C. F. *The Book of Kings*. Biblical Commentary on the Old Testament. Grand Rapids: Eerdmans, 1965.

Kittel, R. *Die Bücher der Chronik und Esra, Nehemia und Esther*. HKAT. Göttingen: Vandenhoeck & Ruprecht, 1902.

———. *Die Bücher der Könige.* HKAT, I/5. Göttingen: Vandenhoeck & Ruprecht, 1900.

Klostermann, D. A. *Die Bücher Samuelis und der Könige.* Kurzgefasstes exegetisches Handbuch zum Alten Testament. Nordlingen: C. H. Beck'sche Buchhandlung, 1887.

Knott. J. B. "The Dynasty of Jehu: An Assessment Based upon Ancient Near Eastern Literature and Archaeology." Ph.D dissertation, Emory University, 1971.

Kraeling, E. *Aram and Israel.* New York: Columbia University, 1918.

Kuyt, A. and Wesselius, W. "A Ugaritic Parallel for the Feast of Ba'al in 2 Kings x:18-25." *VT* 35 (1985) 109-11.

Landsdorfer, S. *Die Bücher der Könige.* HS, III/2. Bonn: Hanstein, 1927.

Langlemat, F. "Pour ou contre Salomon? La redaction prosalomonienne de 1 Rois, I-II" *RB* 83 (1976) 321-79, 481-529.

Levin, C. *Der Sturz der Königin Atalja. Ein Kapitel zur Geschichte Judas im 9. Jahrhundert. v. Chr.* Stuttgart: Katholisches Bibelwerk, 1982.

Lichtheim, M. *Ancient Egyptian Literature. Volume 1: The Old and Middle Kingdoms.* Berkeley: University of California, 1975.

Liverani, M. "L'Historie de Joas." *VT* 24 (1974) 438-53.

Long, B. *1 Kings, with an Introduction to Historical Literature.* FOTL 9. Grand Rapids: Eerdmanns, 1984.

———. "2 Kings III and Genres of Prophetic Narrative." *VT* 23 (1973) 337-48.

Malamat, A. "Kingship and Council in Israel and Sumer: A Parallel." *JNES* 22 (1963) 247-53.

May, H. G. "A Key to the Interpretation of Zechariah's Vision." *JBL* 57 (1938) 173-84.

McCarter, P. K. "Plots, True or False. The Succession Narrative as Court Apologetic." *Int* 35 (1981) 355-67.

———. "The Apology of David." *JBL* 99 (1980) 489-504.

———. "'Yaw, Son of Omri': A Philological Note on Israelite Chronology." *BASOR* 216 (1974) 5-8.

McCarthy, D. J. "II Samuel 7 and the Structure of the Deuteronomic History." *JBL* 84 (1965) 131-38.

———. "An Installation Genre?" *JBL* 90 (1971) 31-41.

McKenzie, J. L. "The Elders in the Old Testament." *Bib* 40 (1959) 522-40.

McKenzie, S. L. *The Chronicler's Use of the Deuteronomistic History.* HSM 33. Atlanta: Scholars, 1985.

Mettinger, T. N. D. *King and Messiah. The Civil and Sacral Legitimation of the Israelite Kings.* Lund: Gleerup, 1976.

Miller, J. M. "The Fall of the House of Ahab." *VT* 17 (1967) 307-24.

Montgomery, J. A. *A Critical and Exegetical Commentary on the Book of Kings.* Ed. Henry S. Gehman. ICC. Edinburgh: T. & T. Clark, 1951.

Myers, J. M. *I Chronicles.* AB 12. Garden City: Doubleday, 1965.

———. *II Chronicles.* AB 13. Garden City: Doubleday, 1965.

Napier, B. D. "The Omrides of Jezreel." *VT* 9 (1959) 366–78.

Nelson, R. D. "Josiah in the Book of Joshua." *JBL* 100 (1981) 531–40.

———. *The Double Redaction of the Deuteronomistic History.* JSOTSup 18. Sheffield: JSOT, 1981.

Nicholson, E. W. "The Meaning of the Expression '*m-h'rs* in the Old Testament." *JJS* 10 (1965) 59–66.

Noth, M. *The Deuteronomistic History.* JSOTSup 15. Sheffield: JSOT, 1981.

———. *The History of Israel.* 2d ed. London: Adam & Charles Black, 1960.

Oded, B. "Judah and the Exile." In *Israelite and Judean History.* Ed. John H. Hayes and J. Maxwell Miller. OTL. Philadelphia: Westminster, 1977, 435–89.

Olyan, S. "*Haššālôm:* Some Literary Considerations of 2 Kgs 9." *CBQ* 46 (1984) 652–68.

Oppenheim, A. "Neo-Assyrian and Neo-Babylonian Empires." In *Propaganda and Communication in World History*, Vol I. Ed. Harrold D. Lasswell, Daniel Lerner and Hans Speier. Honolulu: University, 1979, 111–44.

Parker, S. B. "Jezebel's Reception of Jehu." *MAARAV* 1 (1978) 67–78.

Plein, I. "Erwägungen zur Überlieferung von I Reg 11, 26–14, 20." *ZAW* 78 (1966) 8–24.

Pope, M. H. "Rechab." *IDB* 4.14–16.

Posener, G. *Litterature et politique dans l'Egypte de la XIIe dynastie.* Paris: L'Ecole des hautes Etudes, 1956.

Pritchard, J. B., ed. *Ancient Near Eastern Texts Relating to the Old Testament.* 3rd ed. Princeton: Princeton University, 1969.

Rad, G. von. "The Royal Ritual in Judah." In *The Problem of the Hexateuch and Other Essays.* New York: McGraw-Hill, 1966, 211–16.

———. *Studies in Deuteronomy.* SBT 1/9. London: SCM, 1953.

Rehm, Martin. *Das zweite Buch der Könige.* Würzburg: Echter Verlag, 1982.

Robinson, J. *The Second Book of Kings.* The Cambridge Bible Commentary. Cambridge: Cambridge University Press, 1976.

Rofé, A. "The Classification of Prophetical Stories." *JBL* 89 (1970) 427–44.

Rost, L. *The Succession to the Throne of David.* Sheffield: Almond, 1982.

Rudolph, W. *Chronikbücher.* HAT. Tübingen: Mohr (Siebeck), 1955.

———. "Die Einheitlichkeit der Erzählung vom Sturz der Atalja (2 Kön 11)."

In *Festschrift für Alfred Bertholet*. Ed. W. Baumgartner, O. Eissfeldt, K. Elliger, and L. Rost. Tübingen: Mohr (Siebeck), 1950, 473–78.

Šanda, E. *Die Bücher der Könige: Das Zweite Buch der Könige*. EHAT. Münster: Aschendorffsche Verlagsbuchhandlung, 1911.

Schmidt, K. W. "Prophetic Delegation: A Form-Critical Inquiry." *Bib* 63 (1982) 206–18.

Schmitt, H. *Elisa: Traditionsgeschichtliche Untersuchungen zur vorklassischen nordisraelitischen Prophetie*. Gütersloh: Gerd Mohn, 1972.

Sekine, M. "Literatursoziologische Beobachtungen zu den Elisaerzählungen." *AJBI* 1 (1975) 39–62.

Sellin, E. and Fohrer, G. *Introduction to the Old Testament*. Nashville: Abingdon, 1965.

Skinner, J. *I and II Kings*. NCB. Edinburgh: T. C. & E. C. Jack, 1904.

Sloush, N. "Representative Government among the Hebrews and the Phoenicians." *JQR* 4 (1913) 303–10.

Smith, Clyde C. "Jehu and the Black Obelisk of Shalmaneser III." In *Scripture in History and Theology: Essays in Honor of J. Coert Rylaarsdam*. Ed. Arthur L. Merrill and Thomas W. Overholt. Pittsburgh: Pickwick, 1977, 71–105.

Snaith, N. "The First and Second Book of Kings: Introduction and Exegesis." In *IB* 3.3–338.

Soggin, J. A. "Der judäische 'am-ha'ares und das Königtum in Juda." *VT* 13 (1963) 187–95.

Soleh, A. "The Artistic Structure of the Story of Jehu's Enthronement (2 Kings 9–10)." *Beth Mikra* 28 (1982/83) 64–71.

Spieckermann, H. *Juda unter Assur in der Sargonidenzeit*. Göttingen: Vandenhoeck & Ruprecht, 1982.

Stade, B. "Anmerkungen zu 2 Ko 10–14." *ZAW* 5 (1885) 275–97.

Stade, B. and Schwally, F. *The Book of Kings*. Baltimore: Johns Hopkins, 1904.

Steck, O. *Überlieferung and Zeitgeschichte in den Elia- Erzählungen*. WMANT 26. Neukirchener-Vluyn, 1968.

Sternberg, M. *The Poetics of Biblical Narrative: Ideological Literature and the Drama of Reading*. Bloomington: Indiana University, 1985.

Strange, J. "Joram, King of Israel and Judah." *VT* 25 (1975) 191–201.

Stuhlmueller, C. "The Prophetic Combat for Peace." *Way* 22 (1982) 79–87.

Sturtevant, E. H. and Bechtel, G. *A Hittite Chrestomathy*. William Whitney Linguistic Series. Philadelphia: University of Pennsylvania, 1935.

Sulzberger, M. "The Polity of the Ancient Hebrews." *JQR* 3 (1912–13) 1–81.

Tadmor, H. "Autobiographical Apology in the Royal Assyrian Literature." In *History, Historiography and Interpretation: Studies in Biblical and*

Cuneiform Literatures. Ed. H. Tadmor and M. Weinfeld. Jerusalem: Magnes, 1983, 36–57.

——. "Traditional Institutions and the Monarchy: Social and Political Tensions in the Time of David and Solomon." In *Studies in the Period of David and Solomon and Other Essays*. Ed. Tomoo Ishida. Winona Lake: Eisenbrauns, 1982, 239–57.

Thenius, O. *Die Bücher der Könige*. 2d ed. Leipzig: S. Hirzel, 1873.

Tigay, J. H. "An Empirical Basis for the Documentary Hypothesis." *JBL* 94 (1975) 329–42.

——. *The Evolution of the Gilgamesh Epic*. Philadelphia: University of Pennsylvania, 1982.

Thorton, T. C. H. "Charismatic Kingship in Israel and Judah." *JTS* (1963) 1–11.

——. "Solomonic Apologetic in Samuel and Kings." *CQR* 169 (1968) 159–66.

Timm, S. *Die Dynastie Omri. Quellen und Untersuchungen zur Geschichte Israels im 9. Jahrhundert vor Christus*. Göttingen: Vandenhoeck & Ruprecht, 1982.

Unger, M. F. *Israel and the Arameans of Damascus*. Grand Rapids: Zondervan, 1957.

van der Ploeg, J. "Les Anciens dans l'Ancien Testament." In *Lex Tua Veritas*. Ed. Heinrich Gross and Franz Mussner. Trier: Paulinus, 1961, 175–91.

Veijola, T. *Die ewige Dynastie. David und die Entstehung seiner Dynastie nach der deuteronomistischen Darstellung*. Helsinki: Suomalaisen Tiedeakatemian, 1975.

Weinfeld, M. *Deuteronomy and the Deuteronomic School*. Oxford: Clarendon, 1972.

Welch, A. D. *The Work of the Chronicler: Its Purpose and Its Date*. London: Oxford University, 1939.

Wellhausen, J. *Die Composition des Hexateuchs und der historischen Bücher des Alten Testaments*. 4th ed. Berlin: Reimer, 1963.

Whitelam, K. W. "The Defense of David." *JSOT* 29 (1984) 61–87.

——. *The Just King: Monarchic Juridical Authority in Ancient Israel*. JSOTSup 12. Sheffield: JSOT, 1979.

Whitley, C. F. "The Deuteronomic Presentation of the House of Omri." *VT* 2 (1952) 137–52.

Widengren, G. "King and Covenant." *JSS* 2 (1957) 1–32.

Whybray, R. N. *The Succession Narrative. A Study of II Samuel 9–20; I Kings 1 and 2*. SBT 2/9. Naperville: Allenson, 1968.

Wifall, W. "Bone of my Bone and Flesh of my Flesh—The Politics of the Yahwist." *CurTM* 10 (1983) 176–83.

——. "David—Prototype of Israel's Future?" *BTB* (1974) 94–107.

——. "Genesis 3:15—A Protoevangelium?" *CBQ* 36 (1974) 361–65.

——. "The Breath of His Nostrils: Gen 2:7b." *CBQ* 36 (1974) 237–40.

Wilcoxen, J. "Narrative." In *Old Testament Form Criticism*. Ed. John H. Hayes. San Antonio: Trinity University, 1974, 57–98.

Williams, R. J. *Hebrew Syntax: An Outline*. 2d ed. Toronto: University of Toronto, 1976.

——. "Literature as a Medium of Political Propaganda in ancient Egypt." In *The Seed of Wisdom: Essays in Honour of T. J. Meek*. Toronto: University of Toronto, 1964, 14–30.

Wilson, J. A. "Egyptian Civilization." In *Propaganda and Communication in World History*, Vol I. Ed. Harrold D. Lasswell, Daniel Lerner and Hans Speier. Honolulu: University, 1979, 145–74.

Wiseman, D. J. "Is it Peace? Covenant and Diplomacy." *VT* 32 (1982) 311–26.

Wolf, C. U. "Traces of Primitive Democracy in Ancient Israel." *JNES* 6 (1947) 98–108.

Wolf, H. H. "The Apology of Hattusilis Compared with other Political Self-Justifications of the Ancient Near East." Ph.D. dissertation, Brandeis University, 1967.

Wolff, H. W. "The Kerygma of the Yahwist." *Int* 20 (1966) 131–58.

Würthwein, E. *Der 'am ha'arez im Alten Testament*. BWANT, IV/17. Stuttgart: Kohlhammer, 1936.

——. *Die Bücher der Könige*. ATD. Göttingen: Vandenhoeck & Ruprecht, 1984.

——. *Die Erzählung von der Thronfolge Davids theologische oder politische Geschichtsschreibung?* ThSt (B) 115. Zurich: Theologischer, 1974.

INDEX

THE CATHOLIC BIBLICAL QUARTERLY MONOGRAPH SERIES

Order from:

**The Catholic Biblical Association of America
The Catholic University of America
Washington, DC 20064**